D1636834

Literary Trails of Eastern North Carolina

NORTH CAROLINA LITERARY TRAILS

is a project of the North Carolina Arts Council,

an agency of the North Carolina Department

of Cultural Resources

Wayne Martin, Executive Director, North Carolina Arts Council

PROJECT DIRECTOR: Rebecca Moore, North Carolina Arts Council

literary trails

of
Eastern
North Carolina

A GUIDEBOOK

Georgann Eubanks

Photographs by **DONNA CAMPBELL**

The University of North Carolina Press *Chapel Hill*

Designed by Richard Hendel

Set in TheSerif and Scala Sans types

by Tseng Information Systems, Inc.

Manufactured in the United States of America

The paper in this book meets the guidelines for permanence and durability of the Committee on Production Guidelines for Book Longevity of the Council on Library Resources.

The University of North Carolina Press has been a member of the Green Press Initiative since 2003.

Library of Congress Cataloging-in-Publication Data

Eubanks, Georgann.

Literary trails of Eastern North Carolina : a guidebook / Georgann Eubanks ; photographs by Donna Campbell.

p. cm. — (Literary trails of North Carolina)

Includes index.

ISBN 978-1-4696-0701-6 (cloth : alk. paper)

ISBN 978-1-4696-0702-3 (pbk. : alk. paper)

1. Literary landmarks—North Carolina—Guidebooks. 2. Authors, American—Homes and haunts—North Carolina—Guidebooks. 3. North Carolina—In literature—Guidebooks. 4. North Carolina—Intellectual life—Guidebooks.

I. Campbell, Donna, 1951– II. Title.

PS144.N63E9 2013

810.9′7565—dc23

2012037474

cloth   17 16 15 14 13   5 4 3 2 1

paper   17 16 15 14 13   5 4 3 2 1

CONTENTS

O! those Carolina roads! extending leagues on leagues, with never a crook discernible by the eye, flanked by thick-set pines that have been blazed and scarred by surveyors and tar-makers; level as a house floor, and sometimes as hard; musical at times with the hunter's horn, the hounds in full cry, or the notes of a thousand birds, thrown into fine harmonic relief by the low bass of the wind as it sweeps through the lofty pines.

—From *Bertie: Or, Life in the Old Field, A Humorous Novel*,
  by George Higby Throop (1851).

The forces of nature have written their history on the landscape of eastern North Carolina. Yaupons on Oak Island stand in permanent slant against incessant gales. Dunes at Hatteras are relentlessly sculpted by waves and wind. In the Neuse River Basin, shallow runnels cut by evening rainfall are etched by fresh raccoon prints come daybreak. And in the thickest groves of catbrier and scrub oak in the swamp, the Carolina jasmine climbs the pines toward early spring light, at first as single vines that splay and circle the trunks but soon flowering out like so many Easter skirts.

This is an ancient land of pale sand and darkest muck, of deep rivers and shallow bays—always in motion, always changing, always under threat of weather, and now, human indulgence as well. Early humans survived here for 10,000 years before they were met by strange, weapon-wielding immigrants four centuries ago. Only then did the written story of what came to be called eastern North Carolina begin.

Literary Trails of Eastern North Carolina is the last volume in a series commissioned by the North Carolina Arts Council. The Arts Council's charge was to gather excerpts from our state's finest writers—and in some cases, visiting writers—to build a series of tours west to east, a bridge of letters across the landscape. Using literature as the basis for eighteen tours in each of three volumes, *Literary Trails* invites a new generation of explorers—whether traveling by imagination or by vehicle—to see the state through the eyes of the poets, journalists, novelists, memoirists, and playwrights who have lived here.

The writing gathered in *Literary Trails of the North Carolina Mountains* was shaped by a strong oral tradition and the humbling quality of the mountains themselves. In *Literary Trails of the North Carolina Piedmont*, the story line is progress—in education, transportation, industry, technology, culture, and commerce—and the raw spots that are rubbed up when urban meets rural.

In this volume, eastern North Carolina writers reveal lives long tied to the land and regularly troubled by storms. They tell stories of hardship and hard work, and of the tendency to give fierce attention to hierarchies left over from the stratified societies that first sent these settlers in search of freedom. In this part of the state, native and newcomer, entitled and enslaved, and old ways and new have clashed again and again over the centuries. Habits die hard here, it seems. One hears pure music in the place-names—Gumbranch, Moyock, Chinquapin, Ocracoke, Wagram, Calabash—and some pieces of ground are still so remote that human eyes have seen them only from the air. This part of the state is not entirely rural, however. In its cities (Raleigh, Fayetteville, Cary, Wilmington, Greenville, and Jacksonville) and in towns too big now to be called small (Rocky Mount, Wilson, Goldsboro, and New Bern, for example), sodium lights wash the nighttime sky.

Over the past century, writers and readers of all stripes began flocking to the coast when the weather warmed in search of leisure and restoration by the ocean. Today, they happily keep dozens of quaint bookstores and lending libraries in business with their voracious appetites for pages to turn in the shade of an umbrella.

The shelves hold books about ghosts and more ghosts, and about pirates, of course. That stands to reason. Because the literature about this territory goes back more than 400 years, the history it tells cannot help but be lightened by mysteries and legends. But along with the sea foam are some fine literary surprises from the past and present.

Who knew, for example, that a very young Robert Frost spent a week in the Great Dismal Swamp contemplating suicide after being spurned by the woman he would eventually marry? Or that the setting of *Show Boat*—Edna Ferber's novel, which became a musical and then a movie—was inspired by a floating theater that the author visited while it was docked at Bath? Or that actress Ava Gardner, of Smithfield, a longtime friend of Ernest Hemingway, also spent time with classicist Robert Graves, who composed several poems to honor her?

In the twentieth century, towns in eastern North Carolina spawned more than their fair share of prominent journalists: NBC's David Brinkley, of Wilmington; *New Republic* commentator Gerald Johnson, of Riverton; CBS's Charles Kuralt, who spent much of his childhood in Onslow County; *New Yorker* reporter Joseph Mitchell, of Fairmont; *Wall Street Journal* editor Vermont Royster, of Raleigh; and *New York Times* editor Clifton Daniels, of Zebulon. Horace Carter, of Tabor City, edited that town's newspaper and worked jointly with his colleagues at the neighboring Whiteville paper on a series of stories that earned the first Pulitzer Prize ever awarded to rural newspapers.

Some may say that the literary heart of the state is Southern Pines, the location of the North Carolina Literary Hall of Fame, into which a small group of accomplished writers is inducted every other year. This stellar assemblage is commemorated in what was the library of novelist James Boyd, who often entertained F. Scott Fitzgerald, William Faulkner, and other literary lights at his Weymouth estate, now a center for arts and humanities activity.

The presence of the military in eastern North Carolina gave rise to a variety of novels and memoirs through the twentieth century, including works by Marion Hargrove (Fort Bragg), William Styron (Camp Lejeune), and Pete Hendricks (Cherry Point).

These tours also visit a range of humble home places—Paul Green's in Lillington; Bernice Kelly Harris's in Seaboard; John Charles McNeill's in Wagram; Samm-Art Williams's in Burgaw; Leon Rooke's in Roanoke Rapids; and Eloise Greenfield's in Parmele.

Inland tours take readers to Civil War sites through excerpts from work by William Trotter, Mark L. Bradley, Jeri Fitzgerald Board, E. L. Doctorow, and Rod Gragg. Stories of the Lumbee Indians provide a different view of the Civil War, Reconstruction, and later years. A notable group of African American women in Halifax, Northampton, and Hertford counties have provided strong narratives from the northeastern corridor.

In addition to recognizing the universities and colleges that regularly feature literary events, publish journals, and offer degrees in creative writing, *Literary Trails of Eastern North Carolina* documents some noteworthy gatherings of writers that have occurred over the years. Among these are the first meeting of the North Carolina Writers Conference in Manteo in 1950; the 1977 reunion of Black Mountain artists and writers, hosted by poet Ron Bayes, at St. Andrews College in Laurinburg; and the ongoing performances of music, poetry, and storytelling at the R. A. Fountain General Store near Greenville, hosted by writer Alex Albright.

It would have been, of course, an impossible task for one book to be comprehensive—or even barely representative—of all the works created in this region's forty-five counties. The excerpts provided are generally brief, and the idea is to send you to a library or bookstore looking for more from a writer whom you might meet for the first time in these pages.

The selections have been chosen because they speak to place, offer a fresh view, capture a moment in history, or illuminate a complicated event. Because of the long history of eastern North Carolina, a good many writers long gone and out of print have been given new voice in these pages to help us all remember what has been and continues to be definitive about the region. Some of the stories are tragic. Others are lighthearted.

Poets may give us sharp snapshots of particular places and times, but prose writers—by definition—must traffic in transformation. We can almost always say of a good story that the characters in it will never be the same as a result of the events that come to pass in the course of the narrative. Eastern North Carolina is full of such dramas.

Robert Frost said, "No surprise for the writer, no surprise for the reader." I have experienced many surprises along the way in researching and writing these three books on North Carolina literature. This journey of stories has changed me. I hope the same for you.

Georgann Eubanks

trail one

The Southeastern Corridor: Waters Dark and Clear

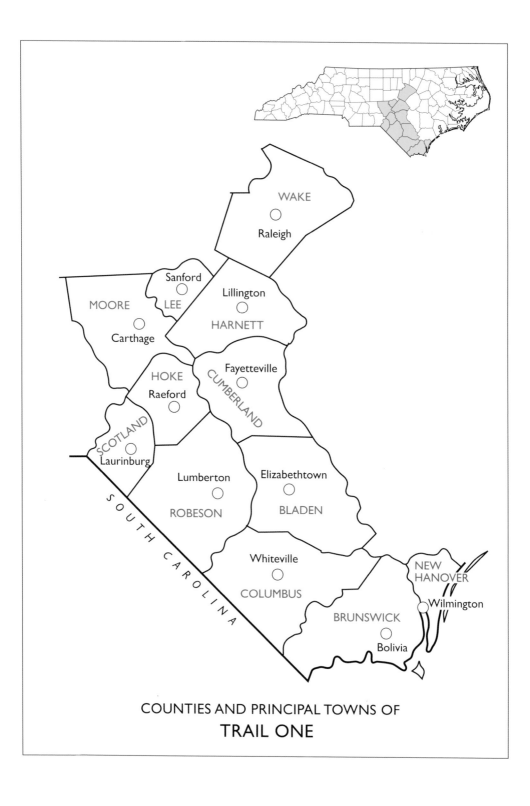

COUNTIES AND PRINCIPAL TOWNS OF
TRAIL ONE

Since it is somewhat changed today, I'm describing our geography from memory. The county has more farms and towns now, more ditches, more roads and bridges and railroad tracks. But back then everything not pinewoods or fields was swamps, fifty of them labeled on the map and more whose names were never known to mapmakers. Some were pocosins, shallow egg-shaped basins landlocked and still, scattered northwesterly as if a clutch of stars had been flung aslant in one careless toss from heaven, leaving bays that sometimes filled with rain and sometimes dried in the sun, growing gums and poplars and one tiny bright green plant found nowhere else on earth, the toothed and alluring Venus flytrap.

In the bigger swamps, miles wide and inches deep, a slow current drew toward the river through thickets of briar and cane and bottle-neck cypress, each tree rising from a little island of its own making. The roots caught silt from the drifting stream, and slowly built a solid ground where none had been before.

—From *Nowhere Else on Earth*, by Josephine Humphreys
(New York: Penguin, 2000), 2.

Novelist Josephine Humphreys writes in the imagined voice of Rhoda Strong Lowrie, a nineteenth-century woman born of a Scottish father from the Isle of Skye and a Lumbee Indian mother—a marriage that mirrors the complex human relations of this region. The book's description of the landscape in southeastern North Carolina remains true.

The seven tours in this trail run from the urban dazzle of Raleigh to the southern coast along a rough-hewn route dictated by the Lumber, Black, and Cape Fear rivers, which permit easy passage only at certain intervals through fields and swamps. These rivers were the principal means of transportation for native peoples and the later settlers who came across the Atlantic and up this swampy corridor from the port city of Wilmington—the last stop on this trail. Commerce in the early days of settlement was all about timber, turpentine, pitch, rosin, and tar—the production of which, by most accounts, led to the designation of North Carolinians as "Tar Heels."

Curiously, in the bay lakes of the region, the shallow waters run clear, while deeper rivers run very dark, filled with tannin leaching from leaves that drop from the tangled canopy above—an image sometimes ominous, always mysterious. These waters and the shape-shifting land between them form the psychological basis for much of the writing along this trail. Menacing stories of cottonmouth moccasins, alligator, bear, and bobcat are common, as are stories of the Ku Klux Klan.

Extraordinary poets have been born here, notably A. R. Ammons, a two-time

National Book Award winner who was raised south of Whiteville, in fields as flat as an iron skillet and just as hot come summer. Guy Owen, a mentor to many writers who came through college at Davidson, Elon, and North Carolina State, also wrote lovingly in poetry and prose of the Clarkton farm where he was raised. Heather Ross Miller, who was brought up in the Piedmont in a large family of serious writers, ended up in this region because of marriage. She put her considerable talents to work documenting daily life in the remote area around Singletary Lake.

The beaches in this section engender a sense of nostalgia for the decades when North Carolina fiercely held to its laws against liquor by the drink. Those laws stifled tourism and left the high-rise condos perched, as late as 1980, on either border—Virginia Beach to the north and Myrtle Beach to the south.

Not just the Venus flytrap but also some fourteen other species of carnivorous plants grow in the remote reaches of the Green Swamp along this trail. North Carolina's literature has been graced through history by strong writers who have been ready to describe a region of the state that is both "toothed and alluring," and certainly like nowhere else on earth.

Raleigh

Visit North Carolina's capital city through the eyes of many writers. Thomas Wolfe called it Sydney in *Look Homeward, Angel*. Novelist Barbara Neely named it Farleigh. Millboro is Lucy Daniel's pseudonym. Regardless of appellation, the city has long been a literary live wire and serves as our gateway to the East.

Writers with a connection to this area: Betty Adcock, Gerald Barrax, Sally Buckner, Kim Church, Anna Julia Cooper, Jonathan Daniels, Josephus Daniels, Lucy Daniels, Angela Davis-Gardner, A. Elizabeth Delany, Sarah L. Delany, Elizabeth Edwards, Charles Frazier, Gail Godwin, Anna Wooten Hawkins, Amy Hill Hearth, Scott Huler, Robert Inman, John Kessel, Susan Ketchin, Carrie Knowles, Richard Krawiec, Armistead Maupin, Margaret Mitchell, Lenard D. Moore, Barbara Neely, Guy Owen, Reynolds Price, William Price, Vermont Royster, Larry Rudner, David Sedaris, Mary Snotherly, Elizabeth Daniels Squire, Anne Tyler, Richard Walser, Thomas Wolfe

For more than two centuries, Raleigh has been a magnet for the rest of the state, drawing farmers with their produce for market, representatives from all one hundred counties to their seats in the legislature, and schoolchildren who come in a string of yellow buses each year to see state government at work and experience the artistic, literary, and natural treasures laid up for them in the capital city. North Carolina has the distinction of having established the nation's first state cultural resources department and the first state-sponsored symphony, art museum, and residential secondary school of the arts. It seems fitting, then, to begin this tour at one of these attractions: the North Carolina Museum of Art. In 1997, the institution asked forty-five of the state's best-known writers to put pen to paper and describe a favorite work in the museum. Raleigh native and *New Yorker* contributor David Sedaris was

tour 1

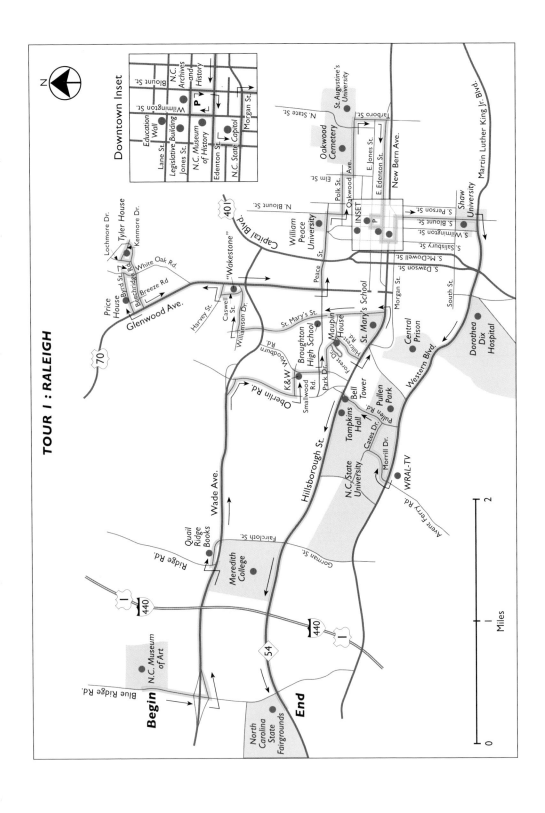

TOUR 1 : RALEIGH

Downtown Inset

N

Education Wall
Legislative Building
Lane St.
Jones St.
Wilmington St.
N.C. Archives and History
Blount St.
N.C. Museum of History
P
Edenton St.
N.C. State Capitol
Morgan St.

70
401
401

Lochmore Dr.
Tyler House
Kenmore Dr.
Price House
White Oak Rd.
Byrd St.
Beechridge Rd.
Breeze Rd.
Glenwood Ave.

Capital Blvd.

William Peace University

St. Augustine's University
Oakwood Cemetery
N. State St.
Tarboro St.
E. Jones St.
Oakwood Ave.
E. Edenton St.
New Bern Ave.

Polk St.
Elm St.
N. Blount St.

Martin Luther King Jr. Blvd.

Peace St.

INSET
P
S. Salisbury St.
S. Wilmington St.
S. Blount St.
S. Person St.
Shaw University

S. McDowell St.
S. Dawson St.
South St.

"Wakestone"
Harvey St.
Caswell St.
Williamson Dr.
St. Mary's St.
Broughton High School
Woodburn Rd.
Maupin House
Forest Dr.
Hillcrest Rd.
St. Mary's School
Morgan St.
Central Prison
Dorothea Dix Hospital

Oberlin Rd.
K&W
Smallwood Rd.
Park Dr.
Bell Tower
Pullen Park
Pullen Rd.
Western Blvd.

Wade Ave.

Quail Ridge Books
Ridge Rd.
Faircloth St.
Meredith College
Gorman St.
Hillsborough St.
N.C. State University
Tompkins Hall
Cates Dr.
Morrill Dr.
WRAL-TV
Avent Ferry Rd.

I 440
I 440

54

Begin
Blue Ridge Rd.
N.C. Museum of Art
North Carolina State Fairgrounds

End

0   1   2
Miles

among those tapped for an essay. Sedaris attended Wake County public schools and visited the museum when it was still downtown, long before its present and magnificent incarnation on the west side of Raleigh.

■ NORTH CAROLINA MUSEUM OF ART

2110 Blue Ridge Road

Each year our elementary school class took a field trip to the North Carolina Museum of Art. To prepare us for our visit, the board of education sent us a roving arts ambassador, a trained cultural cheerleader. To our fifth-grade class this person arrived in the form of one Mrs. Kingman. This was a woman who favored floor-length capes and appeared to wear all of her jewelry at the same time. She had about her the air of a middle-aged man masquerading as a woman and having a very good time doing so. Mrs. Kingman claimed to adore the capitals of Europe, "the very idea of the Far East," and the livers of geese mashed into a paste and served upon crackers. We were enchanted. . . . "This is your cultural clubhouse and you're welcome to visit anytime you like," Mrs. Kingman said. "Each of you deserves to surround yourself with beautiful objects. Just don't touch anything or they'll have one of their goons break off your fingers. While we're at it, I advise you not to scream, shove one another down the staircase, or lean against the wall. You can't eat, drink, spit, or sit on the furniture. Other than that, I want you to make yourselves at home."—From "The Resurrection of Christ," by David Sedaris, in *The Store of Joys: Writers Celebrate the North Carolina Museum of Art's Fiftieth Anniversary*, edited by Huston Paschal (Winston-Salem: John F. Blair, in association with the North Carolina Museum of Art, 1997), 65.

Welcome to Raleigh! The Museum of Art is worth a half day at minimum and features a fine café and a gift shop with many good-looking books, including *The Store of Joys*.

Though bookstores along these literary trails are generally listed at the end of each tour, our next destination deserves a bit more limelight for its contribution to the spirit of generosity and mentorship that has characterized the North Carolina literary community over decades.

From the art museum parking area, turn left on Blue Ridge Road and proceed to Wade Avenue. Head east and turn left at the second traffic light to reach the Ridge Road Shopping Center.

When writer David Sedaris first toured the North Carolina Museum of Art as a grade school student, the facility was downtown on Morgan Street. Today's museum offers more than forty galleries in two buildings and a striking collection of works that are set outdoors around the 164-acre Museum Park on Blue Ridge Road. Courtesy North Carolina Museum of Art, North Carolina Department of Cultural Resources.

■ QUAIL RIDGE BOOKS AND MUSIC

Ridge Road Shopping Center

3522 Wade Avenue

This bookstore does not stop at specializing in the work of North Carolina authors. In ways that go far beyond peddling books, the store's founder, Nancy Olson, has helped any number of the state's best-known writers advance their careers.

When sales of Charles Frazier's *Cold Mountain* were initially slow (apparently because some booksellers did not like the cover), Olson invited Frazier—her friend of ten years—to do an in-store reading. With Olson's enthusiastic

Literary maven Nancy Olson welcomes readers to Quail Ridge Books and Music. The portrait in the background is of novelist Reynolds Price, painted by Beverly McIver, and the books in the foreground are a novel by Charles Frazier.

push, *Cold Mountain* quickly sold 6,000 copies at Quail Ridge alone. Volume orders from other booksellers started pouring in to the publisher.

Raleigh writer Angela Davis-Gardner was struggling to find a publisher for her fourth novel, *Plum Wine*. Olson read and loved the manuscript, so she sent it immediately to a New York City literary agent. Before long, the agent sold it to Random House, which gave the author a two-book contract going forward and arranged to bring her previous novels back into print.

A small Christian house in Indiana published Jan Karon's first book, *At Home in Mitford*. A friend brought Olson the first edition, and after reading it, she sent it along to the same New York agent. The rest, as they say, is literary history. Several subsequent titles in Karon's Mitford series have made their way to the top of the *New York Times* best-seller list.

Olson's eye for excellence led National Public Radio commentator Susan Stamberg to call the store for new book recommendations one year. Novello Press, in Charlotte, had just published Ron Rash's first novel, *One Foot in Eden*. On Olson's suggestion, Stamberg mentioned the book on the radio show *Week-*

end Edition. Instantly, Rash had calls from three major publishing houses and soon landed an agent to represent him.

When Quail Ridge hosts a reading, the audience can swell to more than 500 patrons. Tom Wolfe, Elizabeth Edwards, and Raleigh natives David and Amy Sedaris have been among the writers whom Quail Ridge has hosted to overflow crowds, which leads in a quirky way to our third destination.

Take Wade Avenue east and exit in about a mile at Oberlin Road; turn right and watch for Smallwood Road on the left, leading into Cameron Village. Turn left on Smallwood and then right on Woodburn to reach another literary hotspot, the K&W Cafeteria.

■ K&W CAFETERIA

511 Woodburn Road

Before the days of Starbucks and bookstores with cappuccino machines, there was the cafeteria—the hangout of choice for writers in Raleigh. Carrie Knowles remembers when the K&W wasn't the only cafeteria in Cameron Village. She has a story to tell about Ballantine's, a cafeteria in this neighborhood that closed in 1999.

> When I first moved to Raleigh more than thirty years ago, I was lucky enough to make Virginia Grier's "list." Virginia recruited local writers to be judges for the Raleigh Fine Arts Society Literary Contest for high school students. She was the consummate southern lady with the most genteel of southern drawls. You felt honored to work for her. Plus, if you were a judge, you got to join the winning writers and their families at the banquet in the Confederate Room of Ballantine's Cafeteria in Cameron Village.
>
> Ballantine's was one of those grand southern cafeterias where you could eat fried everything and overcooked vegetables until your heart begged for a cleansing taste of congealed salad or a simple slice of chocolate chess pie. At that first banquet, I embraced the joy of eating chess pie and fried okra with a room full of gifted writers, young and old. The food was worthy of a line or two in a fried chicken poem, but the real treat of the evening was watching the generosity and genuine support the judges offered the young people we were celebrating.
> —Used by permission of Carrie Knowles

With Ballantine's gone, Raleigh novelist and short-story writer Kim Church takes to the K&W as her place of refuge and inspiration. Church's short story

"Cafeteria Lady" is about fear and aging, inspired by Yeats's poem "The Wild Swans at Coole." For Church's narrator, the swans take the form of an elderly hostess modeled after the late Myrna Morton, who worked here for years.

> The cafeteria lady takes my tray. She is old, with hunched shoulders, a feathery mustache, gray hair done up in a net. Her eyes are small and dark, darting, seeing everything at once. She has many jobs. She greets customers, helps them find tables when the room is crowded, which it always is at lunchtime—shoppers, store clerks, tradespeople, retirees from Cameron Village, office workers like me, but never anyone I know, so I'm safe here, no threat of conversation. It's best to avoid conversation after therapy, the same way you don't go swimming right after a meal. You need time to digest.
>
> Some customers need help setting their food on tables. Some expect her to fetch condiments. She can gauge exactly how much attention each of us needs.
>
> She checks my drinking glass. "Sweetened?" she asks, in case I want refills.
>
> "Yes."
>
> I can't imagine a more perfect hostess. Or a more unlikely one. Because all the while she's greeting customers and setting tables and collecting trays and ferrying condiments and tea pitchers, she is also shaking uncontrollably. She has a condition that causes tremors in her hands and arms. Her elbows shudder like baby-bird wings.
>
> —From "Cafeteria Lady," by Kim Church, in *Prime Number Magazine* 11 (2011), http://www.primenumbermagazine.com/Issue11_Fiction_Kim Church.html.

From here, follow Woodburn south through Cameron Street. Cross Clark Avenue and then turn left onto Park Drive and take the third right onto East Forest Drive.

■ **ARMISTEAD MAUPIN HOUSE**

312 East Forest Drive

Writer Armistead Maupin grew up in Raleigh. He lived with his family in this rented house from the age of three until he turned seven, when his parents bought a house in another neighborhood nearby. Maupin graduated from Broughton High School in 1962 and earned his BA from the University of North

Carolina at Chapel Hill (UNC–Chapel Hill), where he wrote for the *Daily Tar Heel.* He served as a naval officer on river patrol in the Vietnam War and later worked for WRAL-TV. At the time, Maupin says, he was on board with the political views of the station manager, who was also a family friend—future senator Jesse Helms. Maupin later disavowed these conservative views and took up the cause of gay rights.

In 1976, after working as an Associated Press reporter in the San Francisco bureau, Maupin began his enormously popular serialized novel set in San Francisco. *Tales of the City* first appeared in the *Pacific Sun* and later in the *San Francisco Chronicle* and eventually grew to six volumes. It was adapted for a television miniseries starring Olivia Dukakis and Laura Linney. Maupin was also one of the first writers to address the subject of AIDS, in his novel *Babycakes*, published in 1983.

Return to Park Drive and turn right. Then take the first right on Hillcrest Road and follow that all the way to Hillsborough Street. Turn left and the next site is on the left.

■ ST. MARY'S SCHOOL

900 Hillsborough Street

The Lay family took meals in the college dining hall, and of course all two hundred girls stared at their visitor. Very self-conscious, Wolfe wrote that, "shot with four hundred arrows," he tried to "slide and sidle" to his place at the table, but in fact, according to Elizabeth Lay, who was also a student at the university, "he didn't seem bothered by it at all. He took everything in his stride." All the Lays liked him, and one of the younger daughters developed a schoolgirl crush on the visitor, particularly admiring "the way his hair curls up front."—From *Look Homeward: A Life of Thomas Wolfe*, by David Herbert Donald (New York: Little, Brown, 1987), 44.

Thomas Wolfe visited Raleigh many times as an undergraduate at Chapel Hill. This passage describes the impact of the lanky six-foot-six-inch man as he tried inconspicuously to share a meal with the entire female student body at St. Mary's. Wolfe came to this campus as the guest of his college roommate, George Lay, whose father was the school's rector. George's sister Elizabeth, mentioned here, would become the wife of playwright Paul Green, and the couple formed a friendship with Wolfe that lasted for the rest of his life. Today St. Mary's is a boarding and day school for college-bound girls.

Among Triangle writers, Anna Wooten Hawkins was a beloved poet. She was born in Kinston, studied at the University of North Carolina at Greensboro, and taught at St. Mary's in the 1980s and 1990s. When she discovered that her life would be shortened by ovarian cancer, she wrote this poem about her connection to the City of Oaks.

BURIAL
You live in a town of trees
under your childhood.
The ground is one star
purpling into violets.
Ants do not know your name.

Then you become acquainted.
Cozy moles greet your bones.
Dirt borrows your skin
like a friendly neighbor,
and soon the whole complex
signals you a resident,
permanent and forever.

For the second time,
you belong.
—From *Pembroke Magazine* 35 (2003): 152.
   Used by permission of Tom Hawkins.

Proceed east on Hillsborough Street and take the first left on St. Mary's Street. In seven blocks, the next stop is on the left.

■ BROUGHTON HIGH SCHOOL

723 St. Mary's Street

Then in my third year of high school, with a record of excellent teachers behind me, I encountered a singular and powerful teacher of literature and composition who ignited my engine and aimed me onward. Her name was Phyllis Peacock, and her method was inimitable. Through some two decades of prior teaching, she'd developed the ability to recognize a young man or woman who was inexplicably fascinated by the working of language. Then she'd give him or her appropriate assignments to stretch present limits, correct the obvious blunders of detail and focus and keep up a steady, if agreeably hard-nosed, line of praise to lure them on.—From *Learning a Trade: A Craftsman's Notebooks, 1955–1997*, by Reynolds Price (Durham: Duke University Press, 1998), xi–xii.

Since opening in 1929, this stalwart institution has trained many fine citizens, but few among its faculty have been so fondly remembered as Broughton English teacher Phyllis Peacock, who taught not only novelist Reynolds Price but also his younger brother, William. At his death in 2011, the *New York Times* called Reynolds Price "one of the most important voices in modern Southern literature."

For his part, William Price spent his career at the North Carolina Division of Archives and History, which, at his retirement, in 1995, was the largest state

Broughton High School was an early influence in the lives of many North Carolina writers. The school was named for Needham Broughton, a prosperous printer and avid supporter of the Wake County Schools at the turn of the twentieth century.

historical agency in the nation. He was involved in the creation of a shelf of books about state history, including the five-volume series *The Way We Lived in North Carolina*, which is now available in a single volume from the University of North Carolina Press.

Nearly a decade after Reynolds Price's graduation from Broughton, Peacock also inspired soon-to-be-novelist Anne Tyler, whose family had moved from Celo, in western North Carolina, to Raleigh. Longtime Raleigh poet-in-the-schools Mary C. Snotherly also had the benefit of Peacock's genius.

From Broughton, turn left on St. Mary's (heading away from downtown). Cross Wade Avenue and turn right at the next intersection onto Williamson Drive. In .3 miles, turn left onto Caswell Street to see a house that once belonged to a most prolific family of writers.

■ "WAKESTONE"

1520 Caswell Street

Josephus Daniels, editor of the *Raleigh News and Observer* and secretary of the navy under Woodrow Wilson, lived in this house from 1920 until his death in 1948. In 1950, the house was sold to the Raleigh Masonic Lodge.

Daniels was the father of essayist and newspaper editor Jonathan Daniels, whose lively works on North Carolina are excerpted in the Mountain and Piedmont volumes of *Literary Trails*. In 1937, he moved his family into the spacious brick house at 1540 Caswell (adjacent to the Masonic parking lot) and lived there except for the years when he served as press secretary to President Truman. He sold the house in 1965 and retired to Hilton Head Island, in South Carolina.

Jonathan Daniels was a classmate of Thomas Wolfe at UNC–Chapel Hill. Daniels reviewed *Look Homeward, Angel* upon its publication, in 1936, and said that while it was vividly written, it was full of "lurid details of blood and sex and cruelty." Daniels had taken offense at Wolfe's criticism of the South, and of North Carolina, in particular.

Wolfe nevertheless came to visit his classmate in Raleigh. According to Wolfe biographer Joanne Marshall Mauldin, the six-foot-six-inch writer "had plunked his bulk in a fragile antique chair, giving his host a tale to tell in perpetuity with more than a hint of malice. Miraculously Daniels's chair had held" (from *Thomas Wolfe: When Do the Atrocities Begin?* [Knoxville: University of Tennessee Press, 2007], 133).

Jonathan Daniels's eldest daughter would have been nine the year Wolfe visited. Elizabeth Daniels Squire became an award-winning mystery writer who lived and wrote in western North Carolina until her death, in 2001.

Jonathan's daughter Lucy was a precocious writer whose first novel, *Caleb, My Son*, was published when she was only twenty-two. She was summoned to New York to appear on the *Today Show* and earned a sheaf of glowing reviews nationwide for her insightful and daring effort to write about the simultaneous fear and excitement in Raleigh's African American community in the wake of the Supreme Court's *Brown v. Board of Education* decision.

Lucy Daniels was undoubtedly familiar with the employees who worked in service to her grandfather at the large house next door. The novel intimately depicts the tragic conflict between Asa, chauffeur to a wealthy white family in "Millboro," and his son Caleb, a railroad worker and clandestine civil rights activist.

> Caleb, himself, never stopped to think what Asa's plans for him might have been. He knew, of course; down in the depths of his soul he knew without even being conscious of it. He never allowed himself to be conscious of things like that.
>
> He did love his parents, too—though he never let himself admit that either. He loved them and, despite himself, he respected them. But at the same time he regarded them—especially his father—with pity. Was it

not painful to be barely able to read, to be forced to dress up like a trained monkey every day, to have to bow and scrape to another man just to keep your family in food and clothes? And what seemed even more tragic to Caleb was the fact that Asa didn't see his own plight; that he did not seek to remedy it, nor even allow others to. He called it the will of God and said it was the colored man's duty to accept without questioning.

—From *Caleb, My Son*, by Lucy Daniels (New York: J. B. Lippincott, 1956), 35.

Following her instant success, Lucy Daniels, like her father before her, earned a Guggenheim Fellowship. She published her second novel, *High on a Hill*, in 1961 and then suffered a long writer's block. To overcome it, she went back to school and dedicated herself to the study of psychology. In 1989, working as a clinical psychologist in Raleigh, she created the Lucy Daniels Foundation to help artists, writers, and other gifted people explore the roots of their creativity through psychoanalysis. Her memoir, *With a Woman's Voice: A Writer's Struggle for Emotional Freedom*, was published in 2001.

■ PRICE AND TYLER HOUSES

2311 Byrd Street and 2512 Kenmore Drive

From here, the tour continues with a drive by the houses where Reynolds Price and Anne Tyler lived as teenagers.

From the Daniels house, continue north on Caswell and turn right on Harvey Street, then left on Glenwood Avenue. In .8 miles, turn right on Byrd Street. The Price house is on the left, past Breeze Road. This is the last place Reynolds Price lived with his family. He left in 1952 to start his freshman year at Duke University, in Durham.

Anne Tyler—who would be among Price's first creative writing students at Duke, where he returned following graduate studies as a Rhodes Scholar at Oxford—lived close by, at 2512 Kenmore Drive, during her high school years. She graduated from Broughton in 1958. Tyler has published more than twenty books and has been honored with the Pulitzer Prize, the National Book Critics Circle Award, and the Pen/Faulkner Award.

Follow Byrd to its end at White Oak Road and turn right. Take the next left onto Beechridge Road and then the first left onto Lochmore. Kenmore is the next street to the right, and the Tyler house is on the right, set high on a hill.

Retrace your route back to Beechridge. Follow it to Glenwood and turn left. Continue on Glenwood south 1.5 miles to Peace Street and turn left. Cross under Capital Boulevard. William Peace University is up the hill on the left.

■ WILLIAM PEACE UNIVERSITY

15 East Peace Street

Formerly Peace College and restricted to women, this institution is front and center in an autobiographical short story by Asheville native Gail Godwin. Though she would graduate from UNC–Chapel Hill, Godwin completed her first two undergraduate years here to be near her estranged father, who lived in Smithfield. In the short story, the narrator, now many years beyond school, is sitting on an airplane next to a chatty woman who designs admissions materials. The woman starts talking about Lovegood without knowing the narrator is an alumna:

> "I've just returned from this junior college in North Carolina that you wouldn't believe," she told me. "In this day and time it's an anachronism, that's what it is. The girls there . . . well, they're still girls, for one thing: they think of themselves as girls. And they're good girls; they walk around that beautiful campus looking too good to be true. I wouldn't be surprised if many of them were still virgins. No I'm not kidding. This school is a hotbed of all the old virtues: you know, duty, loyalty, charity, respect for all the old traditions of religion and society. The place is actually called Lovegood College. 'Love good.' And you should see their graduation ceremony, I was there for it. The 'girls' wear white, off-the-shoulder gowns, with hoops, and each girl carries two dozen long-stemmed roses. It's in the evening, and after they get their diplomas, they go out to the fountain in front of this gigantic old antebellum mansion with columns four stories high, and each 'girl' throws one dozen roses into the fountain. Then she hands over her second bunch to her mother—or some aunt or godmother if the mother is dead—and the mother graciously takes out one single rose and gives it back to her daughter."—From "Old Lovegood Girls," in *Evenings at Five*, by Gail Godwin (New York: Random House, 2004), 163.

Godwin's fiction details precisely the Peace College tradition at commencement. Today, however, men are admitted.

Continue ahead on Peace Street and turn right on North Blount Street. Along this historic lane are a number of elegant mansions, including the governor's, all dating from the 1800s. The social strata exemplified by these houses is the subject of some ridicule by author Barbara Neely, who was born in Pennsylvania but spent significant time in North Carolina working as a social justice activist and writer for *Southern Exposure* magazine and Africa News Service in Durham in the 1970s and 1980s. Her ironically titled *Blanche White* mystery series features a brash African American protagonist with a sense of humor about race and class. In one novel, Blanche picks up some extra cash working with a local catering company:

> Tonight's affair was at the home of Jason Morris and his wife, Nancy. They lived in the Morris clan's ancestral mansion, which along with most of its furniture, had been built by slaves. Everybody in Farleigh knew of the Morris family, its being one of the state's oldest and including such pillars of the South as slavers, Indian-killers, Confederate generals, and diehard segregationists. But Ardell said this generation saw itself as the leaders of the New South. Of course, they still occasionally named their sons Braxton and Zebulon, in honor of their Confederate, slaver ancestors, and they still didn't invite their string of mulatto relatives with the same looks and last name to sit down at the family table.
>
> "New South," Ardell had told Blanche, "means sending their kids to integrated schools—long as ain't no more than one or two colored children present—instead of sending them to all-white Christian academies like they used to do. New South is celebrating Martin Luther King Day without mentioning that their daddies wanted to kill him, and hiring outfits like us for a lot less than they pay the big white caterers."
>
> —From *Blanche Passes Go*, by Barbara Neely (New York: Penguin, 2001), 17.

Turn left on Polk Street and note the Burning Coal Theater at the historic Murphey School. Plays by North Carolina writers are regularly produced and often premiered here.

Proceed to Elm Street and turn right. You are in the Victorian section known as Oakwood. In one block, turn left on Oakwood Avenue, which leads directly into a sprawling cemetery on the left. A map to help you locate the following graves is available at the cemetery office, which is open on weekdays.

■ OAKWOOD CEMETERY

701 Oakwood Avenue

Seven governors and many state and city leaders are interred in this private cemetery, which dates from 1869. One of the most fascinating quasi-literary figures buried here is the first husband of Georgia novelist Margaret Mitchell. Berrien "Red" Upshaw was a Raleigh native who went to college in Atlanta and met the young Miss Mitchell shortly after her social debut. Already known as a gambler, sometime bootlegger, and general scoundrel, Upshaw wooed Mitchell away from another suitor named John Marsh, a newspaper copy editor. Upshaw and Mitchell married in Atlanta in 1922 and honeymooned at the Grove Park Inn, in Asheville.

Because of Upshaw's costly habits, Mitchell soon had to take a job at the *Atlanta Journal Sunday Magazine*, where, once again, she came under the influence of John Marsh, the man who would become her second husband. Mitchell's marriage to Upshaw was short and apparently volatile. After their divorce, he continued his gambling and married twice more. His death in Texas, in 1949, was ruled a suicide.

Seven months later, Mitchell was hit by a speeding taxi in Atlanta while crossing Peachtree Street and killed. Many literary scholars have attributed the traits of the character Rhett Butler in Mitchell's novel, *Gone with the Wind*, to Upshaw, who is buried in Section A.

Josephus Daniels, patriarch of the literary Daniels clan, is also buried in Section A, at the far corner of the cemetery's Oakwood Avenue perimeter.

Vermont Connecticut Royster (cousin of the popular big-band leader Kay Kyser, of Rocky Mount) is buried near the center of the Confederate Cemetery. Royster was a Raleigh native who studied at UNC–Chapel Hill before joining the *Wall Street Journal*, in 1936. There he worked his way up to editor (1958–71) and won two Pulitzer Prizes for his commentaries.

Elizabeth Edwards, wife of former U.S. presidential candidate John Edwards, is buried in the center of the Forest Section. Her literary success came near the end of her life, with her 2009 memoir, *Resilience*.

Lawrence Rudner, a popular professor of journalism, world literature, Holocaust literature, and creative writing at North Carolina State University, is buried in Raleigh Hebrew Cemetery, at 450 North State Street, adjacent to Oakwood. His grave is on the right side of the main drive, about 150 feet down. Rudner wrote two novels: *The Magic We Do Here* (1988) and *Memory's Tailor* (1998). Rudner finished the second novel shortly before he was diagnosed with cancer. He died at the age of forty-eight. Rudner's colleagues, writers John Kessel and Susan Ketchin, edited the book for posthumous publication.

■ ST. AUGUSTINE'S UNIVERSITY

1315 Oakwood Avenue

Continue east on Oakwood Avenue to reach St. Augustine's University, a private, historically black school founded in the Reconstruction era and affili-

Shown here in 1898 with their whole family, Annie Elizabeth "Bessie" Delany and Sarah Louise "Sadie" Delany were more than a hundred years old in 1993 when their best-selling oral history, Having Our Say, *was published. The sisters were raised on the campus of St. Augustine's College, where their father, Henry Beard Delany, was vice president. From* Having Our Say: The Delany Sisters' First 100 Years, *by Sarah L. Delany, A. Elizabeth Delany, and Amy Hill Hearth. Used by permission of Amy Hill Hearth,* © 2012.

ated with the Episcopal Church. It began as St. Augustine's Normal and Collegiate Institute, and one of the earliest and most distinguished students (later a teacher here) was Anna Julia Haywood Cooper. She was born into slavery in Raleigh and ultimately earned a doctoral degree from the Sorbonne. Cooper was a poet, polemical writer, and advocate of women's rights and the rights of African Americans.

Sisters Sarah and Elizabeth Delany grew up on the campus of St. Augustine's. Their 1993 oral history, *Having Our Say: The Delany Sisters' First 100 Years*, written by Amy Hill Hearth, a *New York Times* journalist, became the basis for a Broadway play and a CBS miniseries. Their father, Henry Beard Delany, was the first African American elected bishop in the Episcopal Church and served as a vice president of St. Augustine's. The sisters' oral history depicts Raleigh before and during the Jim Crow era, when they elected to move to Harlem in

New York City as conditions continued to worsen for African Americans in the South.

> Many fine, young colored people graduated from Saint Aug's and went on to share what they had learned with countless others. Growing up in this atmosphere, among three hundred or so college students, reading and writing and thinking was as natural for us as sleeping and eating. We had a blessed childhood, which was unusual in those days for colored children. It was the rare child that got such schooling!
>
> But since we were girls, our every move was chaperoned. All little girls and young women were chaperoned in those days. That's because things hadn't improved much since slavery days as far as the right of colored women and girls to be unmolested. If something bad had been done to us, and our Papa had complained, they'd have hung him. That's the way it was.
>
> —From *Having Our Say: The Delany Sisters' First 100 Years*, by Sarah L. Delany, A. Elizabeth Delany, and Amy Hill Hearth (New York: Dell, 1993), 62.

At the corner of Oakwood Avenue and North Tarboro Street, turn right on North Tarboro. Follow it three full blocks to East Edenton and turn right. Turn right again on North Wilmington Street. To visit the next sites, park in the public lot at the corner of North Wilmington and East Jones streets, adjacent to the North Carolina Museum of History and across from the North Carolina Archives and History building. Plan to spend some time exploring both of these treasuries of state history and literature. (See Literary Landmarks at the end of this tour.)

■ *EDUCATION WALL*

Stroll through or walk around the building that houses the North Carolina General Assembly at 16 West Jones Street, across from the Museum of History and the Museum of Natural Sciences. In the grassy courtyard behind the legislature's headquarters, you can see the thirty-by-ninety-foot *Education Wall*, created in 1990 by Durham artist Vernon Pratt. The wall is a public art project that celebrates the state's Department of Public Instruction, just behind. The pink granite wall and the native stone benches present quotations by North Carolina writers, including George Moses Horton, Reynolds Price ("by example, almost never by words," referring to his teacher Phyllis Peacock), Doris Betts, Jonathan Daniels, Fred Chappell ("You are a child / You are / suitable / to be / awed"), and musical notations by North Carolina jazz great John Coltrane. The

The thirty-by-ninety-foot Education Wall, *created by artist Vernon Pratt, features quotations from North Carolina writers George Moses Horton, Doris Betts, Fred Chappell, and Reynolds Price. The benches in front of the wall present other literary excerpts and information about the wall and its red granite.*

words "teach" and "learn" are at the top of the wall, written in the Cherokee Indian syllabary.

Pratt often played with words through his primary medium of painting. He died in a bicycle accident in 2000. His daughter Jane, a writer, was the founding editor of the popular *Sassy* magazine in the 1980s and *Jane* magazine in the 1990s.

From the parking lot on East Jones Street, turn right. At the next corner, turn right on North Blount Street and in one block, turn right on East Edenton to take in the North Carolina State Capitol building, built in 1840.

■ NORTH CAROLINA STATE CAPITOL BUILDING

1 East Edenton Street

Several novels have included this striking building as a backdrop, and Raleigh nonfiction writer Scott Huler tells the story of the site in a book entirely devoted to the city's infrastructure:

Raleigh's state capitol sits at the top of a slight rise in the terrain, surrounded by a gridwork of streets, largely because an enterprising settler named Joel Lane appears to have gotten some commissioners from the brand-new state of North Carolina drunk enough to buy his property. It's a long story, plausibly true, and beloved by Raleighans. After the Revolution, legislators of the new state needed to plant their capital somewhere that would offend neither the coastal cities in the east nor the Appalachian settlers in the west. The great middle of the state was largely unsettled; Wake County, in 1792, still lacked a town of any description. The local Tuscarora Indians never had a settlement here, and even the European farmers working their way west seem to have found little here of interest: Of the 1,000 acres Lane eventually sold to the state, three quarters were virgin forest.

With six sites under consideration, including several on the Neuse River, the commissioners remained deadlocked until they spent a night at the home of Lane, who allegedly served them a mixture of bourbon, sugar, and cherries called Cherry Bounce. The next morning the commissioners voted to buy Lane's 1,000 acres, which were several miles from the Neuse.

—From *On the Grid: A Plot of Land, an Average Neighborhood, and the Systems That Make Our World Work*, by Scott Huler (New York: Rodale, 2010), 14.

Drive around the capitol building and turn left on Morgan Street and then right on South Blount. The next destination is six blocks south.

■ SHAW UNIVERSITY

118 East South Street

Baptist-affiliated Shaw University is the oldest historically black college in the South. It is the alma mater of Lenard D. Moore, the first African American president of the Haiku Society of America. Moore received the Raleigh Medal of Arts for his service teaching creative writing in public schools and as the founder of the Carolina African American Writers' Collective. He taught at North Carolina State and Shaw and is now on the faculty of Mount Olive College.

RHYTHM

Welcome to Southeast Raleigh,
where the tar-colored night
sifts through the upstairs window

where the square fan
on the sill
agitates the heat.

Welcome to the siren's wail,
the solitary person sitting
on the high-back chair.

The desk touches
the June calendar,
a photo of the sun blazes.

Welcome to the pen
from a local dentist
that drills these words,

pen that sweats
like marbles held too long
in a closed hand.

Welcome to whatever rhythm
swings on the hinges
of the door of this city.
—"Rhythm," by Lenard D. Moore, in *Triangle Lifestyle
Magazine*, March–April 2002, 46.

■ WRAL-TV

2619 Western Boulevard

From South Blount, turn right onto Martin Luther King Jr. Boulevard and follow it until it becomes Western Boulevard. The route passes Dorothea Dix Hospital on the left and North Carolina's Central Prison and Pullen Park on the right. Ahead on the left is Raleigh's oldest television station, WRAL, on which Charlotte writer Robert Inman loosely based the setting of his comedic novel, *Captain Saturday*.

Will worked at his computer in the Weather Center, a spacious room just off the station's newsroom. Putting together a weathercast was part meteorology, part graphic design. Will was not a meteorologist, not in the academic sense of the word, but he had studied and taken correspondence courses and earned the Seal of Approval of the American Meteorological

Association. The best thing he had going, though, was experience. Twenty years on the air in Raleigh, watching the peculiarities of the local weather, the way systems would sweep in from the Midwest and hit the mountains over by the Tennessee line and do strange things. Will didn't always agree with what the meteorologists at the Weather Service said. Usually, he was right. —From *Captain Saturday*, by Robert Inman (Boston: Little, Brown, 2003), 19.

Over the years, the multitalented staff at WRAL (Bill Leslie and Amanda Lamb, for example) have ventured into the world of print.

At the traffic light past the TV station, turn right on Morrill Drive to enter the campus of North Carolina State University, a land-grant institution established in 1887. Take the next right on Cates Drive and follow it to Pullen Road and turn left. Pullen follows the eastern edge of campus and passes some of the oldest buildings here, including the university's Memorial Belltower. Turn left on Hillsborough Street toward the commercial district that caters to State students.

■ TOMPKINS HALL

2211 Hillsborough Street

On the left, past the bell tower, is Tompkins Hall. If this structure looks like a cotton mill, it's because it was built to look like one. But text has replaced textiles in this building for many years now. Tompkins is headquarters to the university's vital creative writing program, which has trained countless novelists, poets, and nonfiction writers, including Kaye Gibbons, T. R. Pearson, Haven Kimmel, Pamela Duncan, and Darnell Arnoult.

This program was built on the shoulders of novelist and poet Guy Owen (see Tour 5) and Richard Walser. For decades, Walser was the state's foremost literary historian. He wrote and edited more than thirty books and pamphlets—notably poetry and short-story anthologies; biographies of Bernice Kelly Harris, Thomas Wolfe, and Inglis Fletcher; and the slim but jam-packed *Literary North Carolina*, which has been a constant resource in the development of *Literary Trails*.

From the 1960s onward, State's creative writing program advanced, hosting on its faculty such talents as novelist Lee Smith, poet Gerald Barrax, and scholars Lucinda McKeithan and James Clark. Today, Jill McCorkle, Thomas David Lisk, Wilton Barnhardt, Dorianne Laux, John Kessel, and John Balaban, among others, continue the strong literary tradition here.

This poem by longtime Raleigh resident Richard Krawiec, a seasoned publisher and writer who has taught in college classrooms, prisons, and homeless shelters across the state, offers a meditation on what it is like to grow older in a town perpetually refreshed by the presence of college students.

CONFLICT OF SEASONS
Winter still fights, won't shed
its icy evenings though March
insists on daytime 60s.

The students I pass
on Hillsborough Street wear
shorts and t-shirts, gather
under stage-sulfur glare
of streetlights, laugh and punch
each other in the arms.

I have become the man
in a sweater who sits quietly
in Stewart Theater, Cup A Joe,
shirt buttoned to the neck
overwear wrapped against
the threat of a chill.

I flex my fingers against
the stiff arthritis of damp ground,
tell myself there is no conflict,
I can still run with the students.
—Used by permission of Richard Krawiec

Continue ahead on Hillsborough Street to see one more important bastion of literary training, Meredith College, two miles ahead.

■ MEREDITH COLLEGE

3800 Hillsborough Street
This Baptist school dates from 1891 and has grown to be one of the largest women's colleges in the nation. It is also known for its graduate program in business, which is coeducational.

For many years, Meredith students had the benefit of studying with poet Betty Adcock, a winner of the North Carolina Award for Literature (the state government's highest honor). Her work is featured in Tour 10. Suzanne Newton, author of young-adult fiction, also taught here. Her work is excerpted in Tour 16. Raleigh essayist Suzanne Britt has been on the faculty for more than two decades. Meredith's annual creative writing workshop for women and the Meredith Young Writers' Camp for girls are popular summer programs on campus. Meredith's Friends of the Library sponsors a spring dinner (a benefit for the Carlyle Campbell Library) that has featured many North Carolina writers as keynote speakers.

From Meredith, continue ahead on Hillsborough Street past the North Carolina State veterinary school to our final stop on this tour.

■ NORTH CAROLINA STATE FAIRGROUNDS

Every October these grounds draw visitors from across the state and beyond. Dorton Arena—with a roof like two dinner plates pitched at opposite angles and leaning on the rim of an invisible sink—is featured among many other familiar Raleigh landmarks in this poem the city commissioned in 1992 from Sally Buckner to celebrate its bicentennial year.

RALEIGH, MOVING THROUGH THE YEARS
The thousand acres purchased from Joel Lane
    now bristle with palatial offices,
    clustered condominiums, sprawling malls
    neighborhoods with Elizabethan names.
From the city's core, freeways stretch long fingers;
    a haze of blue exhaust veils the horizon.
Beneath the glowing globe of the Capitol dome,
    pigeons perch on Zeb Vance's shoulder,
    then rise, feathery iridescent blur,
    and swoop above the jaunty bronze Sir Walter
    presiding at the Civic Center doorway.
Briggs Hardware, a nineteenth-century sentinel
    mirrored in twenty-first-century towers,
    now houses artifacts of the city's story.
Oakwood's porches gleam in candlelight.
    The Auditorium shimmers, a rhythmic dazzle.
Where thousands gather in autumn celebration,
    Dorton Arena's curves carve the skyline.

Meanwhile, children cavort on the Pullen carousel.
    while raucous students caper on Hillsborough Street.
In sleek, sun-lit alabaster cubes,
    legislators swap their jokes and votes.
Saris and turbans mingle with jeans and suits;
    Dixie drawls, with Hispanic and Asian accents.
After too many years, black and white
    can share a meal, formulate a deal.
But the brisk pace of professional steps up the ladder
    is muffled by the scuffed shoes of the homeless.

In the ringing cacophony of grace and glitter,
    tradition and change and contradiction,
this city stands poised on the brink of tomorrow.
—Used by permission of Sally Buckner

North Carolina Museum of History

5 East Edenton Street

919-807-7900

http://ncmuseumofhistory.org

In addition to its permanent exhibition on the complete history of the state, this facility sponsors lectures, readings, and other special events of interest to readers and writers. The museum store has an excellent collection of books in all genres pertaining to the state's history and people.

North Carolina State Archives

109 East Jones Street

919-807-7310

http://www.archives.ncdcr.gov

Photographs, maps, films, organizational records, and even a statewide cemetery survey make this trove of materials a source of priceless information online and on-site for anyone interested in North Carolina lore.

Wake County Public Libraries

http://www.wakegov.com/libraries/

Literary activities (book clubs and writing workshops, for example) are scheduled year-round at the branches of the Wake County Public Library system. Check the website for listings and locations.

Reader's Corner

3201 Hillsborough Street

919-828-7024

This book and music store, like its affiliate in Asheville, has been around long enough to collect some amazing finds in used books. Jammed with bargains and first-edition surprises, it also benefits from proximity to North Carolina State.

Cary : Apex : Holly Springs : Fuquay-Varina : Angier : Buies Creek : Lillington : Sanford : Southern Pines : Aberdeen

Journey to the source: The North Carolina Literary Hall of Fame at the Weymouth Center for the Arts & Humanities, in Southern Pines. Explore the extraordinary literary connection between Cary and Aberdeen. Go deeper with a canoe trip on the Cape Fear.

Writers with a connection to this area: Malaika King Albrecht, Sherwood Anderson, Doris Betts, James Boyd, Mary Belle Campbell, Tim Downs, Clyde Edgerton, William Faulkner, F. Scott Fitzgerald, John Galsworthy, Paul Green, Ernest Hemingway, Patricia Hickman, David T. Manning, John P. Marquand, Jill McCorkle, Tim McLaurin, Hoke Norris, Walter Hines Page, T. R. Pearson, Sam Ragan, Leon Rooke, John Rowell, Sarah Shaber, Stephen E. Smith, Alexandra Sokoloff, June Spence, Julia Montgomery Street, Thomas Wolfe

We begin in Cary—currently North Carolina's seventh-largest city and one of the state's most culturally diverse communities. The town's growth spurt began in the 1960s, with the establishment of the Research Triangle Park, where pharmaceuticals, biotechnology ventures, and other innovative enterprises came together to tap the collective resources of nearby universities. Many bright and affluent researchers followed, and Cary is their hub.

Cary's old town tells a different kind of story. It is the birthplace of one of the most important figures in twentieth-century publishing.

Walter Hines Page, the eldest son of the town's founder, Allison Francis "Frank" Page, was born in 1855. His adult life was haunted by his boyhood memories of the coffins of Civil War casualties arriving regularly at the Cary train station and, later,

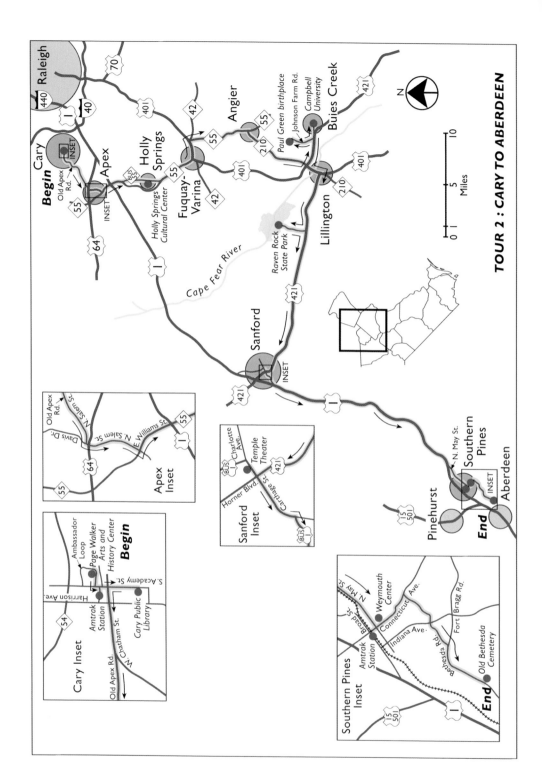

TOUR 2 : CARY TO ABERDEEN

N

Miles

0   1   5   10

Raleigh

440
70
1
40
I
55
64

Begin Cary
Old Apex Rd.
INSET

Apex
INSET

55
BUS 55
Holly Springs
55
Holly Springs Cultural Center

Fuquay-Varina
42

401

42

55

55

Angier

Paul Green birthplace
Johnson Farm Rd.
Campbell University

210

Buies Creek
421
421

401
Lillington
210
401

Raven Rock State Park

Cape Fear River

I

421

Sanford
421
INSET

421

I

Pinehurst
15
501

Southern Pines
N. May St.
INSET
End Aberdeen

Apex Inset
Old Apex Rd.
N. Salem St.
Davis Dr.
N. Salem St.
E. Williams St.
1
55
64
55

Begin
Cary Inset
54
Ambassador Loop
Page Walker Arts and History Center
Harrison Ave.
Amtrak Station
Cary Public Library
S. Academy St.
W. Chatham St.
Old Apex Rd.

Sanford Inset
BUS 1
Charlotte Ave.
Temple Theater
421
Horner Blvd.
Carthage St.
BUS

Southern Pines Inset
15
501
I
Broad St.
N. May St.
Amtrak Station
Weymouth Center
Connecticut Ave.
Indiana Ave.
Bethesda Rd.
Fort Bragg Rd.
End
Old Bethesda Cemetery

Town of Cary founder Allison Francis Page, father of writer and publisher Walter Hines Page, built this structure as a hotel in 1868. It was restored and converted in 1985 to serve as the Page-Walker Arts and History Center in the heart of downtown.

of William Tecumseh Sherman's troops coming to his family's home, hunting for the spoils of war.

Following studies at Trinity College (now Duke University), Randolph-Macon College, and Johns Hopkins University, Page pursued a career in journalism in the Midwest and in New York City. He returned to his home state in 1882 and bought the newspaper that would eventually become the *Raleigh News and Observer*. Page wrote passionate articles urging the South to overcome its losses in the Civil War and get on with the business of improving education and welcoming industry. He also involved himself in the establishment of an institution devoted to practical disciplines: the school that would become North Carolina State University.

Unfortunately, Page's editorial messages did not sit well with local readers, and he once again relocated, eventually to Boston, where he took the reins at the *Atlantic Monthly*. He soon doubled the magazine's readership.

In 1899, with his literary star in ascendance, Page cofounded Doubleday, Page and Company, a major international publishing house that claimed Rudyard Kipling in its early stable of writers. He also launched *World's Work*, a news magazine considered innovative for its early adoption of photojournalism. Through all these venues, Page continued to champion education for citizens of all races and urged a more progressive agenda for the South, though he deliberately avoided the muckraking tactics of other prominent writers of his era.

In 1913, Page left publishing to assume the U.S. ambassadorship to Great Britain and soon found himself urging Woodrow Wilson and Congress to declare war on Germany. The stresses of wartime diplomacy likely contributed to his death, only a month after World War I ended.

During his lifetime, Page published three books—the last, a novel. His collected letters, posthumously edited, earned Pulitzer Prizes—the first volume in 1923 and the second in 1929.

Page writes vividly about the Wake County landscape of his childhood through the narrative voice of his semiautobiographical novel, which chronicles the struggles of a Harvard-educated man who rejects Confederate nostalgia and strives to reform his home state. Here, Page describes a night when the central character, Nicholas Worth, comes home on horseback from a visit in Raleigh with his grandfather:

> The night and the earth and the pine forest—when you come in direct contact with all these at once, you feel yourself akin to fundamental things, especially if you are a boy and your alert imagination is quickened by every sound and perfume. And you will carry the odour of the earth and of the trees in your memory at whatever distance you may live from them and however many years thereafter. Go into the woods at night now, if you are old, and you will be likely to recall a road and a wood that gave forth the same odours half a century ago; and you may even conjure up some particular night and recall with distinctness all that happened then.—From *The Southerner*, by Walter Hines Page (New York: Doubleday, Page, 1909), 29–30.

■ PAGE-WALKER ARTS AND HISTORY CENTER

119 Ambassador Loop off North Academy Street
919-460-4963

Located east of the Cary city hall in the heart of old town, the Page-Walker Hotel was built in 1868 by Walter Hines Page's father. It has been restored and furnished with Page family memorabilia to serve as the town's heritage museum and art gallery and as a conference and wedding venue. The only other surviving building from the Page estate—a smokehouse dating from 1840—was moved to the site from elsewhere and is surrounded by a native herb garden.

Explore Cary's old town and its charming collection of historic buildings and contemporary public art. Then head south on Academy Street, noting the restored Amtrak station on the right. Cross Chatham Street. In the Cary Public Library, at 310 South Academy, you can find at least nine novels by present-day Cary writer and cartoonist Tim Downs, whose Bug Man novels center on the exploits of Nick Polchak, a forensic entomologist from North Carolina State who travels the country solving murders and other mysteries using his knowledge of insect behavior.

Head out of town to the west on Chatham Street, which soon turns south and becomes Old Apex Road. As you take in the handsome yards along the way, keep in mind this fantastical poem about North Carolina's state bird by David T. Manning, a distinguished Cary poet and stalwart of the Friday Noon Poets group, which has been meeting weekly in Chapel Hill for years:

AT THE SPRING
Before she could drink from the garden hose
a cardinal landed on her wrist
and plunged its beak into the clear bubbling.

She froze in scarlet presence
but managed to gentle the nozzle's flow.
Never so close to a wild thing,

she was soaked but held rock-still
as the redbird clung to her wrist
tilting its head up and down

as it drank, so close she could see
its tiny tongue. There was a song—
whether in her stunned mind

or from a distant bird, she could not tell.
For a moment nothing died and the winds
lost their ways. The hose chirred

softly like a night-thing's call
and she heard the redbird lisping
as it dipped again and again into the spring.
—From *Rattle* 27 (Summer 2007), http://rattle.com/blog
    /2009/05/at-the-spring-by-david-t-manning/

■ APEX

Old Apex Road becomes North Salem Street as you approach the village of Apex. Stay on North Salem, turning left where Davis Drive comes in on the right and North Salem continues to the left. Cross under US 64 and you are now headed into the old downtown district, an intriguing collection of antique stores, galleries, and eateries.

Writer Julia Montgomery Street was raised here. Street is best known for her popular children's books set across North Carolina. In 1966, she coauthored, with North Carolina State professor Richard Walser, *North Carolina Parade: Stories of History and People*. In short, dramatic chapters, designed for juvenile readers, Walser and Street manage some 400 years of North Carolina history, from the disappearance of Virginia Dare to the career of antebellum African American poet George Moses Horton to the founding of the Research Triangle Park.

From Apex, this tour tracks south to yet another pearl in the necklace of historic towns that surround the capital city. Continue on South Salem Street to the intersection of NC 55 (East Williams Street) and turn left. Follow 55 Business (not Bypass) to reach Holly Springs.

■ HOLLY SPRINGS

Wake Forest College alumnus Hoke Norris, who began his newspaper career in Elizabeth City and continued it in Raleigh, was raised here. After service in World War II and a Nieman Fellowship in journalism at Harvard, Norris became literary editor at the *Chicago Sun-Times*. In 1956, he published *All the Kingdoms of Earth*, the first of his two novels, both of which mirror the landscape and people he remembered from his Holly Springs youth. Norris's sympathetic story is peopled by two generations of hardscrabble African Americans who persevere against natural disasters and white supremacy in a place called Crooked Creek, North Carolina.

When the waters rose, Gra'ma took off her shoes, tied the leather thongs in a bowknot and strung them around her neck, so they hung down on her chest; she put her feet in a cane-bottom chair, with her toes wiggling in the air like a pair of blacksnakes; and bending sideways, she scraped some coals from the stone hearth, swept them into an empty snuff can, and set the can beside her knotty ankles. "Ain't goin let no old flood keep me from smoking," she said, giving a fierce look. —From *All the Kingdoms of Earth*, by Hoke Norris (New York: Simon and Schuster, 1956), 3.

A review in *Time* magazine judged the novel "a noble try" and compared it to Alan Paton's *Cry, the Beloved Country*, which had been published in 1948 on the eve of the formal enactment of apartheid in South Africa.

When the American civil rights movement escalated in the 1960s, Norris gave up his editorial post and returned to the South as a reporter for the *Sun-Times*. In 1962, as a counter to the obstreperous voices of segregation, Norris put together an anthology of fourteen essays by social justice advocates—all white Protestants and southern born and raised. Among the contributors were Asheville's Wilma Dykeman and her husband, James Stokely; Raleigh journalist Jonathan Daniels; Mississippi journalist Hodding Carter III; and University of North Carolina playwright Paul Green. *We Dissent*, from St. Martin's Press, was widely reviewed and dismissed or praised according to the editorial stance of the publication on the matter of civil rights.

Today, on the site of the grade school that Hoke Norris attended, the Holly Springs Cultural Center and Public Library share a handsome new theater space and gallery. To visit this innovative center for performing, visual, and literary arts, watch for signs and turn right on West Ballentine Street, which crosses NC 55 in the historic business district.

Continue south on 55 as it turns to the east through Fuquay-Varina.

■ FUQUAY-VARINA

Perhaps because of its irresistible name, Fuquay-Varina (the first word is pronounced few-kway) makes a cameo appearance in a number of works of fiction by North Carolinians, including *The Bug Funeral* by Raleigh writer Sarah Shaber, and *Who Goes There* by Roanoke Rapids–born Leon Rooke. The latter involves the planned heist of a fortune in coins from the U.S. mint traveling by a railroad car that passes through Fuquay-Varina.

Fayetteville writer John Rowell sends his characters looking for wedding outfits in Fuquay in "The Mother of the Groom and I," a short story in his collection *The Music of Your Life*. In *Crash Diet*, Jill McCorkle's narrator in the story "First Union Blues" explains her decision to leave the town and her boyfriend "who went and bought himself a surfboard with no surf whatsoever there in Fuquay-Varina" (66–67). Novelists Michele Andrea Bowen, Clyde Edgerton, Margaret Maron, and T. R. Pearson (who lived in Fuquay-Varina for a while) have also invoked the percussive name in their books.

Continue through town on NC 55, taking a sharp right as 55 turns south toward Angier.

Regina, North Carolina, had been a farming town, but by the time of my raising it was fast becoming what it is now, a bedroom community with residual patches of brightleaf tobacco, to me little more than a blur of white blossom caps along the flanks of a speeding car as me and my friends flung our dregs of soda into the ditches and bewailed the lack of things to do besides ride aimlessly, singing to the radio. Go on diets of Tab, grapefruit and popcorn. Pluck our eyebrows and brown our legs with baby oil and iodine. I thought settling in Regina meant aspiring only to marry young and drive an hour to Raleigh to work someplace you could wear lipstick and hose, quitting when the babies came. *If* your husband could afford it. I carried vague notions of ascent. I trusted that once I got out of Regina, the future would cough up its gems.—From *Change Baby*, by June Spence (New York: Riverhead Books, 2004), 7.

This description is spot on. Raleigh novelist June Spence writes of her parents' hometown of Angier, which, she says, "is a heavily fictionalized version of the town, based on faulty memory, third-person accounts, and my imagination to fill in the rest." The story benefits from multiple narrators and unravels many a family secret as a daughter is forced to return to her rural roots to help care for her mother following a house fire. Spence moved the letters around in Angier to spell Regina. "Change baby" refers to the daughter who was born late, as her mother was moving toward menopause.

In Angier, take NC 210 toward Lillington, and in a little over seven miles you'll reach US 421. Turn left. You are now on the Paul Green Memorial Highway, so named for one of the giants of North Carolina letters. Green's hometown of Buies Creek is ahead.

■ **BUIES CREEK**

Paul Green, born in 1894 on a farm just off US 421, was the first white southern writer to create plays with African American characters—a challenge at the time, because black actors were not allowed on the stage. His Pulitzer Prize—for the tragedy *In Abraham's Bosom* (1927)—came early in a career that spanned six decades.

"Paul Green, for much of his career, was not in the mainstream of the American theater. That is, he avoided gratuitous violence, loveless sex, miserable introspection, ironic ambiguity, sophisticated banter, and fearful despair, as

The birthplace of North Carolina playwright Paul Eliot Green (1894–1981),
in Harnett County, is still surrounded by working farms.

subjects for the stage. Still another reason you may never have heard of him is because he was in his beginning a regionalist," his daughter, Janet, explained in a talk she gave shortly after her father's death, in 1981. "The cultural deprivation of the rural South, the ungodly barbarisms of the primitive religion like the ones that held sway during revivals, the sudden illnesses, and useless deaths, the sick superstitions, the poverty of post–Civil War times, the bitter racism laid their mark on him then and for life."

All of these aspects of life in late nineteenth- and early twentieth-century North Carolina became Green's subject matter and led him to a lifetime of work to abolish the death penalty and improve human rights. Today, the Paul Green Foundation, based in Chapel Hill, carries on the work in his spirit.

Green's generosity toward other writers was also legendary, and he was a ready collaborator with such distinguished writers as Richard Wright and Kurt Weill and with his many students and apprentices. His daughter, Janet, suggested that it was the profound isolation that Green felt as a precocious youth here in Harnett County that led him to work with and support other writers at every opportunity.

"I was as lonely as a one-legged duck, so I made up things in my head," he once said of his childhood. In addition to his bright imagination, Green inherited his mother's musical abilities. "He ordered a violin, Stradivarius Model,

In 1917, before finishing his first year at the University of North Carolina at Chapel Hill, Paul Green enlisted in the U.S. Army and served in World War I. Taken in 1919, this photo shows Green back on campus. Eight years later, he would win the Pulitzer Prize for his play In Abraham's Bosom. *Courtesy of the Paul Green Foundation.*

for $2.45, and, incredibly, taught himself to play it by taking a correspondence course and practicing in the piney woods," his daughter said. It would be this musical capacity that led Green to popularize a new form of theater—the symphonic drama. By definition, these productions, based on historical events that incorporate music, dance, and drama, are performed on the site of the events they depict. Green's best-known play, *The Lost Colony*, was the first such production. It has been presented continuously in Manteo since 1937 (except during World War II blackouts) and has been seen by more than 4 million people.

Remarkably, the farmhouse where Paul Green was born and raised is still standing. Watch for the historical marker at the intersection with Johnson Farm Road on the left side of US 421, three miles east of the intersection with NC 210. Turn left on Johnson Farm Road and proceed 2.1 miles. The house is on the left.

■ CAMPBELL UNIVERSITY

Buies Creek Academy, where Paul Green attended school, is now Campbell University, a Baptist-affiliated private institution just ahead on 421. Known today for its conservative principles, Campbell has another notable literary connection. The university hired former U.S. Air Force fighter pilot and freshly minted Ph.D. Clyde Edgerton to serve on its English faculty, in 1977. When his popular first novel, *Raney*, was published, in 1985, the school's administrators questioned Edgerton about whether his comedic treatment in the novel of the marriage between a Free Will Baptist woman and an Episcopalian academic was furthering the mission of the school. Ultimately, they withheld Edgerton's contract and he resigned. Among his many novels published since, three of them—*Killer Diller* (also adapted for film), *Lunch at the Picadilly* (adapted as a musical), and *The Bible Salesman*—draw mirthfully on his misfortunes in Buies Creek.

■ LILLINGTON

Backtrack on US 421 to Lillington and turn left on 401/210, which crosses the storied Cape Fear River before entering the town center. The Cape Fear runs through a great many works of North Carolina literature, and here is our first put-in, a site that Fayetteville-born Tim McLaurin writes about in his memoir, *The River Less Run*: "As we pushed off from shore beneath the bridge we had to get quickly into midstream. There, I could line us up with the chute that spilled down the ledge to the slow, deep water. I wondered how low the canoe would ride with all this gear. If we were to swamp, she would not blame the white water and the rocks; she would blame me" ([Asheboro, N.C.: Down Home Press, 2000], 26).

McLaurin's life and work are considered ahead in Tour 3, but for the time being, literary adventurers might be interested in following McLaurin's route downriver. Canoes and kayaks are available at Howard's Barbecue and Canoe Rentals, on the far side of the bridge. It is possible from here to travel only two miles south to SR 2016 or on to the NC 217 bridge in Erwin, a distance of ten miles.

In his memoir, McLaurin also mentions another uncommon landmark some six miles upstream. Raven Rock is a massive outcropping at the easternmost edge of the Piedmont, where it meets North Carolina's coastal plain. Now protected by a thousand-acre state park that surrounds it, the rock itself stretches more than a mile along the river and rises 150 feet high. It is accessible by a 2.6-mile-loop trail in the park. Follow US 421 east and watch for signs to the park.

■ SANFORD

To reach the next point on this tour, follow 421 from Raven Rock Road into Sanford—a distance of sixteen miles. Turn right on Carthage Street to have a look around this historic town, which includes a transportation museum in the restored train station, a renovated Coca-Cola bottling plant, and the renowned Temple Theatre, built in 1925 by the owner of the Coca-Cola plant. Launched as a venue for vaudeville, the theater has survived several transitions, from movie house to National Historic Site, and is now the cultural center of Lee County. Productions by the North Carolina Shakespeare Festival and performances by touring musicians keep the theater's regular main stage lit, and black box productions feature local professional and amateur artists.

Sanford was home in the 1960s to novelist Doris Betts, who is also featured in volumes 1 and 2 of *Literary Trails*. Betts raised her children here while commuting to Chapel Hill to teach creative writing at the university. Her husband, Lowry, was a local attorney who was eventually appointed to the bench. While in Sanford, the Betts family owned two off-road motorcycles, and Doris told an interviewer who visited her at home in 1969 that her true dream was to own an enormous Triumph motorcycle that she could "open up" on the highway. The Betts family lived at 535 Bracken Street, and it was here that Doris wrote a number of short stories (including her best-known, "The Ugliest Pilgrim") and *The River to Pickle Beach*, the only one among her six novels that is set on the North Carolina coast, in Brunswick County.

From Sanford, follow 421 through town to US 1 and head south toward North Carolina's Sandhills, a region unlike any other in the state, famous for its many golf courses, temperate weather, sandy landscape, and the *Pinus palustris*, the longleaf pine—a tree that can live 300 years and which tops out at 100 feet.

■ SOUTHERN PINES

As the years passed, the pine woods were slowly drained of their turpentine. The trees were still mighty, but each dark trunk bore a long pale herringbone scar, stretching as high up as the pullers would reach, at its bottom a little rough-hewed slot into which the precious sap oozed down every spring. The supply was failing, and the demand as well, for the iron and steel ships they were building now had small use for naval stores.—From *Old Pines and Other Stories*, by James Boyd (Chapel Hill: University of North Carolina Press, 1952), 6.

By 1850 nearly all U.S. naval stores were produced from North Carolina's pines. The trees were used to produce masts for tall ships. The byproducts of tar, pitch, and resin were used as sealants, and the turpentine was used as a solvent and fuel for lighting. After the introduction of the railroad to the Sandhills in the 1870s, most of the virgin stands of these longleaf pines were harvested. They had nearly disappeared by the early 1900s—the era in which author James Boyd's grandfather, a steel and railroad magnate, bought 1,200 acres here to save the last of the longleaf pines from logging.

To reach the Boyd estate, take US 1 and drive 23.5 miles from Sanford to the intersection with North May Street. Turn left and in 3.3 miles, turn left again onto East Connecticut Avenue and look for the entrance to Weymouth, flanked by stone columns topped by concrete hunting dogs.

■ WEYMOUTH CENTER FOR THE ARTS & HUMANITIES

555 East Connecticut Avenue, Southern Pines

This grand residence once belonged to novelist James Boyd, who was born and raised in Pennsylvania, attended Princeton, studied English literature at Cambridge, and then landed a job as an editor for *Country Life in America*, a magazine published by Walter Hines Page's firm, Doubleday, Page and Company in New York. After serving with the U.S. Army Ambulance Service in World War I, Boyd moved to his grandfather's Weymouth estate with his bride, Katharine Lamont, the daughter of Grover Cleveland's secretary of war. He divided the house and moved half across the street to create the Campbell House, where his brother lived. After making some improvements to Weymouth, Boyd moved into the house to write full time and nurse his poor health. His first novel, *Drums*, set in Edenton, profoundly raised the bar for the genre of historical fiction, according to critics. Boyd was praised for his accuracy in historical detail and the novel's insightful perspective on the American Revolution. N. C. Wyeth provided the dust jacket illustration, and Scribner's sold 50,000 copies in the first year of publication.

Although he lived like a country squire and had a deep affection for horses and fox hunting, Boyd also hosted many grand literary evenings at Weymouth, bringing in friends such as William Faulkner, the editor Maxwell Perkins, F. Scott Fitzgerald, Ernest Hemingway, Sherwood Anderson, Paul Green (who vigorously championed Boyd's work), Thomas Wolfe, John P. Marquand, and British novelist and playwright John Galsworthy, winner of the 1932 Nobel Prize in Literature. Boyd would use these literary connections in 1940 to organize the

This portrait of James Boyd (artist unknown) hangs in the dining room of the house in Southern Pines where Boyd did most of his writing and entertained other well-known poets, novelists, and playwrights of his era. Courtesy of Weymouth Center for the Arts & Humanities.

Free Company of Players, a group of playwrights that included Orson Welles, William Saroyan, Paul Green, Archibald MacLeish, and Stephen Vincent Benét, whose pieces were recorded by a troupe of actors led by Burgess Meredith and broadcast on CBS radio. Boyd's impetus was to encourage free expression and creativity in a period when pre–World War II propaganda was rampant.

Fighting illness throughout his life, including a bout with polio at the age of twenty-six, Boyd still managed to write five novels, a book of poetry, and a story collection before he died, at the age of fifty-five. His wife, Katharine, inherited Weymouth and the *Pilot*, the regional newspaper that Boyd had bought and re-vitalized in 1941, three years before his death.

In 1963, Katharine donated some 400 acres of wooded land to North Carolina to create Weymouth Woods, the first natural area in the state's park system. Then, in 1969, she sold the *Pilot* to poet and journalist Samuel Talmadge Ragan, who had served as the state's first secretary of art, culture, and history (now cultural resources), a position in the governor's cabinet. Writing in the *Pilot*, Ragan covered literary events statewide with passion. In 1982, Governor

Sculpted by Gretta Lange Bader, North Carolina poet laureate Samuel Ragan's bronze likeness overlooks the North Carolina Literary Hall of Fame, which is housed in James Boyd's former study at the Weymouth Center for the Arts & Humanities.

James Hunt appointed him North Carolina's poet laureate, a position he would hold for the rest of his life.

Upon Katharine Boyd's death, Weymouth House became the property of Sandhills Community College, but in 1977 the college could no longer manage the estate and put it up for sale. Sam Ragan and Elizabeth Stevenson (sister of American statesman Adlai Stevenson) marshaled a large group of supporters to create the nonprofit Friends of Weymouth and hosted a grand event that featured Lady Bird Johnson, the widow of President Lyndon Johnson, as special guest. They leveraged enough money to buy the house.

Throughout his life, Ragan served as Weymouth's guardian angel and dogged promoter. He established a program that invited accomplished writers, musicians, and artists to work on projects for a week at a time in residence (a practice that continues today). Lectures, readings, and plays in the main hall and concerts on the lawn keep audiences coming back. Poet and short-story writer Stephen E. Smith is now one of the keepers of Ragan's legacy. He chairs the Ragan Writers at Weymouth and covers literary events for the *Pilot*.

In 1993, the North Carolina General Assembly authorized the establishment of the North Carolina Literary Hall of Fame, and in 1996 the first inductees (including Boyd) were celebrated at Weymouth. A year later and only a week after his death, Sam Ragan was also inducted. Today, housed upstairs in James Boyd's former study, the Hall of Fame is filled with photos, books, and memorabilia from the growing ranks of inductees. A bronze bust of Ragan and his trademark fedora enliven the collection in the room that journalist Jonathan Daniels once declared the launching place for "the Southern literary renaissance" of the 1920s and 1930s. Without Sam Ragan's work at Weymouth and his vigilance as a newspaper publisher, the literary lights in the Sandhills would not burn nearly so bright. Ragan was called on to write poems for many occasions, but in this piece, he is simply marking the end of a busy day at his desk:

FINAL EDITION
They have all gone from the city room.
Down the long hall the last footsteps have died away.
The teletypes are quiet,
But in the distance is the rumble
Of the fresh-inked last news.
The sweeper has come and gone.
A green eyeshade lies on the desk—
  And there's no one to answer the telephone.
—From *The Collected Poems of Sam Ragan*, edited by Marsha Warren
  (Laurinburg, N.C.: St. Andrews College Press, 1990), 38.

From the upstairs rooms of Weymouth, visitors can look out over manicured lawns with colorful plantings of magnolia, camellia, azalea, and boxwood. Dozens of poets have written about Weymouth as a source of inspiration, and Raleigh novelist Alexandra Sokoloff pays homage to the estate—calling it the Folger House—in her thriller, *The Unseen*, which is partly based on the work in the 1960s of J. B. Rhine, famous Duke University parapsychologist.

Sokoloff's main character arrives at the estate to conduct a paranormal experiment: "At the foot of the estate the gate already stood open and she drove between the gateposts with their stone dogs, feeling a shiver of anticipation as the wheels crunched over the slate chips of the circular drive" (New York: St. Martin's Press, 2009), 170.

Sokoloff, who divides her time between Los Angeles and Raleigh, did her research in residence at Weymouth with a group of North Carolina writer friends, including Sarah Shaber and Margaret Maron, and she claims to have encountered the resident ghost, whose presence others have felt.

From Weymouth, follow East Connecticut Avenue northwest to the railroad tracks and turn left on NW Broad Street. James Boyd's literary guests usually arrived at this depot in the middle of Southern Pines. Thomas Wolfe liked to take a late-arriving train and would let himself in at Weymouth. The Boyd children reported that they often came downstairs in the morning ahead of their parents to find him snoring on the sofa. Southern Pines is a handsome village to visit. Walk around as Wolfe did and enjoy the feel of so much history among the stately pines.

■ ABERDEEN

Backtrack to East Connecticut Avenue past Weymouth and take the fourth left onto North Bethesda Road. Continue 3.5 miles until you see a wrought iron archway over the road, marking the entrance to the Old Bethesda Cemetery, which is spread out on both sides of the road. Go beyond the old church, take the last driveway on the left, and drive to the top of the hill. We end this tour paying respects at the graves of some of the writers discussed in this tour.

Walter Hines Page, whose father had a hand in the establishment of the village of Aberdeen, where he owned 1,600 acres of timber, is buried in the Page family plot on the left side of the lane at the top of the rise.

A bit farther down on the same side of the lane is the final resting place of James and Katharine Boyd. The site is marked only by a small bronze plaque set atop a low stone wall mostly overgrown with ivy. The wall surrounds a millstone sunk at the center of the enclosure. Three tall pines, alongside plantings of camellia and dogwood, stand nearby as sentinels. The Boyds knew Page, of course, because Boyd had worked at Page's publishing house after his graduate studies in England.

Across the lane, on the right, is North Carolina poet laureate Sam Ragan, his grave marked by a dramatic, black stone.

Marking this place is a poem by Malaika King Albrecht, who lived in Pinehurst for some years and founded *Redheaded Stepchild*, an online magazine that only accepts poems that have been rejected elsewhere.

GRAVE RUBBING WITH MY DAUGHTERS AT BETHESDA CEMETERY
Some things break, my youngest says,
after the charcoal stick snaps in her hand.

I hold her hand beneath mine
and glide our hands over a winged hourglass.
I tell Serena the image means that time flies.
She laughs, *Time's not a bird, mommy.*

My eldest daughter beside us
presses paper along the next stone.
Like she's brushing her hair,
Amani slides the charcoal in long strokes
down the surface until the space
between images and letters
fills gray as dark clouds.

A daisy barely visible beneath lichen
appears, and sunken images reveal
themselves through absence.
Like a secret message, Amani says.
Her name was Mary Elizabeth.

The child's birth and death day are the same.
A mother and her child though I don't say so.
It hasn't occurred to my youngest
that a child can die.
An expression swift as a bird's shadow,
crosses Amani's face. Something in me
kneels, familiar as a childhood prayer.
—Used by permission of Malaika King Albrecht

■ **LITERARY LANDSCAPE**

Barnes and Noble

Cary Commons
760 SE Maynard, Cary
919-467-3866
This store hosts local author events, regular story times for children, and meetings of the Screenwriters' Group, based in Raleigh.

Nâzım Hikmet Poetry Festival

303 East Durham Road, Suite F, Cary
919-608-5815

Cary's Turkish community created this festival in 2009 to honor Turkish poet, playwright, and novelist Nâzım Hikmet Ran. The daylong festival features readings, a poetry competition, and workshops.

Lazy Lion Used Books and More

601 East Broad Street, Fuquay-Varina

919-552-9639

This easygoing establishment has regular open mic nights for poets and prose writers and will also take used books in trade, by appointment.

Paul Green Festival

http://www.paulgreen.org/festival/

Sponsored in the first year by Campbell University, the Friends of Harnett County Public Library, the North Carolina Humanities Council, and the Paul Green Foundation, all of Harnett County takes a weekend to celebrate its beloved wordsmith through film, readings, lectures, plays, music, ice cream, and baseball—just as the multitalented Paul Green would have wanted it.

Country Bookshop

140 NW Broad Street, Southern Pines

910-692-3211

Since 1953, this locally owned shop has featured an exceptional array of books, particularly North Carolina and regional works. Catering to retirees and visitors from around the world, it's a great stop if you're interested in reading more about Moore County. A noteworthy choice is Manley Wade Wellman's *The Story of Moore County*.

Sandhills Community College

3395 Airport Road, Pinehurst

910-692-6185

http://www.sandhills.edu/events/creativewriting.php

This community college has played a stalwart role in the literary arts of the Sandhills. It was here that Whispering Pines poet Mary Belle Campbell taught creative writing. She also founded Scots Plaid Press and Persephone Press and bequeathed funds to support a number of literary endeavors across the state. Novelist Patricia Hickman, author of *The Pirate Queen*, leads the creative writing program today.

Palustris Festival

Arts Council of Moore County

Campbell House

482 East Connecticut Avenue, Southern Pines

910-692-2787

http://www.mooreart.org

The annual Palustris Festival showcases the visual, literary, and performing arts in Moore County. It is a collaborative venture of the Arts Council of Moore County; the Convention and Visitor's Bureau of Pinehurst, Southern Pines, and Aberdeen Area; and *PineStraw* magazine.

Fayetteville

Even before Sherman's devastating visit, writers were pondering the impact of the military on this town, now a colorful community of tremendous vitality, where Cross Creek meets the Cape Fear.

Writers with a connection to this area: Tanya Biank, Walter Blackstock, Richard Brodhead, Charles W. Chesnutt, Michael Colonnese, Robin Greene, Marion Hargrove, Pete Hendricks, Tony Hoagland, Ahmad Kenya, Catherine Lutz, Carson McCullers, Joe McGinnis, Tim McLaurin, Roy Parker Jr., David Rowell, John Rowell, Omar ibn Sayyid, Robert Strange

■ FORT BRAGG

Fayetteville is a sprawling, blue-collar town and contrasts strangely with adjacent Fort Bragg Army Base, where the 82nd Airborne Division and the Green Berets train. Over four wars, natives and soldiers have bought and sold from each other, flirted with each other's wives and daughters, and fist-fought in bars whenever two or more fellows needed to prove that the uneasy truce between town and base was kept up out of strength rather than weakness.—From *The Keeper of the Moon: A Southern Boyhood*, by Tim McLaurin (Asheboro, N.C.: Down Home Press, 1991), 15.

As Fayetteville writer Tim McLaurin explains, the military has an enormous influence on this area of North Carolina. The base makes its presence felt well beyond the city limits of Fayetteville, in fact, because it reaches into not only Cumberland but also Hoke, Moore, and Harnett counties—covering a total of more than 250 square miles. Fort Bragg has made this region North Carolina's most internationally diverse, by virtue of the many people in service who find husbands and wives during

tour 3

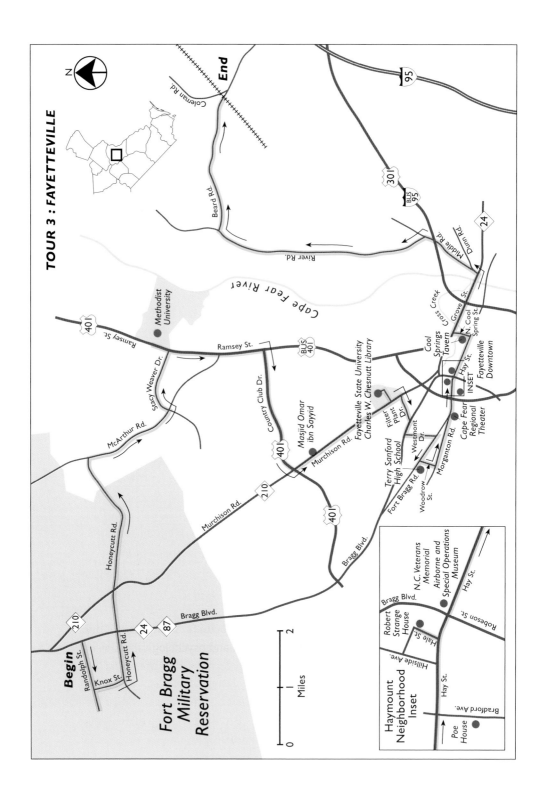

TOUR 3 : FAYETTEVILLE

N

End

Coleman Rd.

95

301

BUS 95

24

Beard Rd.

River Rd.

Middle Rd.

Dunn Rd.

Cape Fear River

Cross Creek

Methodist University

401

Ramsey St.

Ramsey St.

Stacy Weaver Dr.

BUS 401

Cool Springs Tavern

N. Cool Spring St.

Grove St.

McArthur Rd.

Country Club Dr.

Masjid Omar ibn Sayyid

Fayetteville State University
Charles W. Chesnutt Library

Hay St.

INSET

Fayetteville Downtown

Murchison Rd.

401

Filter Plant Dr.

Westmont Dr.

Cape Fear Regional Theater

Terry Sanford High School

Fort Bragg Rd.

Woodrow St.

Morganton Rd.

Murchison Rd.

210

Honeycutt Rd.

210

Begin

Randolph St.

Knox St.

Honeycutt Rd.

24

87

Bragg Blvd.

Bragg Blvd.

401

Fort Bragg Military Reservation

Miles

0   1   2

Haymount Neighborhood Inset

Bragg Blvd.

N.C. Veterans Memorial Airborne and Special Operations Museum

Robert Strange House

Hale St.

Hillside Ave.

Robeson St.

Hay St.

Hay St.

Bradford Ave.

Poe House

foreign tours of duty and bring them back to set up house near the base. Often as not, their extended families immigrate, too, and put down roots.

Enter the base at the Randolph Street entrance off Bragg Boulevard (NC 87). (All vehicles are searched.) From here, you can follow Randolph to the impressive statue of "Iron Mike." Fanning out in every direction from the traffic circle where Mike stands his ground are handsome tan Spanish Colonial officers' houses with terra-cotta roofs. In spring, the azaleas and dogwoods make this part of Fort Bragg look more like a 1940s country club than a military installation.

Novelist Carson McCullers grew up in Columbus, Georgia, near Fort Benning, so when she and her husband, Reeves, moved to Fayetteville from Charlotte in 1939, this setting was familiar. After hearing about the arrest of a Fort Bragg solider for voyeurism, she wrote a novella about a murder committed on an army base. Her grotesque and violent *Reflections in a Golden Eye* (1941) begins:

> An army base in peacetime is a dull place. Things happen, but then they happen over and over again. The general plan of a fort in itself adds to the monotony—the huge concrete barracks, the neat rows of officers' homes built one precisely like the other, the gym, the chapel, the golf course, and the swimming pools—all is designed according to a certain rigid pattern. But perhaps the dullness of a post is caused most of all by insularity and by a surfeit of leisure and safety, for once a man enters the army he is expected only to follow the heels ahead of him.—From *Reflections in a Golden Eye*, by Carson McCullers (New York: Houghton Mifflin Harcourt, 2000), 3.

Sadly, Fort Bragg, especially in the Vietnam era and thereafter, has made headlines as a place of frequent domestic violence, which has, in turn, prompted many books, the best known of which is surely *Fatal Vision*, in which Joe McGinnis tells the story of Jeffrey McDonald, a Green Beret surgeon convicted of the murders of his wife and two young daughters. In a more scholarly but very readable book about Bragg called *Homefront*, Catherine Lutz, an anthropologist, considers the challenges for spouses left behind in times of war and for soldiers who often return with both physical and psychological scars—in particular, post-traumatic stress syndrome. Tanya Biank's *Under the Sabers: The Unwritten Code of Army Wives* is another thoughtful treatment of the lives of those left on base when soldiers deploy to far-flung conflicts.

Contemporary poet Tony Hoagland was born at Fort Bragg and, like so many children in military families, lived a transient life. His father was an army physician deployed to bases all over the south. Hoagland now serves on the faculty of the master's degree program in creative writing at Warren Wilson College, in Swannanoa. His prize-winning work often reflects on the military culture and its cost to families.

JET

Sometimes I wish I were still out
on the back porch, drinking jet fuel
with the boys, getting louder and louder
as the empty cans drop out of our paws
like booster rockets falling back to Earth

and we soar up into the summer stars.
Summer. The big sky river rushes overhead,
bearing asteroids and mist, blind fish
and old space suits with skeletons inside.
On Earth, men celebrate their hairiness,

and it is good, a way of letting life
out of the box, uncapping the bottle
to let the effervescence gush
through the narrow, usually constricted neck.

And now the crickets plug in their appliances
in unison, and then the fireflies flash
dots and dashes in the grass, like punctuation
for the labyrinthine, untrue tales of sex
someone is telling in the dark, though

no one really hears. We gaze into the night
as if remembering the bright unbroken planet
we once came from,
to which we will never
be permitted to return.
We are amazed how hurt we are.
We would give anything for what we have.
—From *Donkey Gospel*, by Tony Hoagland (Graywolf Press, 1998), 3.

Much of the literature about army life from earlier decades was comic. One writer who saw it that way was Mac Hyman, who studied at Duke University in the 1940s and wrote a novel, *No Time for Sergeants*, that became a one-hour

Shortly after his enlistment in the U.S. Army in 1942, North Carolina photographer and conservationist Hugh Morton was photographed in uniform reading See Here, Private Hargrove, *about basic training at Fort Bragg. Courtesy of the Hugh Morton Collection of Photographs and Films, North Carolina Collection, Wilson Library, UNC–Chapel Hill.*

television drama, then a Broadway play, and finally a film starring Andy Griffith. Marion Hargrove, who was born in Mount Olive and trained at Fort Bragg, also made light of his military service, at least before World War II began. Hargrove's book *See Here, Private Hargrove*, about his experiences in basic training, sold well and was made into a movie in 1944 with Robert Walker and Donna Reed. Hargrove would go on to write for television and films from the 1960s to the 1980s.

> By the time Congress says I may go home and be a mere civilian again, I suppose I'll be the best soldier at Fort Bragg. At least I seem to get more individual attention than anyone else. Private tutoring, I always tell the boys.
> The sergeant was putting us through our paces. To be quite frank, the precise way the other citizen-soldiers were doing their part got me confused. Every time I held the rifle at one place, it would seesaw over and finally wind up with a thud on my best toe. The sergeant was quite patient

for a while, but he finally called a halt and walked over to me slowly, clenching his fists desperately to control himself.

"Hargrove," he said with infinite sweetness. "where is the balance of your rifle?"

"This is all the supply sergeant gave me, sir," I said. "I thought it was all here."

—From *See Here, Private Hargrove*, by Marion Hargrove (London: Hodder and Stoughton, 1943), 34–35.

From Iron Mike, travel all the way around the traffic circle and backtrack on Randolph to Knox Street and turn right. At the next intersection, turn left on Honeycutt Road and continue 4.1 miles to McArthur Road, where you will turn right. In 1.7 miles, turn left on Stacy Weaver Road, and in another half mile, turn left on Ramsey Street. The campus of Methodist University is ahead on the right.

■ METHODIST UNIVERSITY

5400 Ramsey Street

This liberal arts institution is highly regarded in literary circles for its biannual Southern Writers Symposium—a showcase for emerging writers—and as the home of Longleaf Press. This nonprofit publishing house sponsors a poetry chapbook competition open to writers from the southeastern United States who have not published a full-length collection. Writers Michael Colonnese and Robin Greene, both of whom teach creative writing at Methodist, manage the press. (Greene's poetry is featured in *Literary Trails of the North Carolina Piedmont*.)

Atlanta-born poet Walter Blackstock, who studied with Archibald MacLeish at Harvard and won several North Carolina prizes for his work, chaired the English department here from 1966 to 1972. He went on to teach at Elizabeth City State University until the end of his career. He published this poem while in Fayetteville:

TIME REMAINS ASKEW

Time remains askew;
The toppling shanties across the tracks
Are not yet uprooted by alabaster hate.
Time's Face stays out of joint:
A gnarled, beetle-gnawed tree

Leers from a roadway, syphilitic with lust and shacks.
This is Hallowed Ground:
Mary Magdalene,
Lazarus,
Cain, the Poet-Son,
Are munching the succulent mandrake;
All of them dream,
Pillowed on a Golgotha stone,
Time has not joined the Yew with the Rose:
A Cross glows not from Calvary,
But from Ishmael's yard,
Long after the Crusaders ride away home,
Stopping first for short beers at Pilate's place.
—From *Leaves before the Wind: New and Selected Poems
from Two Decades*, by Walter Blackstock (Fayetteville, N.C.:
Methodist College Press, 1966), 10.

Head south again on Ramsey Street. In 2.2 miles, turn right on Country Club Drive; in another 2.2 miles, turn left on Murchison Road.

■ MASJID OMAR IBN SAYYID

2700 Murchison Road

As it turns out, the mix of diverse cultures in today's Fayetteville actually long precedes the presence of the U.S. Army. A 177-year-old autobiography reveals another angle on Fayetteville's multicultural history.

Omar ibn Sayyid was a Muslim born around 1770 near the Senegal River, in Futa Toro. This learned man was captured by slave traders and shipped to the port of Charleston, South Carolina. He managed to escape and was eventually arrested in Fayetteville.

In his jail cell, Sayyid began writing on the wall from right to left in a script unknown to his jailers—Arabic.

Sayyid was eventually sent to a Bladen County farm to live with the Jim Owen family. There he wrote his autobiography in Arabic. He was most likely buried in the Owen family cemetery, near Clarkton. In 2010, a historical marker was placed here on Murchison Road in front of the mosque that is named for him. A play, *The Life and Times of Omar ibn Sayyid*, written by Washington, D.C., playwright and actor Ahmad Kenya, has recently toured the country.

From here, follow Murchison south to the entrance of Fayetteville State

The Omar ibn Sayyid Mosque in Fayetteville is named after a West African man who was captured and brought to Charleston, South Carolina, to work as a slave. He spent the latter years of his life in North Carolina writing an autobiography, which was discovered in 1995.

University, on the left. Follow the signs to the campus library. A display in the library lobby offers more information about the writer for whom this building is named.

■ **CHARLES W. CHESNUTT LIBRARY**

Fayetteville State University

1200 Murchison Road

One of the most important African American literary voices of his era, Charles Waddell Chesnutt was born in 1858 in Ohio, the son of free black parents who had left their home in Fayetteville to escape the Civil War. The family returned after the war and Chesnutt spent his formative years here. He was quintessentially American in his determination to succeed, says Duke University president and literary scholar Richard Brodhead. He writes that Chesnutt was a "compulsive achiever" and "self-disciplined toward future attainment, of which Ben Franklin is the national archetype" (*The Journals of Charles Chesnutt*, edited by Richard Brodhead [Durham: Duke University Press, 1993], 2).

Fayetteville by the time of the Chesnutt family's return had been a stop on Sherman's march through North Carolina. The local economy was suffer-

Charles W. Chesnutt's nuanced fiction tackled the topics of Reconstruction and racial identity. His parents ran a grocery store in Fayetteville. Today the library at Fayetteville State University is named for him. Courtesy of Special Collections, Charles W. Chesnutt Library, Fayetteville State University.

ing along with that of the state. Chesnutt, an eager student during this bitter period, was often denied opportunity, but, as Brodhead tells us, not all of Fayetteville's mainstream institutions were equally observant of the color line. Chesnutt had access to a white-owned bookstore, and he managed to learn German from a local Jewish merchant, despite the social penalty for such a cross-racial relationship at the time.

Chesnutt also attended the progressive Howard School, which was perhaps the best free school open to blacks in the state. Financed in part by northern philanthropy, Howard was also championed by a local group that included Chesnutt's father, who helped buy the land on Gillespie Street where Howard's successor, Fayetteville State University, is located today. According to Brodhead, "The availability of the Howard School was the most decisive fact of Charles Chesnutt's early life" (8).

As a young adult, Chesnutt left Fayetteville for Cleveland, Ohio, but his writing continued to focus on the South. His short stories were somewhat popular and collected in two books, published in 1899: *The Conjure Woman and Other Conjure Tales* and *The Wife of His Youth and Other Stories of the Color Line*. Chesnutt's first novel, *The House behind the Cedars*, published in 1900, was set in Fayetteville and dealt with the issue of people of mixed race "passing" as white, a condition that Chesnutt, who was light-skinned, experienced personally. *The Marrow of Tradition*, his second novel, from 1901, focused on an episode of racial violence that occurred in Wilmington in 1898. Chesnutt's sympathetic New York editor for the novels was Walter Hines Page, of Cary (see Tour 2).

In this passage, Chesnutt describes a familiar landmark in Fayetteville:

There was a red brick market-house in the public square, with a tall tower, which held a four-faced clock that struck the hours, and from which there pealed out a curfew at nine o'clock. There were two or three hotels, a courthouse, a jail, stores, offices, and all the appurtenances of a county seat and a commercial emporium; for while Patesville numbered only four or five thousand inhabitants, of all shades of complexion, it was one of the principal towns in North Carolina, and had a considerable trade in cotton and naval stores. This business activity was not immediately apparent to my unaccustomed eyes. Indeed, when I first saw the town, there brooded over it a calm that seemed almost sabbatic in its restfulness, though I learned later on that underneath its somnolent exterior the deeper currents of life—love and hatred, joy and despair, ambition and avarice, faith and friendship—flowed not less steadily than in livelier latitudes. —From *The Conjure Woman and Other Conjure Tales*, by Charles W. Chesnutt, edited by Richard Brodhead (Durham: Duke University Press, 1993), 32.

From here, return to Murchison and proceed south to the first street on the left—Filter Plant Drive—and turn left. Take the second left onto Westmont Drive, which ends at Fort Bragg Road. Turn right to reach the next destination.

■ TERRY SANFORD HIGH SCHOOL

2301 Fort Bragg Road

Named for North Carolina's progressive governor and senator, who was instrumental in the establishment of many organizations dedicated to arts and culture in the 1960s, this school figured in the lives of two important Fayetteville writers, brothers John and David Rowell. Their family home was behind the football bleachers and their mother taught at the high school.

Today, David is deputy editor of the *Washington Post Magazine* and has taught journalism at American University and creative writing at the Harvard

Extension School. He published a novel in 2011—*The Train of Small Mercies*, about the funeral of Robert F. Kennedy. He gives credit to his older brother, John, for his literary career. David told an interviewer that before he started kindergarten, John taught him to read and pushed books and musical soundtracks on him. As a result, David said, "it would never have occurred to me to study business in college or medicine or anything like that." Both brothers studied at the University of North Carolina at Chapel Hill with short-story master Max Steele.

After college, John Rowell left Chapel Hill for New York to pursue an acting career. His collection of stories, *The Music of Your Life*, came out in 2003. John now teaches at a prestigious preparatory school in Baltimore. He explained in an e-mail interview that he rode his bike every day between third and fifth grades from the house behind the Terry Sanford bleachers to nearby Van Story Elementary School.

> Richie desperately longed to be invited into the teachers' lounge—he imagined himself to be the first student in Coble Road Elementary history to be afforded such a privilege. On that day, he would wear his Sunday school shirt and his favorite blue clip-on tie, which featured a picture of a waterskiing couple holding up a banner that read: "North Carolina: Variety Vacationland!" He would be invited to sit on the couch between Mrs. Peet and Miss Hambrick as Mr. Thaddeus Lattimore worked the mimeograph machine.—From "The Teachers' Lounge," by John Rowell, in *Long Story Short*, edited by Marianne Gingher (Chapel Hill: University of North Carolina Press, 2009), 157.

From Fort Bragg Road, take Woodrow Street, beside the high school complex. When it ends at Morganton Road, turn left and follow Morganton, which will become Hay Street. You are now in Fayetteville's Haymount neighborhood— a tony district of handsome residences, several good restaurants, and the Cape Fear Regional Theatre. This part of Fayetteville was high cotton in comparison with the Cumberland County farming community where writer Tim McLaurin was raised. Billy, the protagonist of McLaurin's first novel, was uncomfortable here:

> Billy wandered in that cloud nearly an hour through the silent streets of Haymont, past brick houses with drawn curtains, night lamps framing the windows with light. No dogs barked, they were sleeping too in their fancy kennels or close to their masters' feet. Billy walked mechanically, eyes

Fayetteville's Edgar Allan Poe House did not belong to the gothic poet but to a prosperous brickyard owner who shared his name. Tours are available. The house is close to Hay Street at 206 Bradford Avenue, next door to the Museum of the Cape Fear.

straight ahead, between the nice houses and apartments of the west side of town.—From *The Acorn Plan*, by Tim McLaurin (New York: W. W. Norton, 1988), 126.

Just beyond the overpass for US 401/NC 87, watch for Hale Street on the left and turn left. The next stop is at the end of the street on the right.

■ ROBERT STRANGE HOUSE

114 Hale Street

This was the in-town residence of North Carolina's first published novelist, U.S. senator Robert Strange. His work, *Eoneguski, Or, the Cherokee Chief: A Tale of Past Wars*, is excerpted in *Literary Trails of the North Carolina Mountains*. Strange's other Fayetteville residence—sitting at what was once the center of his 500-acre Myrtle Hill Plantation, on the Cape Fear River—is off Ramsey Street, beyond the Veterans Administration Hospital at the end of Kirkland Drive.

Continue downhill on Hay Street to the intersection with Bragg Boulevard. Turn left to reach the parking area for the next site.

■ AIRBORNE AND SPECIAL OPERATIONS MUSEUM

North Carolina Veterans Memorial

100 Bragg Boulevard

This museum commemorates the conflicts in which the U.S. Army's 82nd Airborne Division and its Special Operations Unit have played a pivotal role. Outside, behind the museum, is another casting of Iron Mike and behind him, the North Carolina Veterans Memorial. This striking and multifaceted public artwork was dedicated in 2011 to honor military personnel in the state—men and women—from all branches.

This complex could take an entire day to experience fully. Before your trip, you might want to obtain a copy of *The Best of Roy Parker Jr.—Reliving Fayetteville's Storied Military History*, published by the *Fayetteville Observer* and available for purchase online from the newspaper.

Parker's long and prominent career in North Carolina journalism began in 1953, when he served as editor of three family-owned weekly newspapers in Hertford, Bertie, and Northampton counties. After years as a reporter for the *Raleigh News and Observer*, Parker came to Fayetteville in 1973 to be an associate editor of the *Fayetteville Observer*, later becoming the editor of the newly established *Fayetteville Times*, which was published until 1990. Today, the *Fayetteville Observer*, which merged with the *Times*, is the oldest family-owned newspaper in the state.

From the front of the museum, proceed down Hay Street to the traffic circle at Market Square, Fayetteville's most familiar landmark, as described earlier by Charles Chesnutt. Continue ahead on Person Street, the second street around the circle. At the next traffic circle, take the third right onto North Cool Spring Street.

■ COOL SPRINGS TAVERN

119 North Cool Spring Street

The white house on the left before you reach the bridge over Cross Creek is the oldest standing structure in Fayetteville, once a tavern and boardinghouse. In 1938, Carson and Reeves McCullers rented a spacious but rundown upstairs apartment here. On warm days, McCullers sat before her portable typewriter on the upstairs veranda and wrote, taking occasional breaks to play her landlady's piano in the downstairs parlor for all the neighbors to hear.

McCullers finally finished *The Heart Is a Lonely Hunter*, the novel she had begun in Charlotte. In a two-month spurt, she then wrote the novella *Reflections in a Golden Eye*.

Believed to be the oldest building in Fayetteville, Cool Springs Tavern housed the state delegates who came to town in 1789 to ratify the U.S. Constitution. Novelist Carson McCullers moved to an upstairs apartment in the building with her husband, Reeves, in 1939 and finished her debut novel, The Heart Is a Lonely Hunter. *She also wrote* Reflections in a Golden Eye *here.*

According to McCullers's biographer Virginia Spencer Carr, the novella, which was published a year and a half later in *Harper's Bazaar*, offended many officers' wives at Fort Bragg and at Fort Benning, near McCullers's hometown of Columbus, Georgia. Upon reading the piece, Mrs. George Patton reportedly cancelled her subscription to the magazine. Eventually the novella was made into a movie starring Elizabeth Taylor and Marlon Brando.

Follow North Cool Spring Street to its end at Grove Street and turn right. After crossing the Cape Fear River, take the first right on Middle Road. Cross I-95 and take the left fork onto River Road, following it four miles to Beard Road, and stop at the railroad tracks. This rural crossroads, now without a country store, was novelist Tim McLaurin's primary inspiration.

■ BEARD STATION

Outside, waiting to be rediscovered each day, lay Beard Station, a few dozen houses and a country store gathered at an intersection. . . . Smells —

Novelist and memoirist Tim McLaurin presents one of his
nonpoisonous, reptilian friends. © Tom Rankin.

honeysuckle, sweet honeysuckle wet with dew. Bite off the end of the flowers and suck out the nectar, only a flash of sweetness, but the flavor cannot be matched in a sugar bowl. Bury your face in the strands of purple wisteria blossom—the fragrance wraps your face like fingers. Don't sniff a bumblebee, for they love wisteria, too. Stand erect and smell the musk of the field that has been turned to seed wheat. The odor is rich, primeval with plants that grew when fishes swam where quail now nest. Catch the scent of bacon—pig meat crackling in its own grease, eggs slowly scrambled in butter. We've been too noisy and Mama is up and cooking breakfast.—From *The Keeper of the Moon: A Southern Boyhood*, by Tim McLaurin (Asheboro, N.C.: Down Home Press, 1991), 16, 18.

Novelist and memoirist Tim McLaurin wrote of Fayetteville and Cumberland County like no one else. Though he served in the Marine Corps and in the

Peace Corps in Tunisia, taught writing at North Carolina State, and traveled the world, this was home. His mother, Darlene, and sister, Karen, are neighbors on the family land on Coleman Road. Tim is buried there, in a tomb whose construction he supervised. Three of his friends built it: fellow novelist Pete Hendricks; Hendricks's wife, Robin; and documentary photographer Tom Rankin.

Tim was crazy about snakes, and when he got cancer, some said it was because he had handled, tended, and been bitten by so many venomous snakes over his lifetime. Once, however, when Tim had been receiving intensive chemotherapy treatments, a black snake bit him and the snake died. Tim carried reptiles to his readings in pillowcases and taught schoolchildren not to fear them. When he died at the age of forty-eight, having published eight books, local North Carolina senator Tony Rand and the state legislature issued a proclamation honoring him. They quoted Tim:

> We are sons and daughters of the land, our heritage tied to fields and woods, the call of hunt, the spiritual transition of the seed that cracks the hard earth and grows into weed, food, flower, or tree. I have carried in my wallet for seven years a plastic sandwich bag filled with plain dirt scooped from the pasture behind the homeplace. It has traveled with me through Africa, Europe, and much of America, a talisman that whispers to me the song of mourning doves, wind in the longleaf pines, the low rumble of thunder from a summer storm that has recently passed and soaked the dry fields. I hope to waltz slowly to that tune the day I lift above this bright land.—From *The General Assembly of North Carolina, Resolution 2003-23, Senate Joint Resolution 608*, http://www.ncleg.net/sessions/2003/bills /senate/html/s608v3.html

■ LITERARY LANDSCAPE

Cape Fear Regional Theatre
1209 Hay Street
910-323-4233 (box office)
http://www.cfrt.org

Begun more than fifty years ago by Herbert and Bo Thorp, this community theater has grown into a regional gem, occasionally premiering work by local playwrights and North Carolina novels that have been adapted for the stage. Casts often include professional actors from New York City and elsewhere. Through its training programs, the theater has also helped launch more than a few Broadway careers.

Purple martin houses made from gourds are a common sight in eastern North Carolina. The birds help to control the mosquito population. This collection hangs near Beard's Crossroads, the childhood haunt of writer Tim McLaurin.

Arts Council of Fayetteville/Cumberland County

301 Hay Street, Fayetteville

910-323-1776

http://www.theartscouncil.com

In addition to the International Folk Festival, its signature event, the arts council has a gallery with exhibitions that rotate frequently, and it funds programs at the Cumberland County Library for both writers and readers.

City Center Gallery and Books

112 Hay Street

910-678-8899

http://www.citycentergallery.com

Used books predominate in this store, which is on the tour route downtown. Paintings and photography by local artists hang on the walls, adding a welcome dimension to the trade. Several book clubs meet here regularly.

Wagram : Riverton : Laurinburg : Maxton : Pembroke : Fairmont : Tabor City

Early spring is an excellent season to take a tour that ranges through the lower Sandhills, in Scotland County, to the Lumber River's widest passage in the land of the Lumbee, in Robeson and Columbus counties.

Writers with a connection to this area: Lewis Barton, Ron Bayes, Horace Carter, Adolph Dial, Josephine Humphreys, Gerald White Johnson, Willie French Lowery, John Charles McNeill, Joseph Mitchell, Howard Owen, Nancy Roberts, Randolph Umberger Jr.

Two powerful strands of North Carolina heritage—the Lumbee Indians and the Scottish highlanders who settled this region—are the storytellers and poets in focus on this tour. We begin in the tiny village of Wagram, seventeen miles south of Aberdeen.

SUNBURNT BOYS (EXCERPT)
I know your haunts: each gnarly bole
That guards the waterside,
Each tuft of flags and rushes where
The river reptiles hide,
Each dimpling nook wherein the bass
His eager life employs
Until he dies—the captive of
You sunburnt boys.

You will not—will you?—soon forget
When I was one of you,
Nor love me less that time has borne
My craft to currents new;
Nor shall I ever cease to share

tour 4

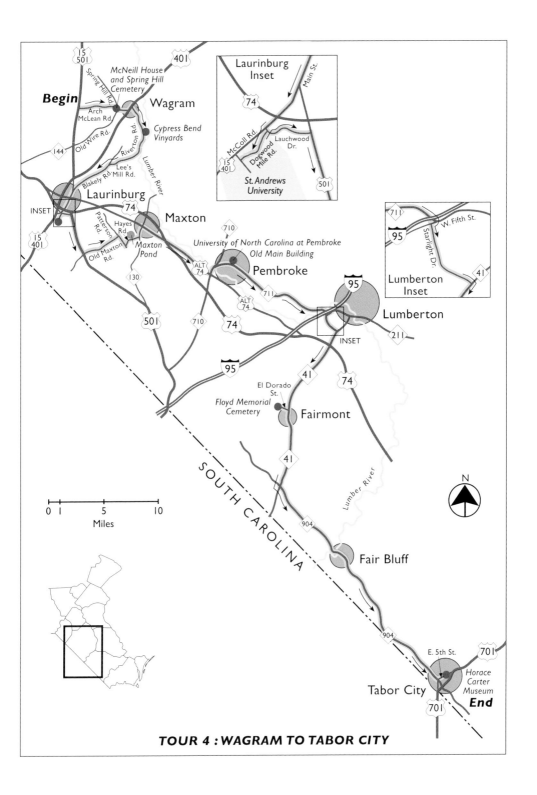

Your hardships and your joys,
Robust, rough-spoken, gentle-hearted
Sunburnt boys!
—From *Songs, Merry and Sad*, by John Charles McNeill
  (Charlotte: Stone and Barringer, 1906, 65).

■ WAGRAM

Poet John Charles McNeill was so popular in his day that many North Carolinians assumed he was the state's poet laureate, though that official designation did not yet exist. McNeill is buried in Spring Hill Cemetery, just outside
Wagram. From US 15/501, take Arch McLean Road, and in 3.5 miles, turn right
onto Spring Hill Road. You'll soon run into Old Wire Road at the Spring Hill Cemetery—a graveyard full of Scottish surnames.

Born in 1874, John Charles McNeill roamed the Scotland County wood-
lands and swam in the Lumber River as a boy. He left for school at Whiteville
Academy, farther south, and then moved on to Wake Forest College, where he
edited the school's literary journal and began writing poetry. Knowing poetry
might not earn him a living, McNeill took a law degree and graduated at the
top of his class. However, he elected to remain on the Wake Forest campus as
an English instructor for a year. He also taught for a time at Mercer College, in
Georgia.

At the age of twenty-six, McNeill finally opened a law practice in Lumberton
and bought a share in the *Argus* newspaper. His poems and stories, grounded
in local lore, were published weekly in the paper, and soon his work was also
making regular appearances in a national publication, *Century* magazine.

Meanwhile, McNeill continued his law practice, moving it to Laurinburg,
where he ran successfully and served a term in the North Carolina legislature, but the poet did not love lawyering. According to literary scholar Richard
Walser, McNeill often snuck off to fish or locked his office door to keep out
clients and wrote poetry instead.

By 1904, he was invited to write a column in the *Charlotte Observer*, which
led to a devoted regional readership and his designation as the first writer to receive the North Carolina Literary and Historical Society's Patterson Cup, for literary excellence. (A bronze bust of McNeill resides in the North Carolina Room
of the main library in Charlotte.)

His first poetry collection, *Songs, Merry and Sad*, was published in 1905. The
next volume of McNeill's work, *Lyrics from Cotton Land*, is largely devoted to

verse written in Negro dialect with a humorous bent that, kindly put, is not favorable to African Americans. The book, though popular in its era, is jarring on contemporary ears.

When he was thirty-three and at the peak of his popularity, McNeill died at his Wagram family home. He was buried near the center of the Spring Hill Cemetery, under a massive longleaf pine. A white marble obelisk marks the grave. McNeill's birthplace, a house called Ellerslie, was moved to a spot across the road from the cemetery in 1967 and restored by the Richmond Temperance and Literary Society Commission. The society's octagonal, brick meetinghouse is set farther back on this appealing property, where Sherman's army passed through on its northern march. The story goes that Sherman's troops blasted to bits the upside-down plaster chalice and Bible that have been restored atop the brick building.

From McNeill's house, we head toward the Lumber River. Turn left on Old Wire Road (NC 144) and left on Wagram's Main Street (US 401). As you enter

The tea-colored Lumber River at Riverton catches sunlight near the shore to reveal the effects of tannin leached from leaves that darken its depths. Local writers John Charles McNeill and Gerald Johnson likely visited this particular swimming hole.

town, note the two historical markers on the left dedicated to McNeill and his kinsman, Gerald White Johnson, one of the most important journalists of the twentieth century, whose boyhood home was nearby.

Watch for Riverton Road and turn right. Though it is not initially apparent, this old road follows alongside the Lumber River. About 2.5 miles beyond the attractive Cypress Bend Vineyards, Riverton Road takes a long leftward curve toward the river. Watch for the No Parking signs on either side of the asphalt, which mark a favorite swimming hole for locals who want to cool off in the dark river—surely a setting that both McNeill and Johnson knew well.

The Lumber flows gently here. Its disarming color is described by Gerald Johnson in his first novel, *By Reason of Strength* (1930), which features a female protagonist: "Through the midst of the swamp usually a sluggish stream meandered, its water stained by juniper roots to the color of strong coffee—sullen, sinister streams, any one of them might have been the dreadful river across which Charon ferried the souls of the dead, or so Catharine thought" ([Laurinburg: St. Andrews College Press, 1994], 23).

Born in 1890, Gerald Johnson, whose mother was a McNeill, also studied at Wake Forest College. His father was the editor of a Baptist publication, and following in his father's footsteps, Johnson established his own newspaper while still in college. He ended up in the newspaper business in Baltimore, writing editorials for the *Baltimore Sun* for nearly forty years. Johnson spent another twenty-five years writing for the *New Republic*. All along, he was also writing biography and accessible histories for children and adults, and his essays were gathered in anthologies—some forty books in all. Charlotte journalist, essayist, and biographer Harry Golden called him one of the greatest stylists in American journalism. Adlai Stevenson, for whom Johnson wrote speeches, called him "the conscience of America."

Johnson went to the same college as Thomas Dixon, the author of a trilogy of novels that presented the Ku Klux Klan as heroic defenders of racial purity (see Tours 9 and 14). Johnson accused Dixon of "asininity" in a column, and he was an unapologetic progressive who wrote blistering critiques of the Jim Crow South. In 1932, he published an essay lambasting the Agrarians at Vanderbilt—a group of writers who suggested that the South should eschew industrialization in favor of "the old way" of life:

> At first blush it seems incredible that twelve men, all born and raised in the South, all literate, and all of legal age, could preach such a doctrine without once thrusting the tongue in the cheek or winking the other eye. . . . Of such a philosophy one can only say that it smells horribly of the lamp, that it was library-born and library-bred, and will perish miserably if it is ever exposed for ten minutes to the direct rays of the sun out in the daylight of reality.—From "No More Excuses: A Southerner to Southerners," by Gerald Johnson, *Harper's*, February 1932, 333.

Johnson grieved at the racial violence that erupted during the civil rights movement. He opposed the Vietnam War and blasted Richard Nixon for the Watergate burglary. He lived a very full ninety years and even took his commentaries to television late in his career. Though his name may not be as familiar as the names of his colleagues H. L. Mencken and W. J. Cash, Gerald Johnson's impact on journalism was indelible.

To reach the next stop in Laurinburg, follow Riverton Road south. It becomes Lee's Mill Road, which ends at a T. Turn left on Blakely Road, which will become North Main Street, in Laurinburg. Turn left to stay on North Main as it merges with US 15/501. In 2.6 miles, turn left onto Lauchwood Drive and then take the first right onto Dogwood Mile Road, to enter the campus of St. Andrews University.

Poets Ronald Bayes and Samuel Ragan at a reading on the campus of St. Andrews College in Laurinburg, around 1980. Courtesy of St. Andrews University.

■ LAURINBURG

This elegant town of older houses surrounded by mature plantings of azaleas and dogwoods has been a center of literary activity since 1961, when St. Andrews Presbyterian College opened. Created by the merger of Flora Macdonald College, in Red Springs, and Presbyterian Junior College, in Maxton, the campus at 1700 Dogwood Mile Road was built without barriers, making it an early leader in serving students with physical disabilities.

At first, St. Andrews's liberal arts curriculum was interdisciplinary and team-taught by a young faculty. As a college established in the 1960s, the school was known for its innovative, socially conscious, and experimental ethos. Out of this culture came St. Andrews Press, launched in 1972 by the school's writer-in-residence and distinguished poet and teacher, Ronald Bayes.

Introducing new or unknown writers to readers has been the press's emphasis through more than 200 published books. The *St. Andrews Review*, the press's literary journal, has likewise given many writers their first publication. In addition, St. Andrews's Fortner Writers Program has sponsored campus readings once a week for nine months every year for forty years, bringing to campus an astonishing array of writers, including Tom Wolfe, James Dickey, Basil Bunting, and Robert Creeley.

In 1977, under Bayes's leadership, St. Andrews hosted a reunion of alumni and faculty of Black Mountain School, founded in the 1930s in the North Carolina mountains (discussed in *Literary Trails of the North Carolina Mountains*). St. Andrews alumni still talk about the reunion, which included presentations by choreographer Merce Cunningham, composer John Cage, and poets Ed Dorn, Fielding Dawson, Jonathan Williams, and Joel Oppenheimer. In honor of inventor and architect Buckminster Fuller, who also came for the reunion, a group of St. Andrews students built a geodesic dome on campus and camped out in it for weeks.

Retrace your path on Dogwood Mile to Lauchwood Drive and turn right. Follow Lauchwood nearly a mile past Scotland Memorial Hospital to US 501 South and turn right. In about four miles, turn left on Old Maxton Road. In 3.7 miles, turn right on Patterson Road. Go one mile and turn left on Hayes Road. Though it is unpaved, this rural road is the most direct route to what is now called Maxton Pond, the site of a famous skirmish between a group of Lumbee Indians and the Ku Klux Klan and now a tranquil spot for fishing.

■ MAXTON

In 1958, local newspapers publicized plans by the Ku Klux Klan to stage a rally at Hayes Pond. Klan leader James "Catfish" Cole aimed to speak at length against the "mongrelization" of whites and Indians in the area. As it turned out, on the night of the assembly, Lumbee and Tuscarora tribesmen outnumbered Klansmen ten to one. Gunshots rang out, and the Klansmen fled into the swamp. No one was injured, and the event ended with the Indians helping "Catfish" Cole liberate his car from a ditch. He was never seen again in these parts. This story, told and retold by generations in the area, was similar in many ways to the Klan buffoonery depicted in a short story by *New Yorker* magazine contributor Joseph Mitchell, whose hometown is ahead on this tour.

Howard Owen, born on the edge of Fayetteville, writes vividly about Scotland County in several novels, and he might well have had Maxton Pond in mind in this passage from his best-selling book, *Littlejohn*:

Before the loggers, they used to tap these pine trees for turpentine. Somebody's always tried to find some kind of use for this sad old country back here. A few years ago, they tried to make Maxwell's Millpond into a re-

Formerly known as Hayes Pond, today Maxton Pond is a popular fishing spot. Lumbee Indians famously interrupted a Ku Klux Klan rally held here, in protest of the proceedings. A short story by Joseph Mitchell, a writer for the New Yorker *magazine who was born in Fairmont, finds the burlesque in the incident.*

sort, like White Lake. They built them a road in from the other side and sold a few lots. They drained all the tea-colored water out and tried to pump clear water in from the East Branch and the natural springs down here. It seemed like it was working for a while, but the old water come back like a bad penny, darker than ever, and Sandy Spring Lake is Maxwell's Millpond again.—From *Littlejohn*, by Howard Owen (New York: Random House, 1992), 11.

Beyond the pond, bear right. Where Hayes Road meets NC 130, turn left to reach downtown Maxton, originally known as Shoe Hill. The first institution of higher education in North Carolina to grant degrees to women, Floral College, was established here by Presbyterians in 1841.

Nancy Roberts was a prolific writer who spent her summers in Maxton as a child. The stories she heard fed a lifelong fascination with local history. She writes of her Maxton grandfather in the preface to her book *Civil War Ghost Stories and Legends*: "During my childhood years I knew him as the one who presided over the twilight depths of an immense general store fragrant with the odors of hoop cheese, country hams, seeds and fertilizer. The shelves were laden with bolts of fabric and black patent Mary Janes and over the front of the store a sign bore the name McRae Company in tall antique gold letters" ([Columbia: University of South Carolina Press, 1992], ix).

Roberts's career as a writer began with a series of ghost stories published in the *Charlotte Observer*, which prompted a letter from Carl Sandburg, writing from his North Carolina mountain home in Flat Rock. His encouragement, Roberts wrote, was a critical boost at a time when she might otherwise have stopped writing. The book quoted above was Roberts's twenty-first.

From the town formerly known as Shoe Hill, we proceed to a village once called Scuffletown—now Pembroke—the site of more Lumbee lore. At the intersection of NC 130 and M. L. King Jr. Drive (US 74 Business East) in Maxton, turn right. Continue onto Alternate US 74 East for 5.3 miles and turn left onto NC 710 West. The next stop, the University of North Carolina at Pembroke (UNC-Pembroke), is on the left. Cross the railroad tracks on University Drive to park and roam the campus.

◾ PEMBROKE

WAY DOWN PEMBROKE WAY (EXCERPT)
Gladiolas sway with blossoms,
Children laugh and play.
'Simmon trees are hung with 'possums
Way down Pembroke way.
Shake my hand and keep on squeezing!
Folks all specialize in pleasin'
Way down Pembroke Way!
—From *Beside the Trickling Brook: A Collection of Poems by Lewis Barton* (Pembroke, N.C.: Barton House, 2001), 37.

Though he was legally blind, Lumbee poet, historian, editor, and newspaper publisher Lew Barton was the patriarch of a literary family. His children continue his work in their own writing and publishing aimed at the preservation and promotion of Lumbee history.

Here on the UNC-Pembroke campus, Old Main Building, prominently facing the railroad tracks, is a central repository of Lumbee history. It was headquarters to the Indian Normal School, the nation's first state-supported institution of higher education for Native Americans. Its proud history is documented in a book by Lumbee historian Adolph Dial—*The Only Land I Know.* Today, as part of the University of North Carolina system, Pembroke houses the Museum of the Native American Resource Center, inside Old Main—a splendid collection of artifacts and information.

Some anthropologists have speculated that the Lumbee people are the racially mixed descendants of the Lost Colony—the English settlers sponsored by Sir Walter Raleigh who disappeared from North Carolina's Roanoke Island in 1590. In its struggle for federal recognition, the tribe has suffered a number of indignities. Because of blurred racial identities in Robeson County among Indians, whites, and blacks, the authenticity of the Lumbee tribe has often been questioned.

Given this history, it was a bold undertaking for writer Josephine Humphreys, a white woman from Charleston, South Carolina, to attempt a novel based on a central figure in Lumbee lore. Humphreys's novel *Nowhere Else on Earth* is an imagined account of the life and death of Henry Berry Lowrie, a tribal hero in these swamplands during the Civil War era. Humphreys assumes the voice of Lowrie's wife, Rhoda Strong Lowrie.

The book was inspired by a chance encounter with a beautiful Lumbee bride whom Humphreys met on a train trip through the region in 1962, a year before she entered Duke University as a freshman. Humphreys had no knowledge of the Lumbee, but the bit of Lowrie family history that the girl conveyed on their train ride inspired Humphreys to become a writer. She studied creative writing at Duke with Reynolds Price, but it would take the experience of writing and publishing three novels before she dared undertake the Lumbee story, which involved a decade of research.

In the following passage, Rhoda Lowrie talks about the welcome advent of the railroad and how it temporarily broke down the routine practice of segregation in Robeson County:

The WC&R [Wilmington, Charlotte & Rutherford] was a stroke of luck for us when it opened—the longest straight run of track in America, eighty miles without a curve. . . . I have to say the train was from its first day down to now the only place in Robeson County (if a moving train can be called

In Pembroke, local actors Melton Lowry and Hope Sheppard appeared as Henry Berry Lowrie and Rhoda Lowrie in Strike at the Wind, *the outdoor drama depicting Lumbee history in the region. The play was written by Randolph Umberger Jr., with music by Willie French Lowery. Courtesy of the Mary Livermore Library, UNC–Pembroke.*

a place) where I ever saw all these people at once, and the odd thing was they seemed to enjoy being thrown in together. Why life in Robeson could not be run on the same principles as the railroad stumped me. The only ones who held back were Miss McCabe's Shoe Heel aunts, safely huddled behind the glass partition of the Ladies' Compartment with the windows closed to avoid contamination, while in the general section, jugs of lemonade were passed from one bench to another and everyone drank and nobody cared. I saw Ben Bethea's little coal-black boy rap on the Ladies' glass, and the Shoe Heel aunts opened their wrist-string pouches to give him a penny. And then they came out from behind the glass to stand in the aisle and watch his jig, and they started breathing the air the rest of us

were breathing. Through the open top half of the windows blew in the hot Robeson County smells of pine and mud and pigs, and the Shoe Heel aunts flushed pink, their eyes sparked, and they struck up conversations with people they ordinarily disdained. Maybe this was because they were on a moving train—a ride does not last forever, and it's not likely there will be any copulation of the races on a railroad bench, not in a full car anyway.
—From *Nowhere Else on Earth*, by Josephine Humphreys (New York: Penguin, 2000), 114, 115–16.

To reach Fairmont, the birthplace of *New Yorker* magazine writer Joseph Mitchell, take NC 711 ten miles toward Lumberton and after crossing I-95, turn right onto West Fifth Street. Then take the first left onto Starlite Drive, which runs into NC 41. Head south on 41 for 7.6 miles, and as you are approaching Fairmont, watch for El Dorado Street. Turn right there and then left onto Marion Stage Road. Pull into the Floyd Memorial Cemetery on the right.

■ FAIRMONT

If you stand with your back to the highway, the Mitchell family plot is 180 degrees around the rotary, on the right side of the graveyard and at the far left corner of the lane that next crosses the main drive.

Joseph Mitchell never completed his degree at the University of North Carolina, but his clever and unadorned writing for the *New Yorker* magazine earned him election to the American Academy of Arts and Letters. This is a rare accomplishment for a reporter, according to Mitchell's *New Yorker* colleague Calvin Trillin, who wrote the foreword to the latest edition of Mitchell's collected works, *Up in the Old Hotel*, published in 2000.

Mitchell wrote mostly about the people he met daily on the streets of Manhattan, but one short story, written in 1939, eerily anticipates the 1958 clash of the Klan with other members of the community in nearby Maxton. In fact, Mitchell's fictional Ku Klux Klan leader is also nicknamed "Catfish," and his effort to terrorize the citizens of "Black Ankle County" is such an embarrassment that the wives of the local Klansmen in the story end up cutting up their husbands' robes to use for pillowcases and aprons. Here is Mitchell's characterization of Catfish:

There was certainly nothing frightening about Mr. Giddy, the Führer of the local Klan. His full name was J. Raymond Giddy, but he had a mustache on his plump face which he treated with beeswax and which stuck out

New Yorker *magazine*
writer Joseph Mitchell
was born in Fairmont,
where this pleasant park
commemorates the town's
war veterans.

sharply on both sides, and consistently he was almost always referred to as Mr. Catfish Giddy, even in the columns of the weekly Stonewall News. He was rather proud of the nickname. He used to say, "I may not be the richest man in Black Ankle County, but I sure am the ugliest; you can't take that away from me." Mr. Giddy was a frustrated big businessman. Before he got interested in the Klan, he had organized the Stonewall Boosters and a Stonewall Chamber of Commerce, both of which died after a few meetings. He was always making speeches about big business, but he was never much of a big businessman himself. —From "The Downfall of Fascism in Black Ankle County," in *Up in the Old Hotel*, by Joseph Mitchell (New York: Pantheon, 1992), 347.

A historical marker honoring Mitchell, placed by the citizens of Fairmont, stands on Main Street, near the public library. From the cemetery, take the first left off Marion Stage Road, which is North Main Street, and follow it south to town.

A poem by A. R. Ammons sings, "How I wish I were over by Fair / Bluff where the old Lumber River snakes under overhanging / cypress-moss, black glass going / gleamy deep and slow."

To reach our last stop, stay on NC 41 for seven miles to the intersection with NC 904. Turn right, and in eight miles you will reach the good-looking town of Fair Bluff, worth a quick tour just to witness the hanks of Spanish moss in the live oak as they sway over the Lumber River. Continue on 904 another fifteen miles to Tabor City. Watch out. One wrong turn and you're in South Carolina.

■ W. HORACE CARTER MUSEUM

1108 East Fifth Street, Tabor City

910-653-3153

Tabor City brings up one more story of the Klan and the valiant journalist who fought them here. W. Horace Carter, born in Albemarle, was the first in his family to graduate from high school. He went on to edit the *Daily Tar Heel* while attending the University of North Carolina at Chapel Hill. After his service in World War II, Carter worked for the merchants' association in Tabor City and then founded the local newspaper, the *Tribune*. On a Saturday in 1950, the Klan staged an enormous parade in town to recruit new members. Carter took offense and launched a three-year series of reports and editorials about local Klan activities, which led to an FBI investigation and more than a hundred prosecutions of Klansmen, including the region's "grand dragon."

Read all about it: This detail from a bronze sculpture outside the W. Horace Carter Museum, in Tabor City, celebrates the town's most distinguished newspaper editor.

During this period, Carter and his family were constantly subjected to death threats. Advertisers sympathetic to the Klan pulled out of the newspaper. Locals shunned Carter's family. Carter's colleague Willard Cole, of the *News Reporter*, in nearby Whiteville, stood with Carter and joined in the effort to publicize Klan violence.

In 1953, these two newspapers and their editors shared the first Pulitzer Prize awarded to a rural publication. Carter, who died in 2009 at the age of eighty-eight, is now celebrated in Tabor City at the museum that bears his name. There you can see copies of his editorials and examine the printing equipment of the era.

■ LITERARY LANDSCAPE

Storytelling and Arts Center of the Southeast

131 South Main Street, Laurinburg

910-277-3599

http://www.storyartscenter.org

Founded in 2006, this storefront organization puts on a storytelling festival each April in Laurinburg and sponsors workshops and other activities throughout the year that are related to the spoken word.

North Carolina Indian Cultural Center

638 Terry Sanford Road, Pembroke

This important cultural center has a replica of Henry Berry Lowrie's cabin and a museum with artifacts from the Lumbee Tribe. The outdoor drama *Strike at the Wind* was also performed here in the summer for many years. With music by Lumbee composer Willie French Lowery, the play—written in 1976 by Randolph Umberger Jr.—tells the story of Rhoda and Henry Berry Lowrie.

Pembroke Magazine

http://www.uncp.edu/pembrokemagazine

Founded in 1969 by the late Norman Macleod, editor and publisher of many fine literary journals, this little magazine has grown from a student publication to a 300-page annual of international scope.

Lumberton : Elizabethtown : White Lake : Singletary Lake : Clarkton : Whiteville : Lake Waccamaw : Green Swamp

Venture deep into the swamp or stay on the paved road and read the writers who understand the call of the wilderness and have mastered the lay of the lowlands.

Writers with a connection to this area: A. R. Ammons, William Bartram, Kaye Gibbons, William Hooks, John Manuel, Joanne Martell, Jill McCorkle, Millie-Christine McKoy, Heather Ross Miller, Guy Owen, Tim Pridgen

■ **LUMBERTON**

To read Jill McCorkle is to get acquainted with Lumberton, sometimes called Fulton and sometimes Marshboro in her stories and novels. Winner of the North Carolina Award for Literature, McCorkle was born in this town, which, according to its visitors' bureau, "is known as the halfway point between New York and Florida." McCorkle attended the University of North Carolina at Chapel Hill, where she met Louis D. Rubin Jr., the founder of Algonquin Books of Chapel Hill, and later earned an MFA in creative writing from Hollins College. In an unprecedented debut, Rubin published McCorkle's first two novels simultaneously, in 1984. She has since written six more books and taught at her alma mater and at Tufts, Brandeis, Harvard, and Bennington. She is a frequent instructor at the summer Sewanee Writers' Conference in Tennessee. McCorkle lives in Hillsborough and teaches graduate-level creative writing at North Carolina State.

Though Lumberton has a long and rich history, McCorkle has mostly offered up the town of her childhood and youth as it was in the late 1960s and 1970s. Flanked by the Lumber River

tour 5

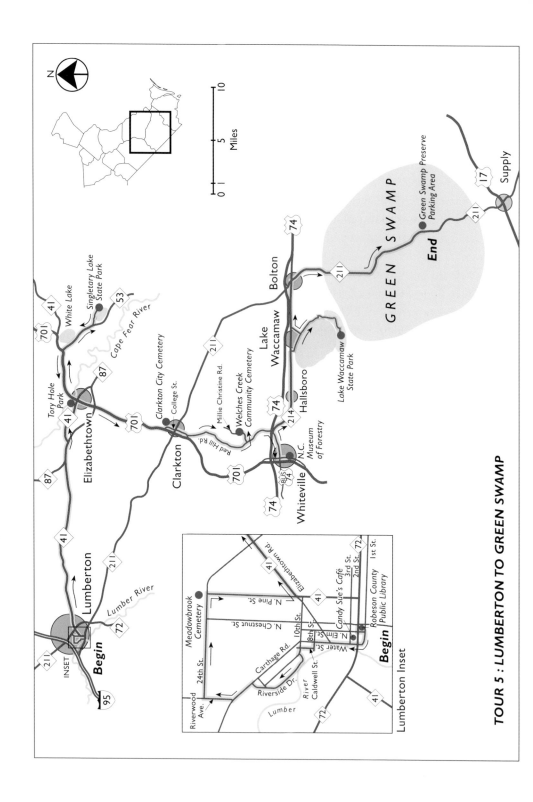

TOUR 5 : LUMBERTON TO GREEN SWAMP

and I-95, Lumberton tends to bring curious people to town who are on their way elsewhere, as McCorkle's fiction attests.

Downtown and near the river is the Robeson County Public Library at 101 North Chestnut Street. Here the stacks still bear signs from the era in which tobacco was dominant, warning patrons: "No Smoking While Shelving Books." To the south of the library, across First Street, is the Robeson County History Museum, at 101 South Elm. Both of these institutions are good places for you to get your bearings before you continue this tour.

From here, proceed west on First Street to Water Street and turn right, following the Lumber River as it sidles along the downtown district. When you reach Eighth Street, turn left.

We used to all come outside when the streetlights came on and prowl the neighborhood in a pack, a herd of kids on banana-seat bikes and mini-bikes. The grown-ups looked so silly framed in their living room and kitchen windows. They complained about their days and sighed deep sighs of depression and loss. They talked about how spoiled and lucky children were these days. We will never be that way, we said, we will never say those things. We popped wheelies in pursuit of the mosquito truck, which was a guarantee on humid summer nights. We rode behind the big gray truck, our laughter and screams lost in the grinding whir of machinery, our vision blurred by the cloud of poison. We were light-headed as we cruised our town—the dark deserted playground of the elementary school, the fluorescent-lit gas stations out on the service road of the interstate that scarred the rural landscape, past the run-down apartment complex where transient military families lived, past houses that were identified by the histories of death, divorce, disaster.—From "Billy Goats," in *Creatures of Habit*, by Jill McCorkle (Chapel Hill: Algonquin Books of Chapel Hill, 2001), 1–2.

Turn right on Caldwell and left on Tenth Street, following it to Riverside Drive. Turn left. Where the Lumber River bends away from town, a lush city park rests in the crook of land below the road. It's a good place to take a walk, but beware, as McCorkle writes in the short story "Snipe": "Our mosquitoes are so big," her daddy was famous for saying, "they roll up your pants legs to bite you" (*Creatures of Habit*, 33).

This sometimes forbidding river appears again in McCorkle's novel *Carolina Moon*:

Future novelist and short-story writer Jill McCorkle demonstrates her early angling expertise in Robeson County. Photo by John McCorkle Jr., courtesy of Jill McCorkle.

When people are missing in Marsh County, the river is one of the first places to go. This was something Robert knew even before he came to work in this town. The men down at the station regularly drag nets up and down through that twisting brown river, one man in the boat designated to watch the branches of the live oaks for snakes that might sense the warmth of bodies below and drop onto them. —From *Carolina Moon*, by Jill McCorkle (New York: Random House, 1996), 113.

Continue on Riverside Drive to Carthage and turn left. In three blocks, turn right on Riverwood Avenue. Jill McCorkle's childhood home sits at the corner of Twenty-fourth Street and Riverwood. As a child, she rode her bicycle east from here all the way across town to the Meadowbrook Cemetery, where her grandparents are now buried. McCorkle says that while you're in the neighborhood, you should have a meal at Candy Sue's Café, 111 West Third Street (910-739-8430).

From Meadowbrook Cemetery, follow North Pine Street south, back through the downtown district, and turn left onto Elizabethtown Road (NC 41 North/ East), to reach our next destination.

■ ELIZABETHTOWN

This proud and lively town of fewer than 4,000 citizens sits on a high bluff above the Cape Fear River and serves as the seat of Bladen County. Melvin's, on West Broad Street, is a hot dog and hamburger stand that has been beloved by travelers and townspeople since 1938. Around the corner from the grill is an enormous mural of NASA astronaut Curtis Brown, who was born here.

Beyond downtown, under the high bridge over the Cape Fear River, is a significant historical site, worthy of a hike through the lovely understory along the river's edge. From the center of town, turn left onto US 701 toward the river. The entrance to Tory Hole is on the left, marked by a sign.

Tory Oath, a novel by Tim Pridgen, recounts the conflict in North Carolina in the late 1700s between the Scots who sided with the Revolutionaries and those who remained loyal to Britain. In 1781, rebellious Whigs overcame Tory forces in a battle that sent the British running into this low spot, which thereafter came to be called Tory Hole. Imagine trying to travel these swamplands on foot or oxcart, as Pridgen's characters did.

Across the swamp came the faint creak of wooden axles in hubs. Somewhere, down under the green, a yoke of oxen strained at a cart. The load was golden yellow split heart pine, cut from the logs in the islands. Gillie Black, the slave lad, hauled it in to the kilns. The trail was black mud, half-spoke deep, and as the oxen groaned and heaved, gobs of ooze slopped down the spokes of the creeping wheels and dropped back to the ground. Duncan saw that as though he were there.

He looked long and intently, not at the blue-green shadow which flowed from the cloud upon the swamp, nor at the proud cypresses which here and there lofted their green feathered leaves above the trees, but to listen to the distressed cart hubs.

—From *Tory Oath*, by Tim Pridgen (Garden City, N.Y.: Doubleday, Doran, 1941), 4.

■ WHITE LAKE

Continue on 701 across the Cape Fear River toward White Lake. One of North Carolina's inland bays, White Lake is aptly named. The bright sand on the bottom is visible even at the clear lake's deepest point, which is about seven feet. One theory holds that meteorites struck the earth, creating the series of shallow inland ponds in this vicinity. Of course, that notion begs the question, where are the meteorites now?

White Lake, once pristine and undeveloped, was known as Bartram Lake when the family of writer and naturalist William Bartram owned property in the vicinity in the eighteenth century. It was also the honeymoon destination for Kaye Gibbons's protagonist in *A Cure for Dreams*, her novel set during the Depression. Today, houses, trailers, and campers, row upon row, radiating out from shore, surround it. The land is all privately owned, save for a Future Farmers of America camp. Small motels in a string along the southern shore provide the only practical access a visitor can find to dip a toe in the water.

■ SINGLETARY LAKE STATE PARK

From US 701, turn right on NC 53 and follow it along the shoreline of White Lake to reach Singletary Lake State Park—a natural preserve several miles south. Poet and novelist Heather Ross Miller lived here for thirteen years during her marriage to Clyde Miller, a park ranger she met in her native Stanly County. Her memoir of the period, *Crusoe's Island*, is a powerful account of her life as she raised young children in the profound isolation of the swamp. The book's title refers to an actual community farther south and east of Singletary Lake, but Miller liked the reference to Daniel Defoe's novel *Robinson Crusoe*, because she did at times feel stranded in this place.

> We walked out to the big flat deserted lake and heard wild ducks and geese honking somewhere on the far shore. Out in the middle, the birds moved like hundreds of dark spots, settling and resettling. Their delicate fluff and pale feathers floated along the pier pilings, caught in pondweed and juniper. The clean fragrance of longleaf pines hung over everything. Warm enough to be spring, the air so soft it stroked my face. Yet it was late December, almost Christmas, 1961. The baby grabbed at things in the white sand, sticks and long brown pine straw, an old gray seashell. It seemed all right there. It smelled good.
>
> And Clyde asked me, as he had back in the Piedmont on our snowy wedding day, Do you think you can stand this? His voice patiently questioning, his eyes a curious blue. [...]
>
> I came to know Crusoe was not a place for everybody. A person from Raleigh or Charlotte might well go a little crazy there in the silence and the solitude of those trees, that whispering sand. Suspicious of the thick

This giant pine stands sentinel in Singletary Lake State Park, where writer Heather Ross Miller found inspiration for her memoir, Crusoe's Island: The Story of a Writer and a Place.

peace gliding in every evening over the tops of pines and oaks, pouring like breath through the low scrub.

A person might well curse the isolation as beautiful and remote as the moon, and hurry back to her bustling, impersonal traffic, her solid pavement impervious to any Aeolian effect, and hide beneath the piquant smell of crowds.

—From *Crusoe's Island: The Story of a Writer and a Place*, by Heather Ross Miller (Wilmington, N.C.: Coastal Carolina Press, 2000), 9, 25.

Among many memorable scenes, Miller's delicate and glowing memoir describes the experience of a total eclipse of the sun here in 1970 and her frequent confrontations with wildlife and rarer encounters with local families who had a long attachment to the place.

Clyde Miller died of pancreatic cancer some five years after the family left Singletary. Miller and her children brought his ashes back to scatter here. Miller writes: "The park taught us too much of health and good humor and stubborn love. The children and I never lost the adventure of Crusoe's Island any more than we lost Clyde" (207).

Retrace the route along NC 53 north to US 701, turn left back toward Elizabethtown, and continue on 701 south to Clarkton. As you near the town limits, turn right on North College Street to visit the business district.

■ CLARKTON

Poet and novelist Guy Owen is buried in the Clarkton City Cemetery on the left as you come into town on North College Street. As you enter the cemetery's main entrance, his grave is on the far right side near the stand of pines that flanks the only other driveway that leads out of the graveyard.

By all accounts, Owen was a marvelous teacher and salient influence on his students, among them Betty Adcock, Sally Buckner, and Robert Morgan. Owen taught at Davidson, Elon, and North Carolina State and founded the literary journal *Southern Poetry Review*. His apprentices often quote his rule of specificity in descriptive prose: "Never write flower," he would say. "Write rose or marigold or chrysanthemum."

As noted on his gravestone, Owen is best known for *The Ballad of the Flim-Flam Man*, a novel that was made into a movie in 1967. But he was also a masterful formalist poet, and many would argue that his best novel was his last, *Journey for Joedel*, first published in 1970 and reissued in a fortieth-anniversary edition by Winston-Salem's Press 53.

In lyrical language that captures this landscape and its history, the novel presents the semiautobiographical coming-of-age story of a thirteen-year-old boy in the 1930s. Son of a white father and a Lumbee mother, Joedel lives in the little town of Clayton, a stand-in for Clarkton. He sometimes misses school to help his father with the cotton and peanuts crops, but in the course of the novel, he finally is allowed to make the journey to tobacco market with his father to witness the cutthroat business of the buyers and sellers.

> Tobacco was not like any other crop under the sun. It wasn't like cotton or corn or sugar cane. All that care and labor, and in the end it went up in smoke. Exhaled from somebody's lungs, or else spat out in nasty snuff spit by old women. Sometimes he would pause in the field and wonder if maybe Jean Harlow would smoke a cigarette made from one of their stalks. Somewhere was the girl he was going to grow up to marry; maybe in a few

years she would inhale into her body some of the very leaf he had plowed and cured.—From *Journey for Joedel*, by Guy Owen (Winston-Salem: Press 53, 1970, 2010), 57.

From the cemetery continue into town on North College Street, noting the historical marker on the left commemorating the Clarkton home, long gone now, that belonged to the mother of painter James Whistler, who was born in Wilmington but lived here for a time. Owen mentions this in the novel.

His mother kept only the parlor clear of newspaper, pasting a color picture of Whistler's Mother above the mantel. This she saved from the cover of *The Progressive Farmer* because Clinton had told her that the painter's mother had lived near Clayton, in a house that was now torn down except for the main chimney. Joedel knew the place well because once the fourth grade had gone there on a picnic and the teacher had made a little talk about Mrs. McNeill and how she ran the Yankee blockade at Wilmington to join her famous son in Europe (49).

A general store dating from 1917 and a handsome public library are the town's main attractions. Continue through Clarkton on South College. Watch for Red Hill Road and turn right.

■ **WELCHES CREEK CEMETERY**

Follow Red Hill Road for 6.5 miles to Millie Christine Road and turn left. Follow the road for a mile and watch for the small green sign on the right that marks the entrance to Welches Creek Community Cemetery. Turn into the dirt lane. The grave of interest is in the first row fronting the dirt road at the far end from the entrance.

A century ago, Millie-Christine McKoy, conjoined female twins born into slavery in 1851, died in their home community near here after a full life of touring and performing for audiences around the world, including President Abraham Lincoln and British and European royalty.

As toddlers, the twins were sold away from their mother to an unscrupulous promoter. Their first exhibition as an oddity of nature took place at the Agricultural Fair in Raleigh. They were later kidnapped by another opportunist and transported to Canada and then to England. For a time, they worked for circus man P. T. Barnum. However, Millie-Christine would eventually control their own

Conjoined twins Millie-Christine McKoy spoke five languages and entertained audiences around the world with their poetry and songs. Shown here in their prosperous retirement, they returned to Columbus County and built a ten-room house in Welches Creek, the community where they were born into slavery in 1851. A 2000 biography by Southern Pines writer Joanne Martell tells their story. Courtesy of the North Carolina Office of Archives and History, North Carolina Department of Cultural Resources.

fate, earn a substantial income, speak five languages, sing beautiful duets, and comport themselves with enormous sophistication and grace.

According to their biographer, Joanne Martell, of Southern Pines, the twins never lacked self-esteem and considered themselves one:

Two heads, four arms, four feet,
All in one perfect body meet.
—A poem by the twins, quoted in *Millie-Christine:*
Fearfully and Wonderfully Made, by Joanne Martell
(Winston-Salem: John F. Blair, 2000), 3.

Friends reported that each sister could be carrying on a wholly separate conversation with acquaintances when suddenly a sentence or phrase would come out of both mouths in unison.

When they were fifteen, Millie-Christine toured with North Carolina's more famous conjoined twins, Chang and Eng Bunker, of Mt. Airy, who were by then fifty-five. "In their younger days," Martell writes, "the brothers had performed amazing gymnastic feats on the stage. Now, they merely wandered about, weary old men answering questions they'd heard a thousand times.... Chang was tipsy much of the time, and Eng had to hold him steady" (121).

Millie-Christine retired to their birthplace in Welches Creek Community and built a grand Victorian house with ten rooms. They doted on their many nieces and nephews in the area and were faithful churchgoers.

In 1912, Millie contracted tuberculosis and would soon die from it. Knowing that Christine, whose separate lungs were still clear, would nevertheless succumb eventually, the twins' doctor rushed a message to the North Carolina governor for permission to help Christine die peacefully with the help of morphine once Millie died. Consent came, but it would take another seventeen hours for Christine to go. Hence, on the gravestone the twins' deaths are listed on consecutive days.

Return to Red Hill Road and turn left to pick up US 74 Business west into Whiteville.

■ WHITEVILLE

Whiteville is the seat of Columbus County and the county's only city. The film adaptation of *Bastard Out of Carolina*, the novel by South Carolina writer Dorothy Allison, was shot here.

If you would like to learn more about local natural history before entering the Green Swamp at the end of this tour, you may want to have a look around the North Carolina Museum of Forestry, at 415 South Madison Street, downtown.

Two important North Carolina writers hail from Whiteville. William H. Hooks, dancer, choreographer, and editor, was also the author of more than fifty children's books. Hooks left Whiteville to earn two degrees in Chapel Hill. He became a consultant to CBS for the *Captain Kangaroo* television series and then worked in children's programming for ABC and NBC before settling on Franklin Street in Chapel Hill. Hooks's best-known book is *Pioneer Cat*. He died at the age of eighty-six in 2008 and is buried at Western Prong Baptist Church, in Whiteville.

Two-time National Book Award winner Archibald Randolph Ammons (or A. R. Ammons as he was known in print) grew up in a large tobacco-farming

Poet A. R. Ammons was also an accomplished watercolorist. This self-portrait is among the writer's artifacts and papers housed at East Carolina University. Reid and Susan Overcash Literary Collection: A. R. Ammons Papers (#1096), East Carolina Manuscript Collection, J. Y. Joyner Library, East Carolina University, Greenville, N.C. Reproduced courtesy of Phyllis Ammons.

family south of town. Many of his relatives are buried at New Hope Baptist Church (252 Rough and Ready Road, five miles south of town off US 701).

Ammons served in the U.S. Navy in World War II, studied at Wake Forest College, and then became a principal and teacher at Hatteras Elementary School, on the coast. He also worked for a time as an executive in the manufacture of biological glass and then earned a graduate degree at the University of California at Berkeley.

All along, Ammons was writing poetry. He published his first collection in 1955, but his breakthrough to national recognition came in 1971, when Yale literary critic Harold Bloom placed his work in the company of Emerson's, Whitman's, and Dickinson's. By this time, Ammons had been teaching for seven years in what was to have been a temporary position at Cornell University in Ithaca, New York. He stayed there for three-and-a-half decades.

Ammons published twenty-seven books of poetry and one book of prose during his long career. He and North Carolina poet and novelist Robert Morgan were the powerhouses of creative writing at Cornell until Ammons's retirement, in 1998. Ammons's work earned him a host of awards, including a MacArthur Fellowship (the "genius grant," bestowed for the first time the year

Ammons won it), the Bollingen Prize, the Wallace Stevens Award, the Robert Frost Medal, and a National Book Critics' Circle Award, among others.

The subjects of his work range widely but are solidly anchored in the landscapes and colloquialisms of his Columbus County upbringing. East Carolina University writer Alex Albright collected Ammons's North Carolina poems in a single volume. This poem, the last in the book, touches on many names familiar to local residents all along this tour.

ALLIGATOR HOLES DOWN ALONG ABOUT OLD DOCK
Lord, I wish I were in Hallsboro, over by the tracks,
or somewhere down past the Green Swamp around Nakina, or
traipsing, dabbling in the slipping laps of Lake Waccamaw:

how I wish I were over by Fair
Bluff where the old Lumber River snakes under overhanging
cypress-moss, black glass going

gleamy deep and slow, 'gator easy and slow:
I bet a mocking bird's cutting loose a Dido in wisteria
vine or mimosa bush over there right now: if I were

down by Shallotte, the fish fries, scrubby sand-woods,
the beach dunes nearby: or Gause's Landing:
Lord, I wish I were home—those pastures—where I'll

never be again: Spring Branch Church, South
Whiteville, New Brunswick: mother and father, aunts,
uncles gone over, no one coming back again.
—From *The North Carolina Poems: A. R. Ammons*, edited by Alex Albright
    (Rocky Mount: North Carolina Wesleyan College Press, 1994), 116.

Proceed east on US 76 Business out of Whiteville and turn right on NC 214 (Sam Potts Highway) southeast to Hallsboro and on to Lake Waccamaw.

■ LAKE WACCAMAW

This egg-shaped lake, another shallow bay of mysterious origin, is settled all around with mostly modest houses. Lake Waccamaw State Park, at the southeastern end, offers good sites for camping and hiking. North Carolina nature writer and memoirist John Manuel, who prefers to tour North Carolina by canoe, has this advice:

If you're longing for a true wilderness experience, consider taking a canoe trip down the Waccamaw River. From the south end of the lake, this narrow stream winds through some of the wildest reaches of the Green Swamp. Red shouldered hawks, water moccasins, and alligators are frequently seen along the river. Black bears and bobcats also prowl the swamp though they are rarely observed. Approximately six miles south of the lake, the river passes the community of Riverview, once known as Crusoe Island. Though now connected to the outside world by a paved road, this once isolated place is thought to have been settled in 1790 by French citizens who fled Haiti during a war between the French and black slaves. Some members of this community still make canoes of cypress logs in the fashion of traditional swampers.—From *The Natural Traveler along North Carolina's Coast*, by John Manuel (Winston-Salem: John F. Blair, 2003), 309–10.

To experience the Green Swamp by car, continue east on NC 214 to Bolton and turn right on NC 211.

■ THE GREEN SWAMP

They rode Highway 211 to the beach—flat miles of swamp and stripped timber. They often went miles without seeing another car, past the homemade-ice-cream shop and farm stands, and past Lockwoods Folly, an area named for a man who once built a big beautiful ship and then had no way to get it to the ocean.—From "Driving to the Moon," in *Going Away Shoes*, by Jill McCorkle (Chapel Hill: Algonquin Books of Chapel Hill, 2009), 175–76.

Some twenty years before McCorkle wrote this passage, the Green Swamp seemed much more forbidding down this narrow road. Today aggressive timbering and settlement have tamed the passage to the state's southernmost beaches, but all fourteen of the carnivorous plants that grow in North Carolina are still represented in the North Carolina Nature Conservancy's Green Swamp Preserve. Five and a half miles before the town of Supply, look for the entrance to the preserve. Primitive trails and hunting sites fan out from the parking area if you want to see the swamp up close.

North Carolina's Green Swamp is one of the best examples of longleaf pine savannas, bay forests, and pocosin ecosystems remaining on the planet. North Carolina nature writer John Manuel unlocks the swamp's treasures in his 2003 book, The Natural Traveler along North Carolina's Coast.

■ LITERARY LANDSCAPE

River Way Outdoor Adventure and Education Center

600 Kingsdale Boulevard, Lumberton

910-736-5573

http://www.riverwayadventure.org/

Located on the river in downtown Lumberton, this nonprofit organization offers trips for children and adults down the Lumber River conducted by guides who tell stories about local history and ecology. Boats are provided and on-site camping is available.

Calabash : Sunset Beach : Shallotte : Holden Beach : Oak Island : Southport : Bald Head Island : Fort Fisher

North Carolina's southernmost beaches have personalities as varied as the writers who love them. Start with some Calabash shrimp and work your way up to the fort named for the father of one of North Carolina's nineteenth-century mountain writers.

Writers with a connection to this area: Jacqueline DeGroot, Christy Judah, Susan S. Kelly, Robert Hill Long, Tim McLaurin, Rebecca Pierre, Dannye Romine Powell, John Rowell, Robert Ruark, Sarah Shaber, Jim Shumaker, Frances Fisher Tiernan, Marybeth Whalen, Charles Whedbee, Emily Herring Wilson, Lee Zacharias

THE OTHER LIFE
The one by the ocean,
upstairs room with a view,
second row, an outside wooden stair . . .
I could have chosen that one,
climbing each night after work,
as a waitress maybe or clerk,
gauzy skirt whispering
at my ankle. Inside, one lamp
left burning, I settle cross-legged
on the bed, emptying quarters
into silvery pools, rolling them
into rounds of fives for the rent,
ten for the train trip to Arizona
next winter. Before supper,
filling the tub as the curtain drifts out
over the TV, revealing stars,
scattering last night's ashes.

tour 6

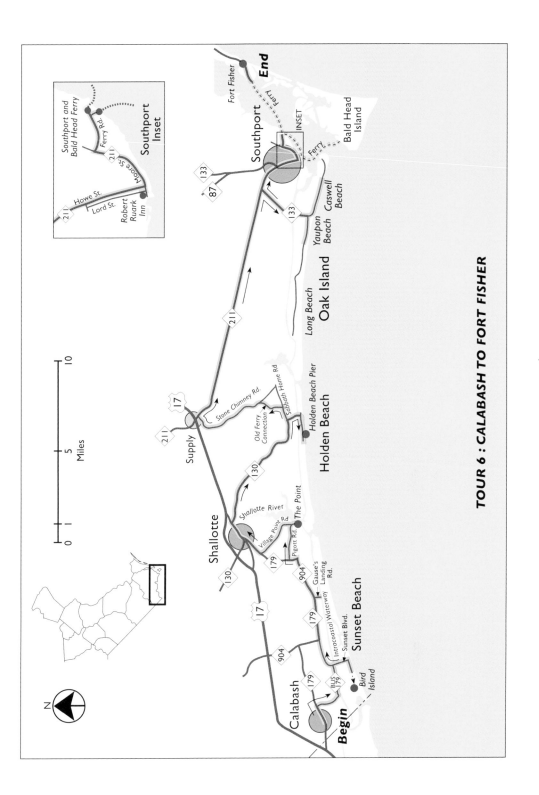

TOUR 6 : CALABASH TO FORT FISHER

Miles

N

Southport Inset

Southport and Bald Head Ferry

Ferry Rd.

211

Moore St.

Howe St.

Lord St.

Robert Ruark Inn

211

Fort Fisher

End

Fort Fisher Ferry

INSET

Bald Head Island

Southport

133

87

133

Ferry

Yaupon Beach

Caswell Beach

Long Beach

Oak Island

211

Stone Chimney Rd.

Supply

17

211

Old Ferry Connection

Sabbath Home Rd.

Holden Beach Pier

Holden Beach

130

Shallotte River

The Point

Shallotte

Village Point Rd.

130

Pigott Rd.

179

Gause's Landing Rd.

904

17

904

179

Intracoastal Waterway

Sunset Blvd.

Sunset Beach

130

Calabash

179

BUS 179

Bird Island

Begin

Instead, I live inland
in the yellow house on the corner
across from the park. That's where
I am now, in the white chair
by the upstairs window,
pin oaks splashing the panes.
Don't misunderstand. I'm here by consent.
I was simply trying to remember
the exact dimensions of longing.
—By Dannye Romine Powell, in *New Republic* 219, no. 26 (1998): 44.

■ CALABASH

Sooner or later, a great many North Carolinians entertain the fantasy, embodied in Charlotte writer Dannye Romine Powell's poem, of abandoning the inland life and working for tips where the air is heavy with salt and the best food is fried. And so we begin on Beach Drive (NC 179) in the village of Calabash, a noun that, when used as an adjective, refers to the lightly breaded seafood served here since the 1930s. Calabash's restaurants are clustered near the docks north of the Little River Inlet, northeast of the border with South Carolina. (Locals recommend the menus at Ella's and Seafood Hut as the most authentic, by the way.)

From here, continue up NC 179 to NC 179B and turn right. Follow it to the end at Shoreline Drive West and turn left. You will be traveling along the Intracoastal Waterway, with Bird Island across the water on your right. When you reach Sunset Boulevard, turn right and proceed over the enormous new corkscrew bridge to Sunset Beach—a village called Pearlie Beach in one of Raleigh writer Sarah Shaber's mysteries in the Professor Simon Shaw series:

Pearlie Beach was a small island south and west of Wilmington on the North Carolina coast. It had a town hall, a police department with one chief and two officers, a chapel, a seafood market, a convenience store, a fishing pier, a small apartment building, and about three hundred beach cottages. Every single structure had been built since 1954, when Hurricane Hazel devastated eastern North Carolina, leaving nothing standing on the island. Across the bridge on the mainland, out of the jurisdiction of the conservative Pearlie Beach town council, were a dozen or so restaurants, a water slide, tourist shops, a miniature golf course, a bookstore, an A.B.C. liquor store, two large marinas, and a campground, all of which lined Pearlie Beach Road on both sides until the intersection with NC Highway 17.—From *Snipe Hunt*, by Sarah Shaber (New York: St. Martin's Press, 2000), 20.

Once accessed by a floating pontoon bridge, Sunset Beach finally capitulated to the jam of boats on the Intracoastal Waterway that had to wait in line for cars to stop and the slow bridge to move. In its place, the state erected this new bridge—so lofty that it seems the Queen Mary could pass through.

When you reach the pier at the end of Sunset Boulevard, turn right on Main Street West to reach one of the truly remarkable writing sites in all of North Carolina.

■ BIRD ISLAND

There's public parking at the end of the pavement where a long boardwalk stretches out to the ocean. Take this path on foot or bicycle to see Bird Island, a state preserve that stretches west to the end of the island. Simply follow along the shoreline away from the last of the houses on Sunset Beach. In about a mile you'll come to a flagpole, a park bench, and a mailbox set at the top of a dune. Inside of the mailbox are pens and notepaper ready for any inspiration you might want to add to the bundle of notes, poems, and narratives written by other visitors who have made this hike. (If you should get to the stone jetty, you are in South Carolina and missed the mailbox.) Charlotte novelist Marybeth Whalen describes the experience of finding the mailbox:

Campbell pointed ahead of them. "Come on," he said and tugged on her hand. "I think I see it." He grinned like a little boy. They crested the dune and there, without pomp or circumstance, just as he had promised stood an ordinary mailbox with gold letters spelling out "Kindred Spirit."

"I told you it was here!" he said as they waded through the deep sand. "The mailbox has been here a couple of years," he said, his tone changing to something close to reverence as he laid his hand on top of it. "No one knows who started it or why, but word has traveled and now people come all the way out here to leave letters for the Kindred Spirit—the mystery person who reads them. People come from all over the world."
—From *The Mailbox*, by Marybeth Whalen (Colorado Springs: David Cook, 2010), 21–22.

The mysterious mailbox set on a dune at Bird Island, near Sunset Beach, invites writers to leave messages, poems, and notes for other beachcombers. Photo by Lee Zacharias, courtesy of Laughing Gull Cottage, Sunset Beach.

Amazingly, on the day we came down the boardwalk, Lee Zacharias, novelist and emerita instructor of creative writing at the University of North Carolina at Greensboro, was making her way back from Kindred Spirit on a bicycle. Zacharias was also carrying her camera. A photographer before she was a novelist, Zacharias supplied the photo of the site featured here.

Zacharias generally spends every May on Ocracoke Island, and her writing about that part of the coast appears later, in Tour 17.

From the mailbox, retrace your route down the beach, and when you are ready, go back across the bridge and follow Sunset Boulevard north, which joins up with NC 179/904 (also called Beach Drive). Continue straight ahead, and in another 2.4 miles watch for Gause's Landing Road on the right. Take this short jog into the scrub if you'd like to see a spot where President George Washington spent the night in 1791, a point also mentioned in A. R. Ammons's poem in Tour 5. The tunnel of ancient oaks draped with moss makes a magnificent frame through which to view the sound. The tour continues on NC 179 past the airport and into the inland village of Shallotte (pronounced shuh-'lote). The road takes a sharp curve left. In a half mile, turn right on Pigott Road. Follow it all the way to its end and turn right on Village Point Road, which leads to a beautiful spot overlooking the Shallotte River that locals call "the point." On

This Quercus virginiana, *or live oak, near the town of Shallotte, is reputed to be more than 2,000 years old. It stands near the healing waters that writer Charles Whedbee describes in* Legends of the Outer Banks.

the way in, look for an enormous oak tree on the left, which is said to be more than 2,000 years old. Behind the tree are the Healing Water Apartments. Writer Charles Harry Whedbee explains the origin of the name, which has been applied over the years to any number of businesses and sites:

> Present in this particular watercourse is a peculiar type of rush or reed that grows nowhere else, so far as is known, but grows here in abundance. In the center of the reed is found a substance that looks for all the world like bread. At last report the growth had not been pinned down other than being generally classified as of genus Juncus in the family Juncaceae. It is thought, however, that this plant is not unique to Shallotte's Inlet. Such a thing would be a rarity, indeed, in botany.
>
> It has been definitely established, however, by careful observation and repeated experiment, that when these reeds become inundated with salt water from the sea, as frequently happens, a sort of mould develops on the

breadlike substance and then washes off in large quantities until the water in the vicinity assumes a rather milky appearance. It is this milky water which has been present in all cases where infectious ailments and other ills have been reported as cured.

—From *Legends of the Outer Banks*, by Charles Harry Whedbee (Winston-Salem: John F. Blair, 1966), 44.

Charles Whedbee served as a judge in Greenville for more than thirty years and still found time to write five folklore collections about the North Carolina coast. He died in 1990, but his work is in print and remains popular.

If you are at the point between Thursday and Sunday, consider a stop at the Inlet View Bar and Grill. Village Point Road will carry you all the way back into the commercial district of Shallotte. US 17 is Main Street. Follow it northwest to Holden Beach Road (NC 130) and stay on NC 130 all the way to Holden Beach.

■ HOLDEN BEACH

"Holden Beach is proud of what we do not have," the town's website declares. This community along the shore comprises mostly modest older houses, set a bit farther apart than at other beaches on this tour. To walk into the Holden Beach Fishing Pier's store and grill, opened in 1959, is to go back in time. Inside, "Becky's Books on the Beach" is a shelf of dog-eared paperbacks set among the fishing tackle and minnow buckets for sale. A sign explains the process: "Borrow, Read, Return, Repeat." The book return is a pasteboard box set near the pinball machine.

EASTER AT HOLDEN BEACH FISHING PIER
Light rides the waves and breaks
to morning. The bleached pavilion's
silent as water, as light.

Now the pier walks long-legged
into the deep,
narrows to the sky.

Where the beginning
flames out
radiance and day.

—From *Solomon's Seal*, by Emily Herring Wilson
(New Braunfels, Tex.: Cedar Rock Press, 1978), 35.

As old-fashioned as the friendly village it serves, the Holden Pier has survived many a rugged storm. A poem by Winston-Salem writer Emily Wilson describes the pier as it "walks long-legged / into the deep, / narrows to the sky."

Winston-Salem poet Emily Herring Wilson has a second home in Swansboro further up the coast, and she has documented her experiences over many years up and down the North Carolina shoreline.

From Holden Beach, cross the bridge on NC 130, and in a mile, turn right on Sabbath Home Road. In .7 miles, turn left onto Old Ferry Connection, which becomes Stone Chimney Road. In 5.5 miles, turn right on NC 211. To visit Oak Island, turn right on NC 133.

■ **OAK ISLAND**

HAMMOCK
This hammock, connecting
tree to tree, becomes a
suspension bridge for ants
who travel the rope that

borders the edge. Focused,
they never lose their way,
never deviate into the web
of highways, the tempting
byways of the green
knotted network that forms
the bed. While live oak branches
bow in an elegant sweep
to the ground, pieces of sky
hide among the leaves overhead.
A blue jay startles herself
by landing too close to
the hammock. A mockingbird,
so enraptured by his own song,
lifts straight up from a fence post
at intervals in his singing.
A grey squirrel sits in
a patch of sun, holds
a toadstool in her paws,
turning it with her delicate
fingers as she eats her
way around the edge. This
is the business of the world.
Our business is not to miss it.
—Used by permission of Rebecca Pierre

Rebecca Pierre is a clay artist and poet who lives on Oak Island (aptly named, because it is still heavily wooded). The island encompasses the beaches Long, Yaupon, and Caswell.

Fayetteville-born short-story writer John Rowell places one of his character-istically funny and poignant stories down east on "Duck Island," a setting that seems suspiciously similar to Oak Island:

Between the hollowed out places through the trees, where little roads have been built, you can see, in the distances, the ocean on one side, the Intra-coastal Waterway on the other. Two years ago, Highway 17 was named in the Guinness Book of World Records as the site of more roadkill per mile than any other highway in the Southeastern United States. And the Duck Island Chamber of Commerce, bless their hearts, actually quoted that in brochures, as if that might be some kind of attractive feature to entice vacationers to come to Duck Island!—From "Wildlife of Coastal Carolina" in *The Music of Your Life*, by John Rowell (New York: Simon and Schuster, 2003), 233.

Though Oak Island made no such claims on roadkill and US 17 is not very close by, Rowell confesses that for this story he drew upon memories of Long Beach, where his uncle owned a house. Long Beach is also the thinly disguised setting of Greensboro writer Susan S. Kelly's novel *The Last of Something*, which has scenes at Figure Eight Island outside Wilmington, too.

For many years, Caswell Beach was home to retired newspaperman and Chapel Hill journalism professor Jim Shumaker. He was the inspiration for Jeff MacNelly's comic strip "Shoe." When Shumaker died, one of his many successful students, Tim McLaurin (discussed in Tour 3), said, "Jim Shumaker proved to me that it was okay for men to write. He wrote beautifully and used his words to make sense of the world, to illuminate and rectify wrongs. On a paper of mine in his editorial class, he once wrote: 'What you don't know about grammar, spelling, syntax and the like—and that is considerable—can be excused in the name of real writing talent.' I could not have received a higher compliment, nor motivation." McLaurin would go on from Shumaker's class to write many vivid descriptions of the eastern North Carolina he knew.

As might be expected on Yaupon Beach, the eponymous tree is everywhere. Native Americans from western North Carolina traveled great distances to acquire yaupon leaves in this vicinity. They used the leaves to brew a caffeinated tea for male purification rituals. Poet Robert Hill Long, who lived for some years just north of Oak Island, in Wilmington, writes from the point of view of an old man in these parts who, like the Indians before him, brewed the tea:

THE RED AND THE WHITE (EXCERPT)
[...] Months when oysters
aren't toxic, he roasts them by the bushel
and tosses shell scraped of oozy muscle

on a piled monument he knows himself by.
He eats like the old ones who summered here,
whose tongues manipulated language remote

as the Lord God bird, when lightning harvested
the starved undergrowth of pine barrens,
where children were assigned to shinny up

the oldest yaupons to pick the youngest leaves
to roast and grind into a tonic against costive winters.
It's the one boyish pleasure he permits himself

behind the house—to chin up, swing bare feet
on a bough, climb as far up and out
as he can without snapping something, to fetch

a tea that can't even explain the past. [...]
—From *10x3 Plus* 6 (2011): 40–42.

From Oak Island, return on NC 133 to NC 211 and drive east, all the way into Southport.

■ SOUTHPORT

If you look at a coastal map, this is the corner, the place where North Carolina's coastline takes a sharp curve and the east-west beaches become north-south beaches. Southport, the fishing village at this convergence, nearly always bustles. Residents of deluxe resort developments and nearby Wilmington have swelled business and traffic, but the charms of Southport's nineteenth-century residential section prevail. Wilmington film studios often use the town as a location for television and movie scenes, so if you visit most any café or restaurant here, you're likely to catch the buzz about which Hollywood actor might be coming to town this week.

Southport's literary legacy is significant. Writer Robert Ruark, born in Wilmington, spent his summers here during the 1920s. The pleasant house at 119 North Lord Street belonged to his beloved maternal grandfather, Edward Adkins, a former river pilot. It is now a bed-and-breakfast called the Robert Ruark Inn (910-363-4169).

As a boy, Ruark hung on his grandfather's every word and learned how to navigate the waters and woods all around:

I could throw a cast net, shoot a gun, row a boat, call a turkey, build a duck blind, tong an oyster, train a puppy, stand a deer, bait a turkey blind (illegal), call the turkey to the blind, cast in the surf, pitch a tent, make a bed out of pine needles, follow a coonhound, stand a watch on a fishing boat, skin anything that had to be skun, scale a fish, dig a clam, build a cave, draw a picture, isolate edible mushrooms from the poisonous toadstools,

Robert Ruark based his book The Old Man and the Boy *on his remembrances of summers spent with his maternal grandfather, Captain Edward Adkins, at this house, now a bed-and-breakfast inn in Southport.*

pole a boat, identify all the trees and most of the flowers and berries, get along with the colored folks, and also practice a rude kind of game conservation.—From *The Old Man's Boy Grows Older*, by Robert Ruark (New York: Henry Holt, 1993), 13.

Not unlike Hemingway in ruggedness, disposition, and simplicity of syntax, Ruark got his start writing for newspapers in Sanford and Hamlet. He soon left the state to become a hard-drinking, chain-smoking world traveler whose journalistic exploits in Africa led to a novel about the Mau Mau uprising called *Something of Value*. The book was banned by the British and Kenyan governments but nevertheless became his first best seller. Ruark also wrote, directed, and narrated a film called *African Adventure*.

His most enduring works, however, have been *The Old Man and the Boy* and its sequel (quoted above). The books were collected from regular columns of the same name that Ruark wrote for the magazine *Field and Stream*. They inspired generations of boys and years later motivated North Carolina writers Tim McLaurin and Pete Hendricks to offer up their own unadorned tales of hunting and other southern lore in novels and memoir.

In his later years, Ruark alienated some Southport folks with his ostentations. He sported around town in a Rolls Royce he'd shipped from London to Wilmington, but mostly people faulted him for his unwillingness to support his struggling parents, who were both alcoholics by then, as was Ruark himself.

Ruark died in 1965 and is buried in Spain, where he spent the last years of his life. He was inducted into the North Carolina Literary Hall of Fame in 2000 and the North Carolina Journalism Hall of Fame in 2009.

■ BALD HEAD ISLAND

You can take a pedestrian ferry from Southport to Bald Head, an island whose stubby lighthouse is within sight of Southport. Bicycles are also permitted on this ferry, because Bald Head has no automobiles—only service vehicles, golf carts, and bikes for conveyance. Take note: If you stay after dark on one of the beaches, the road back to the island's small commercial district (and ferry launch) is very dark, so bring a flashlight. However, a night visit to the beach is strongly recommended. The ocean plankton here are often luminescent, lighting up the waves like waterborne fireflies.

Bald Head is also a haven for turtles. Just as Robert Ruark did with his grandfather, it is possible to study these ancient reptiles as they nest on the beach, an adventure best accomplished under the supervision of the Bald Head Nature Conservancy's Sea Turtle Protection Program (910-457-0089).

> We only walked about a mile when we came on some fresh turtle tracks. The flipper marks were still crumbly on the sand, and there were no other marks leading back down to the ocean. We followed the tracks—as easy as following a tractor—and came to where the dunes started, where the sea oats quit growing, and there she was. She was durn near as big as the dining room table.—From *The Old Man and the Boy*, by Robert Ruark (New York: Henry Holt, 1993), 20.

Make a day of it on Bald Head. The ferry leaves from the same parking lot as another ferry this tour takes, which goes to Fort Fisher. To ride this particular ferry was a fanciful dream that Fayetteville writer Tim McLaurin had when he visited Carolina Beach as a boy with his family in the 1960s.

This gull breaks the rules on the ferry to Fort Fisher. The fort is named for the father of Frances Fisher Tiernan, who wrote many novels set in the North Carolina mountains under the pen name Christian Reid.

I always hoped that one day we might take the ferry across that wide water; a school friend had told me that hovering sea gulls would pluck bread from your hand at the rear of the boat. I had never been on a boat, unless I counted the cypress logs my brothers and I lashed together and floated upon in our irrigation pond.—From *The River Less Run*, by Tim McLaurin (Winston-Salem: John F. Blair, 2000), 102.

■ FORT FISHER

The ferry lands at this Confederate stronghold, which was built in 1861 and overtaken by Union forces in 1865. It was named for Charles F. Fisher, a colonel in a North Carolina regiment, who was killed at the battle of Manassas. He was the father of writer Frances Fisher Tiernan, of Salisbury. Her pen name was Christian Reid. Many of her romantic novels were set in the North Carolina mountains, where she coined a phrase, "The Land of the Sky," that stuck. Her only play, *Under the Southern Cross*, tackled the tragedy of the Civil War.

Pelican Bookstore

1780-10B Chandlers Lane

Village at Sunset Beach, Sunset Beach

910-579-8770

In a strip mall on Sunset Boulevard, near the intersection with NC 179/904, this store is a hot spot for lottery tickets and books self-published by local writers. According to the proprietors, of particular interest to local readers is the steamy *Widows of Sea Trail* trilogy, by Jacqueline DeGroot, which features the actual names of residents who live in the Sea Trails development, near Calabash. Check out the special regional bookcase that's filled with picture books, as well as other offerings by local historians such as Christy Judah.

Lowell's Bookworm

2980 Holden Beach Road SW, Supply

910-842-7380

http://www.lbookworm.com

Lowell's is a house full of finds, including an exceptional collection of mostly used books by North Carolina and southern writers, three friendly cats, and bargain paperbacks. This stop is a must for beach reading.

Books 'n Stuff

Live Oak Village

4961 Long Beach Road SE, #11, Southport

910-457-9017

http://booksnstuffnc.com/

On the way into Southport from Oak Island, this jam-packed bookstore features new and used books, accepts trade-ins, and stays abreast of area writers' latest works.

Carolina Beach : Wilmington : Wrightsville Beach

Elegant, azalea-festooned Wilmington is a city brimming with stories—some difficult, others playful. Although it has been buffeted by hurricanes, pirates, epidemics, the Civil War, and nineteenth-century racial violence, the city and its neighboring beaches prevail today by truth telling and a big menu of annual celebrations.

Writers with a connection to this area: Ellyn Bache, Frederick L. Block, Susan Taylor Block, Wendy Brenner, Ann Preston Bridgers, David Brinkley, David Cecelski, Charles Chesnutt, Emily Colin, Clyde Edgerton, Inglis Fletcher, David Bryant Fulton, Philip Gerard, Thomas Godfrey Jr., Rod Gragg, Virginia Holman, Stephen King, Robert Hill Long, Cash Michaels, Judy Nichols, Jessie Rehder, Anne Russell, John Sayles, Ben Steelman, John Jeremiah Sullivan, Beverly Tetterton, Tim Tyson, Michael White, Kathryn Worth

Wilmington's history is long and deep. For example, poet Thomas Godfrey Jr., of Philadelphia, whose father was a contemporary of Benjamin Franklin, came to Wilmington in 1759 and completed *The Prince of Parthia*—one of only two plays written by an American and produced before the Revolution. It is also the first printed American tragedy. Unfortunately, Godfrey took ill and died at the age of twenty-seven, before seeing his play produced. He is buried in the St. James churchyard, located downtown.

Inglis Fletcher, North Carolina's prolific historical novelist, is buried in the Wilmington National Cemetery. Kathryn Worth, great-granddaughter of Governor Jonathan Worth and kin to O. Henry, based her third young-adult novel, *Sea Change*, here; it tells the story of a teenager's first encounter with religious prejudice. Jessie Rehder, who directed the creative writing program at Chapel Hill in its formative years, was also born and raised in Wilmington.

Given such a span of writers, take the advice of longtime

tour 7

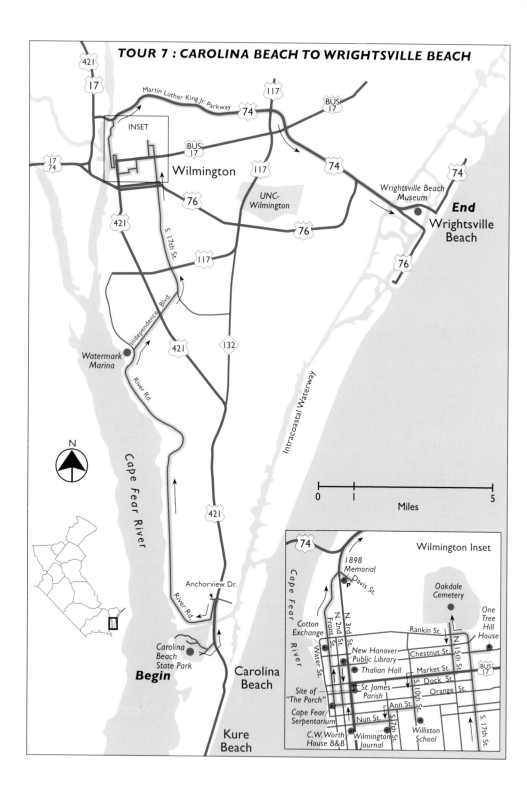

TOUR 7 : CAROLINA BEACH TO WRIGHTSVILLE BEACH

Martin Luther King Jr. Parkway

421
17

117

74

BUS
17

INSET

BUS
17

117

17
74

Wilmington

76

117

74

Wrightsville Beach
Museum

74

End
Wrightsville
Beach

UNC-
Wilmington

421

76

76

S. 17th St.

117

Independence Blvd.

421

132

Watermark
Marina

River Rd.

Intracoastal Waterway

N

Cape Fear River

0   1   5
Miles

Anchorview Dr.

421

River Rd.

Carolina
Beach
State Park

Begin

Carolina
Beach

Kure
Beach

Wilmington Inset

74

1898
Memorial

P   Davis St.

Oakdale
Cemetery

One
Tree
Hill
House

Cape Fear River

Cotton
Exchange

Rankin St.

N. 2nd St.
N. 3rd St.

N. 5th St.

Water St.
N. Front St.

New Hanover
Public Library

Chestnut St.

BUS
17

Thalian Hall

Market St.

S. 10th St.

Dock St.

Site of
"The Porch"

St. James
Parish

Orange St.

Ann St.

S. 17th St.

Cape Fear
Serpentarium

Nun St.

S. 17th St.

Williston
School

C.W. Worth
House B&B

Wilmington
Journal

book reviewer Ben Steelman of the *Wilmington Star-News* and get your hands on a couple of books to extend the scope of this tour, according to your own curiosity. Beverly Tetterton, Wilmington's local history librarian, remembers landmarks long gone in her book *Wilmington: Lost but Not Forgotten*. Poet Susan Taylor Block has created a number of photographic histories of the area. She teamed up with her husband, Frederick L. Block, to produce a memoir of his family, *Tale of a Shirtmaker: A Jewish Upbringing in North Carolina*. Her blog is a trove of still more stories: http://susantaylorblock.com.

Though today's Wilmington is decidedly urban, the natural elements that have shaped it are impossible to avoid. We begin on the outskirts, at Carolina Beach State Park. Pushcart Prize–winner Virginia Holman, best known for her novel *Rescuing Patty Hearst*, is on the creative writing faculty at the University of North Carolina at Wilmington (UNC-Wilmington) and lives close to the park, which is off US 421 on the south side of the Intracoastal Waterway.

> Deep into the woods, the mechanical hum of the world recedes, and something like quiet descends. The tree frogs plonk and the cicadas shirr and I hear a snake race through the tall grass. Out here I can hear each step I take. Here is a place where fox litter the path to their dens with half-gnawed rabbit bones, luring those looking for an unearned feast toward wet teeth. Here the canopy of longleaf pine and live oak grows thick enough to block the Carolina sun. Morning's damp coolness lingers even toward noon. The first waxy stalks of Indian pipe rise from the pine tags, pale as fog. I sit on the forest floor and breathe. The air smells sweet and pure. I stretch out on the ground, watching the pine needles glisten, watching the sky moving slowly beyond them, until I feel I belong here, until I feel small, and my fear, so individual, is claimed by something more vast and powerful than any human. In its place I feel myself filled with longing, with joy, with my satisfaction at being simply three things at once: a woman, alone, in the woods. —From "Three Walks," by Virginia Holman, in *Rambler* (May–June 2008): 36.

The Cape Fear River forms the western boundary of this park and of the city of Wilmington. From here, head north on US 421. Cross the Intracoastal Waterway and watch for Anchorview Drive on the left. Turn left and then immediately left again onto River Road, which will backtrack alongside US 421 the way you've just come and then curve to the right along the waterway. The road rolls thorough the salt marsh northwest toward Wilmington, and the Cape Fear is at your left.

Poet Robert Hill Long was raised in Wilmington and served as the first director of the North Carolina Writers' Network in the mid-1980s. His visceral poems are infused with the natural forces at work along the river he spent his boyhood exploring.

A FLATBOAT ON THE CAPE FEAR (EXCERPT)
This brown-backed river is the biggest alligator
in Carolina, an omnivore. Why else would it carry you
toward its mouth, among spits of sand and crab holes
the ocean licked into place a trillion bones ago?
You're taller than sword grass, not as tall or twisted
as a yaupon tree; the difference is that you try to make
floating alone in a boat mean something. You make marsh flats
tick: crab-claw against grass-hilt, the oblivion clock.
—From *Turnrow* 4, no. 2 (Winter 2005).

Philip Gerard came to the area in the late 1980s and now heads the creative writing program at UNC-Wilmington. An avid boatman, he has written a slew of fiction and nonfiction about the region. In this passage from an essay collection, Gerard explains another natural force to be reckoned with along these waters:

What they don't tell you about hurricanes is that the Big Hit is the beginning, not the end. Fran has swept on up the coast, taking the Weather Channel and CNN with it. On the networks, things are happening in Bosnia, Chechnya, Indonesia.

Here in Hurricanelandia, it's raining eight inches in three hours on top of ten inches that came in with Fran. They predict it will rain for another week. All the low country rivers are cresting, shouldering through the wreckage of human cities toward the sea.
—From *The Patron Saint of Dreams*, by Philip Gerard (Spartanburg, S.C.: Hub City Press, 2012), 8–9.

When you reach Watermark Marina on River Road, turn right on Independence Boulevard. When you reach South Seventeenth Street, turn left. In four miles, you'll cross Market Street. Watch for Chestnut Street and turn right. The house at 1901 will be on the left.

1901 Chestnut Street

A lot of movies and TV shows are shot here, in our adopted coastal home-town of Wilmington, North Carolina—Wilmywood. It started when the late Frank Capra Jr. came here to make *Firestarter* in the early '80s. He liked the place and stayed, and an industry evolved around him. Dennis Hopper bought property. Now half the kids who wait on you downtown are ex-tras, or want to be actors. You'll be in Target and realize you're in line be-hind Val Kilmer. We have studios and a film school, and we're known in the business for our exceptionally wide variety of locations. You can be doing beachy beachy and suddenly go leafy established suburb, go country hayride, then nighttime happening street, pretty much whatever.—From "Peyton's Place," in *Pulphead: Essays*, by John Jeremiah Sullivan (New York: Macmillan, 2011), 347.

National Magazine Award–winner John Jeremiah Sullivan moved his young family from a one-bedroom apartment in downtown Wilmington to this grand neocolonial house. He claims that they would not have been able to afford the place had not the makers of the television series *One Tree Hill* asked to shoot on location here when the Sullivans' loan was being considered. Very shortly after the family moved in, the mortgage was paid in full by the proceeds from mul-tiple shoots.

The moviemaking scene in Wilmington overlaps with the literary life when novels are made into films here. *Divine Secrets of the YaYa Sisterhood*, *The Secret Life of Bees*, *Bastard Out of Carolina*, *Lolita*, *The Road to Wellville*, and *The Mem-ber of the Wedding* are novels that have been shot, at least in part, in the area. Scenes from the 2013 independent film *The Writers*, about a family obsessed with writing, was also shot in town in 2012. Rumor has it that the film includes a cameo by writer Stephen King, playing himself. (*Maximum Overdrive*, the 1986 horror movie that he wrote and directed, was also shot here.)

The presence of the film industry has also influenced Wilmington's theater scene. In 2006, Broadway and television star Linda Lavin and her husband, Steve Bakunas, bought and restored a house here and also renovated an automotive garage at 1122 South Third Street. The building houses the Red Barn Studio, a playhouse that focuses on theater arts and education.

A decade earlier, Tracy Wilkes—a social worker and former marketing ex-ecutive on Broadway—moved to Wilmington and launched the Dreams Center for Arts Education. Through that nonprofit organization, writers and artists from across the country come to provide training in the literary, visual, and performing arts free of charge to children in public housing, after-school programs, and day treatment centers. Among the artists on staff at Dreams is Emily Colin, whose first novel, *The Memory Thief*, was published by Ballantine in 2012 and is partly set in Wilmington.

The net result of all this activity is a thriving and multifaceted city—a growing renaissance that is the sequel to an earlier period of conflict.

Return to Seventeenth Street and turn right. It soon becomes Rankin Street around a curve. Watch for North Fifteenth Street. Turn right and follow it to our next destination.

■ OAKDALE CEMETERY

520 North Fifteenth Street

Burning tar pots were placed on street corners to "purify" Wilmington's air, which was believed to transmit the disease. They spread a stench throughout the city and cloaked its roofs and spires with a dark, ominous-looking cloud of thick, black smoke. The 3,000 residents who remained in the city sequestered themselves inside, closing their doors, boarding their shutters and leaving the streets deserted. An eerie silence gripped the port, broken only by the clatter of doctors' buggies and the creaking of horse-drawn hearses. Daily, burial parties dug trenches in Wilmington's Oakdale Cemetery, and some feared the city's remaining residents would be annihilated. Finally, after 654 recorded deaths, a freak snowstorm hit the city in early November, ending the epidemic.—From *Confederate Goliath*, by Rod Gragg (New York: HarperCollins, 1991), 6–7.

Yellow fever gripped Wilmington in August 1862, as if the Civil War were not already dangerous enough. The plague threw Wilmington into chaos. Drunken brawls and murders were common in the streets. Bodies were often found floating in the Cape Fear River on Sunday mornings. It was also during this period that the 61st North Carolina Infantry was organized in town. Many of these Wilmington boys would fight and die at Bentonville (see Tour 8).

In addition to the yellow fever victims, a few local literary figures are buried in Oakdale. The grave of NBC journalist David Brinkley is in Section R, Lot 6. Ann Preston Bridgers, sister of Elizabeth Bridgers Daniels (wife of writer Jonathan Daniels) is also buried here. She cowrote the play *Coquette*, starring Helen

When she lived in Wilmington, Ellyn Bache wrote Festival in Fire Season, *a suspense novel set during the multihued glories of the city's annual Azalea Festival.*

Hayes on Broadway and Mary Pickford in the screen version (the actress's first speaking role). The movie won an Academy Award.

A map of the cemetery with other stories of townspeople laid to rest here is available in the kiosk outside the cemetery offices, on the right beside the main gate.

Take Fifteenth Street away from the cemetery and turn right in a half mile onto Market Street (US 17). Follow it to Tenth Street, turn left, and proceed five blocks.

■ WILLISTON SCHOOL

401 South Tenth Street

This historic school and community center was founded in 1871 as the first free school for African American children in the city system. After the family of writer David Bryant Fulton moved here from Fayetteville, in 1867, he attended Williston. Bryant later launched his newspaper career in a series of columns about life as a railroad porter for the *Wilmington Record*, the first black-owned newspaper in town. The columns were later published as a collection under the pen name of Jack Thorne. Many years later, basketball star Meadowlark Lemon and tennis great Althea Gibson also attended Williston.

Return north on Tenth to Ann Street and turn left. In three blocks, turn left on South Seventh Street.

■ *WILMINGTON JOURNAL*

412 South Seventh Street

As we shall describe later in more detail, the *Record* newspaper offices were burned down and its editor was run out of town by an angry white mob in 1898. Twenty-nine years later, across the street from the building that was destroyed, R. S. Jervay founded the *Cape Fear Journal*, the predecessor of today's *Wilmington Journal*. Raleigh journalist and film producer Cash Michaels is a regular *Journal* columnist.

Proceed south on Seventh to Church Street and turn right. In four blocks, turn right on South Third. In this block you will pass the C. W. Worth House Bed and Breakfast (910-762-8562). This Queen Anne–style house belonged to the family of Kathryn Worth, an author of young-adult fiction whose work is considered in *Literary Trails of the North Carolina Piedmont*.

Continue north, and just beyond Dock Street, watch for 11 South Third Street, in the same block as St. James Episcopal Church (where Thomas Godfrey, poet and playwright, is buried). This residence is the setting that longtime Wilmingtonian Anne Russell had in mind when she wrote *The Porch*, an award-winning play that takes place in 1946 and is based on Russell's family.

Continue up Third, noting Thalian Hall on the right, a venue completed in 1858 when Wilmington was the largest city in the state. Countless theatrical and musical productions have been staged here since, and it was also the gathering spot where white Wilmingtonians declared their intention to rise up against black property owners, in 1898. Turn left on Chestnut, passing the New Hanover Public Library on the right, and take the next left onto North Second Street. In four blocks, turn right on Orange.

Thomas Godfrey Jr. of Philadelphia came to Wilmington in 1759 and completed The Prince of Parthia, *one of only two plays written by an American and produced before the Revolution. He is buried in the churchyard of St. James parish in downtown Wilmington.*

■ CAPE FEAR SERPENTARIUM

30 Orange Street

One day in 1971 in Wilmington, North Carolina, fourteen-year-old Dean Ripa was at home performing surgery on a cottonmouth snake, and it bit him. This was unfortunate for a couple of reasons. He knew enough about snakes to know he would probably not die, but he did need a ride to the hospital, which meant his parents were going to find out about the fifty snakes he was keeping in their spare room: rattlesnakes, water moccasins he'd caught in local swamps, even several cobras he had purchased via mail-order—he had a king cobra years before he had his driver's license....

Thirty years later, in what might be the ultimate fantasy of young snake-lovers everywhere, Dean Ripa opened the Cape Fear Serpentarium, and, most thrilling of all, to a twelve-year-old acquaintance of mine, he lives there, too.

—From "Love and Death in the Cape Fear Serpentarium," by Wendy Brenner, in *Oxford American* (Winter 2005): 54, 56.

Essayist and short-story writer Wendy Brenner, who also teaches at UNC-Wilmington, made many visits to this 10,000-square-foot facility, which boasts the largest collection of live, exotic venomous snakes in the country, all captured by Dean Ripa, the subject of Brenner's exciting narrative.

Ripa has been featured on *Animal Planet* and the Discovery Channel. He is also a writer. When he was eighteen and working on a children's book, he befriended Beat poet and controversial novelist William S. Burroughs, who continually encouraged Ripa to write about his adventures as a snake collector. Ripa sometimes helped Burroughs with research and is acknowledged in the late writer's work.

From here, you may want to keep your parking spot and walk a block to Water Street, the Wilmington waterfront. Meander along the river toward the Cotton Exchange, formerly a warehouse, now repurposed for retail. A number of eateries and two bookshops are close by (see Literary Landscape). Return to your car and head north on Front Street (one block east of Water) for .7 miles, to the intersection of Davis and North Third, where a parking lot is available for visitors to the next site.

By the morning after African Americans were evicted from their homes and businesses by a mob of white supremacist Democrats in Wilmington, the offices and printing equipment of the Daily Record *—the only African American newspaper in the state—had also been destroyed. Courtesy of the North Carolina Office of Archives and History, North Carolina Department of Cultural Resources.*

■ 1898 MEMORIAL

1018 North Third Street

One hundred years after Wilmington was torn apart by unprecedented racial violence, this bronze and stone sculpture was developed in a community-wide process of storytelling, reconciliation, and healing. The monument's inscription explains the event:

> In 1898 Wilmington's African American majority included members of a growing middle class who served in the municipal government and the city's civil service and in state and federal governmental positions. On November 10, 1898, an armed mob of whites, led by some of Wilmington's most prominent citizens, removed from office the city's duly elected bi-racial government and achieved what historians consider the only successful coup d'état in the history of the United States.

The first African American novelist to address the Wilmington massacre of 1898 was columnist David Bryant Fulton (using the pseudonym Jack Thorne), who immediately wrote *Hanover; or, The Persecution of the Lowly, a Story of the*

Artist Ayokunle Odeleye created six bronze paddles as the focal point of the Wilmington monument that remembers the violent coup d'état in 1898, the only overthrow of a municipal government in U.S. history. Over the past century, the story has been told in prose and poetry. The paddles suggest water—a symbol in African culture of renewal, rebirth, forgiveness, cleansing, and inclusion.

Wilmington Massacre. In 1901, Charles Waddell Chesnutt, of Fayetteville, then brought out his novel *The Marrow of Tradition*, based on careful research. Several of his relatives had lived through the event, and Chesnutt had hoped to provoke a public outcry against Jim Crow and in favor of racial justice. However, the story of the Wilmington massacre slowly faded and was rarely, if ever, covered in the history curriculum for North Carolina schoolchildren in the twentieth century.

More recent scholarship and a range of treatments by white writers across genres have begun to broaden awareness of this North Carolina tragedy. Historians Tim Tyson and David Cecelski offer a thorough nonfiction account in their 1998 book, *Democracy Betrayed: The Wilmington Race Riot of 1898 and Its Legacy.* Philip Gerard's 1994 novel *Cape Fear Rising* and John Sayles's massive 2011 novel *A Moment in the Sun* portray the events leading up to the confrontation. Sayles's treatment in many ways pays homage to Chesnutt's novel.

Poet Michael White, who teaches at UNC-Wilmington, gives an evocative account of the story, which is excerpted here:

COUP (EXCERPT)

(Wilmington, NC)

[...] Sometimes I imagine
10 November, 1898—
the thud of a rifle butt at 8 A.M.

on the door of the *Daily Record*. Post election
Thursday morning. Colonel Waddell backed
by his white mob. You have to expect someone

would knock down lanterns, someone find a match.
The pop and whoosh of upper story windows—
flurries of sparks—then suddenly the crash. . . .

You have to imagine cheers, their soaring hearts.
Therefore the march on Brooklyn—the colored section
whites called "darktown"—where, within an hour

a shout a shot a fusillade let fly
on a group of blacks on the porch of Walker's Store.
Some died where they fell, the others ran away,

but the infantry was called out anyway;
and Captain James, on the 4th Street Bridge to Brooklyn,
told his machine gun squad to "shoot to kill,"

and neighborhood churches, parks, and black-owned houses
everywhere were targets. Panic spread
from block to block like a sheet of wind-fanned flame.

Dan Wright was burned out, forced to run the gauntlet—
forty guns let loose at his back while his
wife, pleading, watched. Josh Halsey, trapped at last,

was forced to run the gauntlet—forty guns
"tore off the top of his head," as someone said,
while his young daughter watched. Imagine a woman

peering out through the drawn blinds of her living
room, as every prayer she had ever known
flits in and out of her mind. . . . Her baby cries,

as just outside, the horse-drawn Gatling crew
takes aim: each burst of rounds like the Holy Ghost,
like the hieroglyphs of stars. So everyone who

could run, ran—four thousand women and children
exiled into swamps and graveyards. Dante
sang of "blackened waters"—city of "wretches

boiled in pitch"—and so Brooklyn became.
By 4 P.M., Waddell was declared mayor.
By 5—gunmetal sundown—what it was

was ghost town: rubble of houses burning, crackle
of sniper fire, a pall of black smoke drifting
down the river. Some of the wounded crawled

beneath their own homes—and were found by the stench
days later. Twenty-five workers, picked off near
the railroad yard, were buried there in a ditch.

But most were left in plain sight: manifestos,
love notes to the future. Streetpole lynchings.
Rigored bodies lying in pools of blood.
[…]
—By Michael White, in *North Carolina Literary Review* 19 (2009): 146–47.

From here, follow North Third Street northeast, away from downtown. It becomes Martin Luther King Jr. Parkway (US 74). Wrightsville Beach is ten miles ahead. Along the way, you may notice Port City Java, a frequent setting in *Tree Huggers*, a mystery by the formerly Ohio-based journalist Judy Nichols, who lives in Wilmington.

■ WRIGHTSVILLE BEACH

Wrightsville sits on an island about a twenty-minute drive from Wilmington. Margaret Mitchell vacationed here for two weeks at the Seashore Hotel, now long gone. One of North Carolina's oldest resort towns, established in 1899, Wrightsville was regionally famous for many years for the Lumina, a grand pavilion once standing at the south end of the island, where Woody Herman, Tommy Dorsey, Guy Lombardo, and Cab Calloway performed with their big bands.

Novelist Clyde Edgerton, who spent his childhood and much of his adult life in Durham, teaches creative writing at UNC-Wilmington. In his 2008 novel, *The Bible Salesman*, the Lumina is called the Electra. It's described through the eyes

15130 –
"Lumina"
Wrightsville
Beach, N. C.

And her name was Maud!
Well how is she coming on anyway
Write to me real soon, Ella Brady

A local landmark and dancing destination for nearly seventy years, the Lumina pavilion at Wrightsville Beach burned in 1973. Clyde Edgerton's novel The Bible Salesman *describes the pavilion in its heyday. Courtesy of the Durwood Barbour collection of North Carolina postcards, North Carolina Collection Photographic Archives, Wilson Library, UNC–Chapel Hill.*

of Henry Dampier, who visits "Swan Island" as a child in 1939. The band plays, the adults dance, and then Henry's family sits on the beach to watch a motion picture projected on a large screen.

> As they watched the movie, a gigantic, full, dull orange moon crept up out of the ocean as if to command armies, and people pointed at it, and Henry felt like it was so close that he could walk to the edge of the water and hold out his hands, palms up, and feel heat from the deep orange glow, then ride out in a rowboat along the path of reflections on the water, hold up an oar, and touch it, feel the oar against the crust. —From *The Bible Salesman*, by Clyde Edgerton (New York: Little, Brown, 2008) 77–78.

To see photographs and learn more about Wrightsville's romantic history, visit the Wrightsville Beach Museum. Bear to the left at the "Welcome to Wrightsville Beach" sign. The museum is at 303 West Salisbury Street—the second driveway on the right.

Lookout Books

Department of Creative Writing

UNC-Wilmington

601 South College Road, Wilmington

http://www.lookout.org

Since 2000, the Publishing Laboratory at UNC-Wilmington has provided students the opportunity to learn the process of editing, designing, producing, and marketing books. *Ecotone*, the literary magazine of the Department of Creative Writing at the university, has also offered hands-on experience to students interested in magazine publishing. Today, Lookout Books marries these two endeavors by serving as the literary imprint of the department. With a new publishing model that splits profits fifty-fifty with its authors, the press, says its website, is dedicated to "emerging and historically underrepresented voices and works by established writers who have been overlooked by commercial houses." During Writers Week in the fall, local readers and university students have a chance to meet writers from the Lookout Books roster. The university also brings in writers in other genres to give readings and teach workshops. The week is a manifestation and celebration of the growth in the university's creative writing program, which began with a handful of teachers and now boasts a large faculty of well-published writers offering courses in fiction, poetry, and creative nonfiction. Students can earn bachelor's and master's degrees and take screenwriting courses in the university's Film Studies department.

Cameron Art Museum

3201 South Seventeenth Street, Wilmington

910-395-5999

http://www.cameronartmuseum.com

In addition to its collection of fine arts, craft, and design by artists from North Carolina and far beyond, the Cameron is often the site of lectures, music, and readings by writers. It is surrounded by the 9.3-acre Pyramid Park, laced with nature trails and an outdoor sculpture exhibition.

Cape Fear Museum of History and Science

814 Market Street, Wilmington

910-798-4350

http://www.capefearmuseum.com

The oldest history museum in North Carolina, founded in 1898, was created to preserve objects and memories from the Civil War. Today the Cape Fear Museum's broad collections represent and interpret the history, science, and cultures of the Lower Cape Fear and provide a valuable perspective on the rich history of the region and its natural assets.

Cape Fear Crime Festival

910-798-6301

This annual confab has drawn scores of mystery and crime writers from afar, in addition to the writers in these genres who live in Wilmington (and there are many). Convened by the New Hanover Public Library, it features workshops, manuscript critiques, and networking opportunities.

Two Sisters Bookery at the Cotton Exchange

318 Nutt Street, Wilmington

910-762-4444

http://www.twosistersbookery.com

If the book is written by a local author, chances are this combination bookstore and gift shop has it. The store is on the ground floor of the Cotton Exchange, facing the river.

Old Books on Front St.

249 North Front Street, Wilmington

910-762-6657

http://www.OldBooksOnFrontSt.com

Since 1982, this chock-a-block bookstore has been selling new and used books with abandon.

Pomegranate Books

4418 Park Avenue, Wilmington

910-452-1107

http://www.pombooks.net

Coffee, tea, comfortable chairs, and a careful selection of North Carolina literature make this charming house a great place to hang out. Near the university, this spacious store hosts workshops, readings, and book signings by local and national writers.

trail two

The Middle Corridor: The Harvest

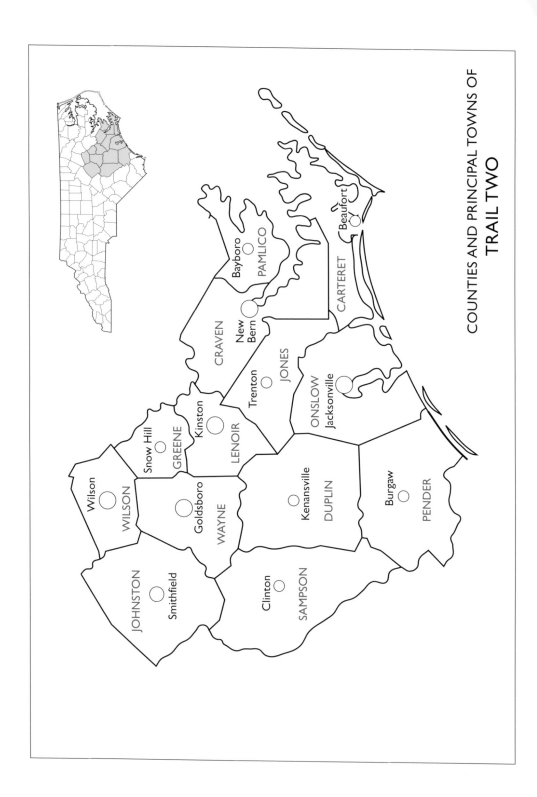

COUNTIES AND PRINCIPAL TOWNS OF
TRAIL TWO

The lower leaves on the green tobacco stalks took on a pale yellow cast. The farm families busied themselves in preparation for the perennial ritual that would consume them for the next six weeks to come. There was an unmistakable urgency in the air. Everyone felt it. It was harvest time.

The simple country folks who inhabited the tobacco farmlands of rural North Carolina, she concluded, seemed to live out their lives wavering between hope and despair. The highs and lows of their existence appeared to fluctuate with the seasons. Their springs, buoyant and anticipating, held the promise of green and growing crops; the long summer days found them laboring mutely, almost mechanically, under sweltering sun rays in hot, dusty fields. But the golden days of autumn, never seeming to reach full glow, left them in a semi-anesthetized state, their quiet stupor brought on by the labor of summer and broken only by guarded whispers about crippling indebtedness, passed along by the men in the fields or the women at the clothesline.

Through it all, they endured, she thought. Yes, the land sapped their strength, stole their youth and faded their dreams. The work was hard. Yet they held steadfastly to the land, rejecting politely the offers of white speculators who would "relieve" them of their burden.

—From "Loose Change," in *Black Butterflies: Stories of the South in Transition*, by
  Sandra Carlton-Alexander (Laurinburg, N.C.: St. Andrews College Press, 1994), 48, 53.

As Warsaw-born writer Sandra Carlton-Alexander implies, the harvest has meant everything in the fertile bottoms of eastern central North Carolina. The land created the livelihoods of every family, whether they farmed or not.

In the late twentieth century, the decline of tobacco and the transition to big corporate farms with mechanized means of planting, tending, and harvesting was a hard adjustment, leading many folks to feel "throwed away," as writer and scholar Linda Flowers, of Faison, put it.

The tours along this trail examine the writing that has grown as surely out of the dark dirt plowed by generations of eastern North Carolina families as has tobacco, cotton, corn, and sweet potatoes—crops more recently augmented by massive operations devoted to raising hogs, turkeys, and chickens.

Though farm reports are less and less frequently heard on AM radio, for those who have lived here for years, the names of market towns that were rattled off every day at noon along with current prices at auction still come to mind in a particular order: "Clinton, Fayetteville, Dunn, Pink Hill, Pine Level, Chadbourn, Ayden, Laurinburg, and Benson."

The adjustment from plantation life to tenant farming to sharecropping to migrant labor and now to global agribusiness is a story line best examined in the lives of those swept along in the swirling currents—a gift from the writers of this region.

McGee's Crossroads : Benson : Dunn : Averasboro : Wade : Spivey's Corner : Newton Grove : Bentonville : Smithfield

From hog killings to hog calling, this tour takes a deep dive into agricultural North Carolina and also visits two of the most significant Civil War battlefields in the state's history.

Writers with a connection to this tour: Jeri Fitzgerald Board, Mark L. Bradley, Doris Rollins Cannon, Allison Adelle Hedge Coke, E. L. Doctorow, Tim Downs, Ava Gardner, Robert Graves, Dorothy Hughes, Margaret Maron, Eric Martin, Melton McLaurin, Michael Parker, Tony Peacock, Lee Server, Shelby Stephenson, William Trotter

■ MCGEE'S CROSSROADS

Fields brown the dozer's tread.
Wood, nails, cement, a pile of bricks—
With every hammer's fall, a cul-de-sac.
My farmboy throws up his hands. . . .
They are farming houses right up to the creeks.
—From "The Farm That Farms New Houses," by Shelby
   Stephenson, in *Rambler* (March–April 2006): 29.

Poet and musician Shelby Stephenson lives in Johnston County with his wife, Linda, on the farm where he was born. Stephenson restored his birthplace, an old plankhouse at 895 Sanders Road. Next door is a more contemporary house, where he now lives. Both are not far from the intersection of NC 210 and NC 50, also known as McGee's Crossroads, a developing village in what might be considered the second concentric ring of "bedroom communities" in the gravitational pull of Raleigh.

Stephenson, who served as editor of *Pembroke* magazine from 1979 to 2010 and received the North Carolina Award for

TOUR 8 : MCGEE'S CROSSROADS TO SMITHFIELD

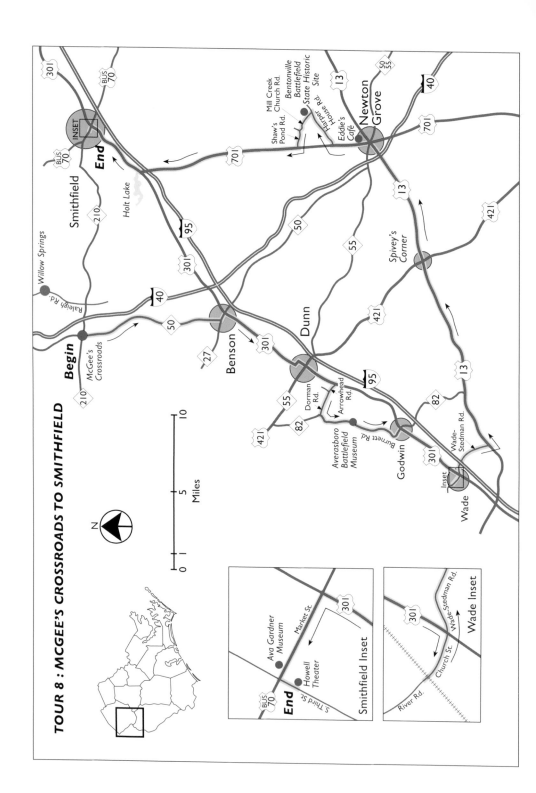

N

Miles
0   1   5   10

Begin
McGee's Crossroads
Willow Springs
Raleigh Rd.
210
50
27
40
301
95
210
BUS 70
301
Smithfield
Holt Lake
End
INSET
BUS 70
Benson
301
55
421
82
Dunn
301
Dorman Rd.
Arrowhead Rd.
Averasboro Battlefield Museum
Burnett Rd.
Godwin
95
82
13
301
Wade-Stedman Rd.
Wade
Inset
50
55
421
Spivey's Corner
13
421
701
Newton Grove
13
50
40
55
701
Shaw's Pond Rd.
Mill Creek Church Rd.
Bentonville Battlefield State Historic Site
Harper House Rd.
Eddie's Café

Smithfield Inset

Ava Gardner Museum
Market St.
Howell Theater
S. Third St.
301
BUS 70
End

Wade Inset

301
Wade-Stedman Rd.
Church St.
River Rd.

Johnston County poet Shelby Stephenson reads from his work in April 2010 during Poetry Month. Courtesy of the North Carolina Arts Council, North Carolina Department of Cultural Resources.

Literature in 2001, has been a stalwart and sonorous voice of agricultural memory, recalling in his poems the place-names and habits of eastern North Carolina farm folks, long before the plantings turned from tobacco to town houses.

The Stephenson family name is attached to any number of enterprises here, notably a historic barbecue restaurant north of McGee's Crossroads, on NC 50. In the following incantation, Stephenson evokes the commonplace brutality of a winter hog killing in Johnston County, vivid enough to give a diner pause over a plate of fresh, local pork:

HOGS
Hog tails hang down after the maul,
unchosen shoats and sows oinking
noses through fencewire on the Bob Higgins line.

Men swill homemade brandy,
rake thick sleeves across their mouths
cutting the sun's slash on the tin barnroof—

taking carcasses, pipes, livers, hearts,
lights into those bloody days,

vatwater roaring above the flames,
women ready to clean chitlins,
tubs emptybellied in ironweedstalks,
gallows poking the sky.

The wrinkly
end of the biggest gut
opens: there's Dwarf Tom Thumb, stuffed, eyeless, propped
up against a washboard:

the sausagestuffer screwed to the eatintable,

sour smell of intestinal slop from stripped hog guts
splattering the washbench, foxhounds' backflung heads
howling in the dogyard at the boy rounding his bellowed
cheeks to puff the bladderballoon tied on a blackgum
stick flitting in the wingblur of gallowsbirds
clapping among drying pig blood,

hunters knowing fresh meat waits on the table when
they remove their boots, put the split floursack towel
back on the 10-penny nail over the washbasin.
—From *Greatest Hits, 1978–2000*, by Shelby Stephenson
  (Johnstown, Ohio: Pudding House Publications, 2002), 9.

Stephenson's cousin, Johnston County novelist Margaret Maron, lives on the opposite side of I-40, in nearby Willow Springs. She also wrestles in her writing with the clash of suburban sprawl and farmstead history, particularly in her mystery series featuring Judge Deborah Knott of fictional Colleton County. In this passage from the novel *Death's Half Acre*, longtime county resident Monica Udell testifies in a hearing over the matter of her free-roaming chickens, one of which has been killed by a newcomer's dog, landing both neighbors in court:

She described how her two acres were all that was left of her grandfather's farm. "You divide the land four or five times every generation and not much is left," she said. "One of my sisters still lives next door, but the others sold out to Crescent Ridge. I've tried to be a good neighbor to these new folks, but I like eggs that have some color to their yolks and aren't full of hormones and stuff and I don't plan to quit just because city's come to the country."
    She admitted that her chickens had originally strayed over to the new-

comers' yards, "but as soon as they asked me to keep them penned, I did. And when she put the law on me about my rooster, I made a big pot of pastry out of him rather than have hard feelings with her."
— From *Death's Half Acre*, by Margaret Maron (New York: Grand Central Publishing, 2008), 57.

"Pastry," known as chicken and dumplings elsewhere, is a staple of eastern North Carolina cuisine, regardless of a family's economic status.

Stephenson's poetry collection *Family Matters: Homage to July, the Slave Girl*, winner of the 2008 Bellday Prize for Poetry, muses on the relationship of the writer's ancestors to the enslaved African Americans who worked their fields.

Maron's novel *Hard Row* speaks powerfully to the relatively recent presence of large numbers of Spanish-speaking people in eastern North Carolina and how, once again, cheap labor and a clash of cultures — this time Anglo and Latino/Hispanic — has created unfortunate power dynamics. The following passage is from the point of view of Judge Deborah Knott, the descendant of white settlers of long ago:

The club was so jammed that the party had spilled out into the cordoned-off parking lot. It felt as if every Hispanic in Colleton County had turned out. I hadn't realized till then just how many there were — all those mostly ignored people who had filtered in around the fringes of our lives. Normally, they wear faded shirts and mud-stained jeans while working long hours in our fields or on construction jobs. That night they sported big white cowboy hats with silver conchos and shiny belt buckles. The women who stake our tomatoes or pick up our sweet potatoes alongside their men in the fields or who wear the drab uniforms of fast-food chains as they wipe down tables or take our orders? They came in colorful swirling skirts and white scoop-neck blouses bright with embroidery. — From *Hard Row*, by Margaret Maron (New York: Grand Central Publishing, 2007), 7–8.

Cousins Stephenson and Maron thus set the stage for this tour, which begins at McGee's Crossroads and avoids interstates 40 and 95 — the arteries that permit passersby to miss the evolving stories in this flat, fertile land.

From McGee's Crossroads, follow NC 50 south through alternating fields and subdivisions toward Benson, once a booming railroad town. Now Benson is home to the annual Mule Days Festival, which celebrates the common beast of burden from times past and draws some 60,000 visitors every September.

From Benson, continue south through the eastern edge of Harnett County on US 301 toward Dunn—once home to a prosperous turpentine distillery, now a village mostly surrounded by strawberry, cotton, and soybean fields. Here the 5.3-mile Dunn-Erwin Rail Trail is a great stop for walking and biking. The repurposed rail corridor crosses the Black River and offers interpretive markers along the way. Restaurants at both trailheads, in downtown Dunn and downtown Erwin, provide weary hikers with nourishment.

■ AVERASBORO

From Dunn, Civil War aficionados can take a side trip off US 301 to visit one of the most written-about Civil War battles in North Carolina. The clash in Averasboro was actually the first calculated resistance to William Tecumseh Sherman's march from Georgia through the Carolinas.

Approximately two miles south of Dunn, watch for Arrowhead Road on the right. Turn right and continue on this road west, which becomes Dorman Road. When Dorman meets NC 82, follow it to the left (south) to the Averasboro Battlefield Museum, at 3300 Highway 82.

Many academic and amateur historians have written page-turners about Sherman's march through the South. One of the most readable accounts about the North Carolina campaign is by William Trotter, whose nonfiction Civil War trilogy inspired him to write two novels about the war. Trotter was born in Charlotte, studied at Davidson College, and now lives in Greensboro.

As Trotter explains, Sherman continued north after securing and plundering Fayetteville in early March 1865. The Confederates, under the command of General Joseph E. Johnston, could not be sure if the general's ultimate destination was Goldsboro or Raleigh, so they prepared for both. Confederate troops under the leadership of General William J. Hardee dug in just east of the Cape Fear River near Averasboro and managed to disrupt the Union's progress, despite a three-to-one disadvantage in troop numbers.

The battle started on March 15 when the two armies made contact at a place just over the Cumberland County line known as the Gypsy Pine. For more than a century, gypsy caravans had parked around that pine tree, holding fairs and tribal conclaves, and plotting nocturnal raids on the barnyards of local plantations. Local legends claim that when the cannons first roared on that rain-misted day, the apparition of a gypsy girl was seen above the tree, outlined against the murky sky and seemingly holding

Simple stones at this North Carolina Historic Site mark the graves of Confederates who died doing battle with Sherman's army near Averasboro and were buried where they fell. Novels by William Trotter and E. L. Doctorow show readers what happened on this ground.

a wand. — From *Silk Flags and Cold Steel: The Piedmont*, by William R. Trotter (Winston-Salem: John F. Blair, 1988), 249.

The battle was bloody. The Confederates lost some 800 soldiers. The Union forces suffered 650 casualties. Meanwhile, according to E. L. Doctorow's well-researched and visceral novel *The March*, Sherman avoided the fray: "Sherman, far back from the battle, sitting by his tent in a pine grove in which odd fragments of grape and canister occasionally dropped, contemplated his tactical options while his staff stood by ready to transmit his orders. He seemed oddly dissociated from the event" ([New York: Random House, 2005], 277).

Among the historic sites along NC 82 that are connected to this battle are three plantation houses, an interpretive museum, and the Chicora Cemetery, where many North and South Carolina soldiers were buried where they fell, marked by stones with such inscriptions as "6 DEAD." The walk through these fields is solemn.

The conflict between Johnston's and Sherman's troops would continue four days later in Bentonville—a destination coming up on this tour. Continue south on NC 82 (Burnett Road) until it rejoins US 301, in Godwin. Turn south on US 301 toward Wade.

■ WADE

Once solely dependent on the cotton gin and sawmill for its livelihood, Wade is a literary destination because of two memoirs that offer accounts of the town, in the same era but from two perspectives—black and white. Dorothy Hughes, the daughter of sharecroppers, was born in Wade in 1936 and spent a number of years living with her grandparents on River Road, just beyond town. Her memoir has a scope much larger than her Wade roots, but the narrative of her early years is revealing.

> On the weekend, my siblings and I had to sweep the yard from side to side and from the front to the back. This was done each week; we did not have any grass and if we did there was no lawn mower. We made our brooms from straw and used them for sweeping the house, but when they wore down some, they were used for outside sweeping. After doing all of the farm work during the week, on Saturdays I had to do the ironing.—From *The Journey Was Not Easy*, by Dorothy Hughes (Bloomington, Ind.: Author House, 2010), 18.

Melton A. McLaurin, an emeritus history professor at the University of North Carolina at Wilmington and former chair of the North Carolina Humanities Council, was born in 1941 and raised in Wade. His book, *Separate Pasts*, is a conscientious account of his own privilege and the quiet rules of segregation that kept him from more than a superficial relationship with his African American neighbors.

> Only the better homes of the village had lawns, not the smooth green lawns of *Better Homes and Gardens* but lawns of several grasses and a variety of weeds, with the greenish-brown hue of army camouflage. Because my father had purchased one of Wade's first lawn mowers, I was hired to cut many of those lawns and came to know them much better. I hated them—the spots of sand that the mower blew against my legs, the sand spurs so tall and thick that I had to wear socks and shoes even on the hottest days, and the clumps of weeds that repeatedly choked

off the mower and forced me to gut at the rope starter. —From *Separate Pasts: Growing Up White in the Segregated South*, by Melton A. McLaurin (Athens: University of Georgia Press, 1998), 10.

To see Wade, turn right off US 301 onto Church Street and drive toward the train tracks where Church becomes River Road, running parallel to the Cape Fear River through dense woods all the way to Fayetteville. To the first-time visitor, Wade today seems much the same as described in the two memoirs, though recent improvements include the addition of long-awaited municipal water and sewer services and a town park.

Backtrack on Church to US 301 and cross the highway onto Wade-Stedman Road. Continue west across I-95 to US 13 and turn left. The route from Wade to our next destination, Spivey's Corner, is 16.5 miles, and it is flanked by rural farmsteads.

■ SPIVEY'S CORNER

For more than forty years, this crossroads has been known as the home of the National Hollerin' Contest. Held every June, the cacophonous competition ends with top prizes for juniors, teens, and ladies and the awarding of the national crown for the best earsplitting performance, whether the contestant is calling hogs, hounds, neighbors, or lost relatives. There are also battles for best whistling and conch-shell blowing.

Such an idiosyncratic tradition has naturally enticed North Carolina writers to bring the town into their stories. Novelist and short-story writer Tony Peacock has written about these contests—he won the hollering championship in 2010 with a rendition of George Gershwin's tune "Summertime."

Michael Parker, winner of the 2006 North Carolina Award for Literature, also couldn't resist a reference in *If You Want Me to Stay*, a heartbreaking family saga set in his native eastern North Carolina: "He had this one favorite T-shirt he got at the National Hollerin' Contest at Spivey's Corner the first year they held it, before it got big-time and the hippie college kids started driving down from Chapel Hill with their pot and their Hacky Sacks" ([Chapel Hill: Algonquin Books of Chapel Hill, 2005], 113).

Cary novelist Tim Downs writes about Spivey's Corner and the phenomenon of CSAs (community supported agriculture), in which local food buyers pay up front to share in the organic produce of a particular farmer. In Downs's novel *Ends of the Earth*, a CSA farmer with customers in Spivey's Corner and Newton Grove discovers that her farm has been infested with a dangerous in-

Sampson County native Tony Peacock, author of the novel Sidney Langston: Giblets of Memory, *is also a hollering champion who took the top prize at Spivey's Corner in 2010. Photo by Emma Tannenbaum, courtesy of the* Fayetteville Observer.

sect planted by an agroterrorist ring—another mystery to be solved by the forensic entomologist who is the hero of Downs's popular Bug Man mystery series (see Tour 2). This tour continues up US 13 from Spivey's Corner to Newton Grove.

■ NEWTON GROVE

US 13 meets NC 50/55 and US 701 at a traffic circle in Newton Grove, which is situated at the core of North Carolina's contemporary farming industry. The town is also a stronghold for Latino/Hispanic advocacy groups intent on helping newly settled farmworkers adapt to life in challenging circumstances.

Various agricultural and migrant labor practices have come under scrutiny as far back as North Carolina writer Edward R. Murrow's 1960 CBS documentary *Harvest of Shame*. More recent stories of pesticide misuse, abusive labor practices, and environmental degradation from animal waste have prompted writers including Johnston County's Margaret Maron to spin out books based on newspaper headlines. Poet Allison Adelle Hedge Coke worked as a farm laborer in North Carolina during the 1970s and 1980s, documenting the difficult circumstances.

THE CHANGE (FOR THE SHARECROPPER I
LEFT BEHIND IN '79) (EXCERPT)
Before the year dusters sprayed
malathion over our clustered bodies,   perspiring
while we primed bottom lugs,
those ground-level leaves of tobacco,
and it clung to us with black tar so sticky we rolled
eight-inch balls off our arms at night   and
cloroxed our clothes for hours and hours
Before we were poisoned   and
the hospital thought we had been burned in fires,
at least to the third degree,
when the raw, oozing hives that
covered ninety-eight percent of our bodies
from the sprays ordered by the FDA
and spread by   landowners,
before anyone had seen
automated machines that top and prime.
—From *Off-Season City Pipe*, by Allison Adelle Hedge Coke
    (Minneapolis: Coffee House Press, 2005), 10.

As a Duke University undergraduate, writer Eric Martin joined a team of students during the summer of 1990 to work with migrant farmworkers and social workers in Johnston County. A decade later, his experience surfaced in his
first novel, *Luck*, about a college activist who tries and fails to improve the lot
of farmworkers in eastern North Carolina. (Student Action with Farmworkers,
now a statewide nonprofit headquartered at Duke, also grew out of the project
that inspired Martin's novel.)

Eddie's Café—Newton Grove's popular barbecue and seafood restaurant
at 502 Main Street (US 701 North)—is mentioned in Martin's novel (where it's
Eddies Bar-N-Q), as is the area health clinic where the writer volunteered and
where the book's central character, Mike Olive, meets Hermelinda Salmeron, his
love interest.

■ BENTONVILLE

Continue north on US 701 for 2.5 miles outside of Newton Grove and turn
right on Harper House Road. Proceed another 2.6 miles to Mill Creek Church
Road and turn left. In .4 miles, look for the Bentonville Battlefield State His-

The annual Bentonville Battle reenactment is one of the largest in the state. It draws scores of visitors to witness a staged version of the last full-scale conflict of the Civil War, which pit Sherman's forces against the weary Confederates under General Johnston's command. Books by Jeri Fitzgerald Board and Mark L. Bradley take us into the minds of the combatants. Courtesy of Bentonville Battlefield, North Carolina Historic Sites, North Carolina Department of Cultural Resources.

toric Site, which interprets the largest Civil War battle in North Carolina. Here Sherman's troops won their final victory in the march from Georgia through the Carolinas. Though the Confederate army did not prevail, its efforts are commemorated by a visitors' center, hiking trail through the battlements, and memorial. A large number of books documenting the complex battle in fiction and fact are sold at the site.

The historic Harper House, where wounded soldiers were brought for treatment, has been furnished as a field hospital and is open to visitors. Early on in her sweeping novel about Johnston County, Jeri Fitzgerald Board, born and raised in nearby Pine Level, imagines the gruesome scene at the Harper House.

A sour taste fills Adaire's mouth as wagons of wounded cross the yard, where the sweet smell of fresh blood hangs in the air. She is startled to see pairs of Negro orderlies in Union Army jackets push through the crowd bearing mud-caked men on stretchers. The wounded beg for water, cry for their mothers, and scream in animal-like sounds that float above the pasture. Adaire spots a young boy whose right arm is missing, a bloody stump signifies its recent amputation. She stares helplessly, her mind else-where. —From *The Bed She Was Born In*, by Jeri Fitzgerald Board (Boone, N.C.: Parkway, 2006), 38.

The Battle of Bentonville was the best and last effort of the Confederate army, which was greatly outnumbered by Sherman's forces. Mark L. Bradley describes the last miserable night in March, before the Rebels made their retreat in morning light:

It is grimly ironic that, because of the proximity of their lines, both the Union and Confederate troops were forbidden to light campfires and had to shiver in the darkness.

For Lt. William Calder of the North Carolina Junior Reserves the inces-sant rainfall was the worst feature of his third night in the trenches near Bentonville. "My feet were soaking wet and my overcoat saturated," he scrawled in his diary. "I laid on the cold wet ground with nothing over me and got a few moments of hurried sleep. I passed a miserable night." On the Federal side of the Sam Howell Branch, a veteran of the 7th Illinois, his poetic impulse undampened by the rain, noted: "The chilling winds make mournful music through the branches of the tall pines."

—From *Last Stand in the Carolinas: The Battle of Bentonville*, by Mark L. Bradley (Campbell, Calif.: Savas Woodbury, 1996), 398–99.

The Civil War in North Carolina would officially end a little more than a month after Bentonville, both sides ragged and exhausted. On April 26, 1865, General Johnston surrendered to General Sherman at Bennett Place in Durham.

When leaving Bentonville, continue ahead on Mill Creek Church Road to Shaw's Pond Road and bear left. US 701 is approximately .75 miles ahead. Turn right on 701 North for ten miles, crossing I-95 and then merging with US 301/ NC 96 North toward Smithfield. Proceed 4.5 miles and turn left on Market Street to see the downtown area.

■ SMITHFIELD

Smithfield, the seat of Johnston County and now home to the Ham and Yam Festival each spring, is also remembered as the site of a disturbing billboard that Eric Martin, early in his novel *Luck*, describes. Central character Mike Olive is leading a caravan of Duke students down US 70 from Durham, past Raleigh and toward the town limits of his hometown of Smithfield, called Cottesville in the novel:

> Once, when Mike was young, there'd been another sign up there with the rest, those simple three K's with the circle and cross, and the chapter number underneath. He remembered the summer when the two state trucks from Raleigh came to take the sign down. Two men coned off a lane and managed the slowed traffic and one man watched and two men unbolted the aging sign from the frame, and finally it was gone. Mike hit the horn as he led his friends into Cottesville for the first time, knowing their eyes were passing quickly over and through the real and phantom signs behind him. He was ashamed. He never told them what they could not see. —From *Luck*, by Eric Martin (New York: W. W. Norton, 2000), 57.

The billboard, which said "Knights of the Ku Klux Klan Welcomes You to Smithfield" and urged North Carolina's white citizens to "Help Fight Communism and Intergration [*sic*]," has hardly been forgotten, but today the visitor can expect a much more intriguing encounter with another part of Smithfield history.

■ AVA GARDNER MUSEUM

325 Market Street, Smithfield

Actress Ava Gardner, the youngest of eight children, was born on a tobacco farm in Grabtown, just southeast of Smithfield, on Christmas Eve, 1922. She often went to the movies at the Howell Theatre, which is still in operation at 131 South Third Street, downtown. Gardner would also rendezvous with her first boyfriend, a local basketball star, out at Holt Lake—now famous for its barbecue and seafood restaurant. It's on US 701 as you come into town from Newton Grove.

Gardner graduated from Rock Ridge High School, in Wilson, and went on to study stenography at nearby Atlantic Christian (now Barton College) until her portrait in the window of her brother-in-law's photo studio in New York caught

A southern delicacy, pickled okra, bears the name of a southern dynamo, Ava Gardner, at the well-designed Smithfield museum that chronicles her life and film career. She was the subject of more than one poem by her friend, classicist Robert Graves.

the eye of a movie scout. Within a year she was in Hollywood and being courted by Metro Goldwyn Mayer and its biggest star, Mickey Rooney, to whom she was soon married.

After a year, Gardner divorced Rooney and spent time in the strange company of millionaire Howard Hughes. She then married jazz musician Artie Shaw, again only for a year. Ultimately, Frank Sinatra was Gardner's true love, and though their marriage also ended quickly, their friendship endured.

In a literary context, Gardner's work in film led her to meet many writers, and literature was a lifetime interest. Her first major film, *The Killers*, was based on the story by Ernest Hemingway. Her friendship with the author led to more parts, in film versions of his short story "The Snows of Kilimanjaro" and his novel *The Sun Also Rises*. Gardner visited Hemingway's compound in Cuba and also toured the bullrings with him in Spain, a country that she eventually made her home for a time before moving to London toward the end of her life.

During the years in Spain, Gardner developed a fast friendship with elderly English classicist, poet, and novelist Robert Graves, whom she visited at his home on the island of Majorca. Graves dedicated several poems to Gardner, and books he gave her are on display in the Smithfield museum.

Ava Gardner wrote a memoir, *Ava, My Story*, which is available at the museum, alongside a short book, *Grabtown Girl*, by local writer Doris Rollins Cannon, who has collected many stories of Gardner's youth and is a cofounder of the museum.

Ava Gardner is buried with her family in Smithfield's Sunset Memorial Park, a mile from the museum.

■ LITERARY LANDSCAPE

Orchard House Booksellers
117 North Third Street, Smithfield
919-938-1511
http://www.orchardhousebooksellers.com

A relative newcomer to Smithfield, Orchard House offers coffee, smoothies, ice cream, chocolates, and pastries. The store also features work by local artists and regular musical events. Loads of Margaret Maron books are on the shelves, as well as the definitive biography of Ava Gardner, by Lee Server.

Goldsboro : Cliffs of the Neuse : Mount Olive : Faison : Clinton : Warsaw : Kenansville : Chinquapin : Willard : Burgaw

The writers in this tour, with few exceptions, left behind their eastern North Carolina roots to experience other worlds, but eventually came home to the landscape that shaped them.

Writers with a connection to this area: Shirlette Ammons, Margaret Boothe Baddour, Jeri Fitzgerald Board, Carolyn Rawls Booth, Sam Byrd, Sandra Carlton-Alexander, Thomas Dixon, Linda Flowers, Kathryn Bright Gurkin, Randall Kenan, Michael Malone, Lenard D. Moore, Michael Parker, David Rigsbee, Celia Rivenbark, Victor Small, William Styron, Emily Weil, Samm-Art Williams

■ GOLDSBORO

HOW WE DEAL WITH DUSK (EXCERPT)
> *Of his bones are coral made.*
> *Those are pearls that were his eyes.*
> > —*The Tempest*

This is the time of evening when
sadness rolls over us like a mower.
The cardinals, who mate for life,
still agitate at last year's nest,
disturbed in the ligustrum, and taunt
the cat. A grey pall coats the plum tree
the quince bushes, the iron love seat
and it's hard to believe the sun shines
somewhere else on earth.
—From *Scheherazade and Other Poems*,
by Margaret Boothe Baddour (Laurinburg, N.C.:
St. Andrews College Press, 2009), 44.

tour 9

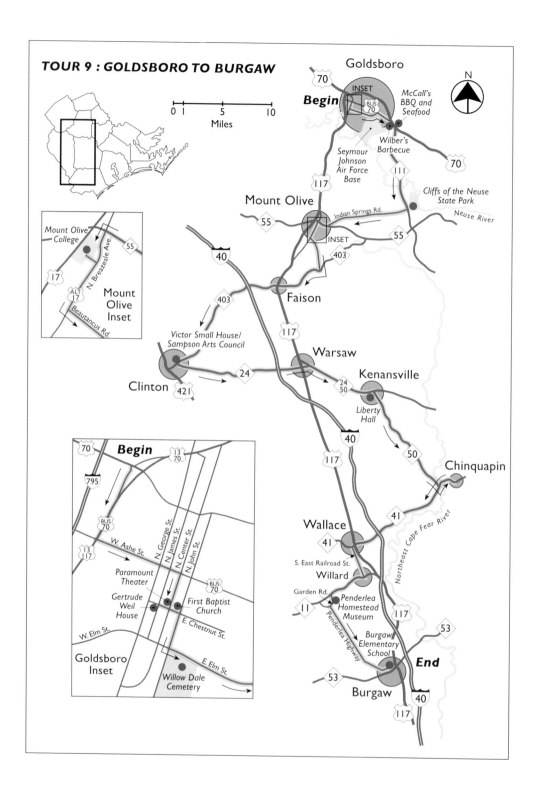

TOUR 9 : GOLDSBORO TO BURGAW

0 1   5   10
Miles

Goldsboro

70

INSET

Begin

BUS 70

McCall's BBQ and Seafood

Wilber's Barbecue

70

111

Seymour Johnson Air Force Base

Cliffs of the Neuse State Park

117

Neuse River

Mount Olive

55

Indian Springs Rd.

55

INSET

403

Mount Olive College

55

N. Breazeale Ave.

17

ALT 17

Mount Olive Inset

Beautancus Rd.

40

403

Faison

Victor Small House/ Sampson Arts Council

403

117

Warsaw

Kenansville

24

24 50

Liberty Hall

Clinton

421

40

117

50

Chinquapin

41

Northeast Cape Fear River

70

13 70

Begin

795

BUS 70

13 117

W. Ashe St.

N. George St.

N. James St.

N. Center St.

N. John St.

BUS 70

Paramount Theater

Gertrude Weil House

First Baptist Church

E. Chestnut St.

W. Elm St.

Wallace

41

S. East Railroad St.

Willard

Garden Rd.

11

Penderlea Homestead Museum

117

53

Goldsboro Inset

E. Elm St.

Willow Dale Cemetery

Penderlea Highway

Burgaw Elementary School

End

53

Burgaw

40

117

This elegiac poem by Goldsboro poet, actor, and humanities instructor Margaret Boothe Baddour sets a fitting tone for a drive through Goldsboro, a town founded in 1787 and incorporated in 1847 as the seat of Wayne County. Baddour's wistful collection, from which this poem is taken, explores the themes of aging and loss.

Goldsboro was overrun with 100,000 Union soldiers under the command of General Sherman following the Battle of Bentonville in 1865, yet many nineteenth-century buildings are still intact. A number of houses in and around the town center have begun to attract newcomers seized with the impulse to renovate the lovely but deteriorating specimens of Victorian, Queen Anne, and Italianate architecture.

If you enter town from the west on US 70, take the Business 70 Exit, which leads to Ash Street. At the traffic circle, take the first right on South Center Street — a boulevard planted with holly trees that runs the length of the downtown district.

In the fall of 1969, the eighty-year-old father of novelist William Styron was married here to his third wife, Goldsboro native Eunice Edmondson. As a young man in 1914, Styron's father had made his first marriage proposal to Edmondson, who turned him down in favor of another suitor. He eventually married Pauline Abraham, who gave birth to the future novelist. Pauline died when her son was a teenager, and William Sr. then married Elizabeth Buxton, who turned out to be a contentious stepmother. (Styron based the unappealing character of Helen Loftis on her in his first novel, *Lie Down in Darkness*.) When Elizabeth died, in 1969, the elder Styron sought out his old flame and found her widowed and living in Goldsboro after years as the wife of a prominent Floridian.

By this time, William Styron Jr. had won the Pulitzer Prize for *The Confessions of Nat Turner*. His wife, Rose, recalled their trip to Goldsboro for the wedding in the foreword to a collection of Styron's letters:

> They married a couple of months later at a church in Goldsboro, North Carolina, where Eunice had an old home — a small, white-pillared house, the last private dwelling on a highway between a Burger King and a Pizza Hut. Pop and Eunice were sitting on the front porch glider when we arrived for the wedding. After the church ceremony, at the Downtowner Motel, where the marquee boasted "Lunch 95¢, Dinner $1.95," guests assembled at a long formal dinner table, but Pop and Eunice sat at a table for two in the corner, holding hands. — From *Letters to My Father*, by William Styron, edited by James L. W. West III (Baton Rouge: Louisiana State University Press, 2009), xviii.

Eunice and William Styron Sr. lived happily into their eighties and are buried in Goldsboro's Willow Dale Cemetery. The Downtowner Motel was on Center Street but has been razed.

Continue ahead to 139 South Center Street, the site of the landmark Paramount Theater, which was recently restored. Built in 1882 by the Weil family, this high Victorian Italianate structure was once the tallest building in town. The Paramount regularly hosts theater and other arts and literary events. Turn right on Chestnut Street. The next destination is one block ahead.

■ GERTRUDE WEIL HOUSE

Corner of James and Chestnut streets, Goldsboro

In *The Bed She Was Born In*, Jeri Fitzgerald Board's sweeping novel of the region that recounts events from before the Civil War to World War II, only one major character bears the name of an actual person. Gertrude Weil, born in this house in 1879, was the first North Carolinian to graduate from Smith College. Like others in her family, she was active in many causes. She helped organize the Goldsboro Equal Suffrage Association and became president of the statewide organization in 1919. She founded the North Carolina League of Women Voters, worked in support of collective bargaining and better working conditions for laborers, and in the 1930s, took on the cause of civil rights for African Americans to protest the practice of lynching. As Hitler rose to power in Germany, Weil and her mother helped Jewish refugees escape from Europe. In Board's novel, Weil has a cameo role when she travels to speak to a group of women in a neighboring town.

Weil died in this house in May 1971, just weeks after the North Carolina legislature ratified the Nineteenth Amendment, affirming at last the state's approval of women's right to vote. (North Carolina was among a handful of states that had refused the original ratification, in 1920.)

Many other assets in Goldsboro derive from the Weil family's philanthropy: among them, the second-oldest synagogue in the state, Temple Oheb Shalom, at 112 West Oak Street (now serving as the community soup kitchen), and Herman Park, an urban refuge where many of the oldest tree specimens in the city still flourish. Local writer Emily Weil, who married Gertrude's nephew David, has published more than a half dozen books on state and local history and lore, which are available from the Wayne County Historical Association.

From here, backtrack on West Chestnut, cross Center, and turn left on South John Street. The next stop is on the left.

One of Goldsboro's most striking historic houses belonged to suffragist and civil rights activist Gertrude Weil. She appears as a character in Jeri Fitzgerald Board's novel The Bed She Was Born In.

■ FIRST BAPTIST CHURCH

125 South John Street, Goldsboro

In 1886, future novelist Thomas Dixon assumed the pastorate of this church. Dixon had already graduated from Wake Forest College and studied political science at Johns Hopkins University, where he befriended future president Woodrow Wilson. He then tried to establish himself as an actor in New York, but failing in his ambitions, he moved back to North Carolina to earn a law degree in Greensboro and then decided to pursue the ministry at the Wake Forest seminary.

Dixon, who opposed slavery but believed in the inferiority of people with dark skin, preached in Goldsboro for only a year, but that year came at the height of recruitment activity by the Ku Klux Klan, which was urging former Confederate soldiers to help suppress newly empowered African Americans in Goldsboro. The long occupation of Goldsboro by Union troops after the war had already stirred local resentment among whites and would influence Dixon's best-selling trilogy of Reconstruction novels—*The Leopard's Spots* (1902), *The Clansman* (1905), and *The Traitor* (1907), which presented fiction as fact. The books were adapted to become the script of the controversial 1915 film *The Birth of a Nation*.

Backtrack on South John to West Elm Street and turn left. You'll pass by the Willow Dale Cemetery, where the Styrons are buried, and continue across the Philip Baddour Bridge (named for poet Margaret Baddour's husband, who represented the district in the North Carolina legislature). On your right is Seymour Johnson Air Force Base, a significant presence in Goldsboro today.

Bear left at the curve where Wright Brothers Avenue merges with Elm and take the second right onto East Ash. (On the way out of town you'll pass two of Goldsboro's most famous eateries—Wilber's Barbecue and McCall's BBQ and Seafood Restaurant.) Turn right on NC 111 and continue 8.4 miles to a left turn on Park Entrance Road.

■ CLIFFS OF THE NEUSE STATE PARK

240 Park Entrance Road, Seven Springs

They are tall straight cliffs, high above the river, and from the tops of them you can see miles across the cypress swamps and bottom land. When Gordon Cherry and I were boys we used to camp there on Saturdays and holidays when there was no school. We'd hide in ambush behind fallen pines and pop off invading enemy forces with our twenty-two rifles as our imaginations swept them around the elbow of the river in driftwood battleships. Once our withering fire almost nipped a real admiral in the form of a fisherman checking his shad traps.—From *Small Town South*, by Sam Byrd (Boston: Houghton Mifflin, 1942), 8.

Cliffs of the Neuse State Park is a bit more grown-up now than Sam Byrd's memoir describes. Camping, hiking, and fishing are still popular activities here, as are the striking views of the Neuse River from the top of the cliffs.

Born in nearby Mount Olive, Sam Byrd was a successful actor before he became a writer. As journalist Bernadette Hoyle tells it, "He made theatrical history as the original ball-bouncing half-wit, Dude Lester, in *Tobacco Road*, and played the role for 1,151 consecutive performances, during which he ate more than a thousand raw turnips to the delight of Broadway audiences" (*Tar Heel Writers I Know*, Winston-Salem: John F. Blair, 1956, 28). Byrd then played Curley in the Broadway production of Steinbeck's *Of Mice and Men*. A chance meeting with a Houghton Mifflin executive at a literary party at the Algonquin Hotel in New York led Byrd to write *Small Town South*, which won the publisher's Life in America prize for 1942.

From Park Entrance Road, turn right onto Indian Springs Road and follow it for 9.6 miles. Turn right on SR 55 (west) to the town of Mount Olive. In 1.1 miles, turn left toward Henderson Street and follow it through the campus of Mount Olive College.

■ MOUNT OLIVE

Mount Olive is the setting for Durham writer Alice Wisler's first novel, *Rain Song*. It is also home to Mount Olive College, where the poets Lenard D. Moore (whose work is considered in Tour 1) and David Rigsbee teach. Rigsbee is known for his literary criticism as well as his elegant poetry. Though he grew up in Durham, his mother's side of the family was from Mount Olive. This intimate poem evokes the complexities of change in the region.

BIG WIND
A big wind blew the Roundup
from a grassy field to my uncle's garden.
He has just finished replanting
the yellow squash and shining cucumber
and pointed out the seared leaves, drooping
but clenched, of the potato plants
he tells me will survive the fallout.
Curled edges are already giving way
to the stain of massed green, against
which defoliant can do no more
than seem insurgent. His wife is probably
losing vision in one eye; neither heart
nor lung reliable: they know the way
to the hospital. He is not sure
waking some days if his legs will

Though this town is better known for its college and for pickled cucumbers, the Mount Olive hog market is a historic facility still put to good use in the land of barbecue and bacon. A novel by Durham writer Alice Wisler—Rain Song—is set here.

hold up his trunk, and if the garden calls,
is it in mockery? Suddenly it must seem
that much else is giving way
that was once beyond question. His sister
is moving. Living with her daughter
up in the mountains and her son-in-law,
both stubborn fundamentalists. Rush
and *Focus on the Family* will be her fare.
He wonders whether this is one
of the secret meanings of *giving*.
I remember the ease with which she posed
like Grable in a bathing suit,
my mother next to her, the farm behind,
out of focus. On the way back, an unfledged bird
stirs in the dirt on our path beneath
an old chinaberry. "Caint put it back,"
he says, looking up. "I guess

I could stomp it," he adds and peers at me
to see the effect. "But I won't."
—From *The Pilot House*, by David Rigsbee
    (New York: Black Lawrence Press, 2011), 38.

From the campus gates, take the second right onto North Breazeale Avenue (US 117 Alternate), and in 1.3 miles turn left onto Country Road, which soon becomes Beautancus Road, so named for a small crossroads where poet, singer, and songwriter Shirlette Ammons was raised. In this musical poem, Ammons introduces her colorful family and the hardships of rural living.

LIVING WILL
Uncle Buddy went before his hog's last feedin,
Uncle Johnny behind a discount cigarette;
Cut'in Citty Ruth withered just before
Hookin her last bait
Three jobs for twelve mouths
Made Grandaddy's heart explode

Gramma, too tired to keep up, asked I
Swathe her feet with camphor;
I prepped her bruised embers,
Seen em crumble to soot as I massaged

Aunt Lou's the youngest of the old,
She comes home to fireworks on the Fourth,
Pig pickins and prodigal patriot bouquets;
She is the lobelia Beautancus planted in Peoria
Savin obituaries, savorin Budweisers
Like flimsy bookmarks in *Our Daily Bread*

On the fifth, she packs her seventies Samsonite,
Back to frying family recipes for Illinois Gamma girls;
No homefolk can see her now
Hovering over that sorority house stove;
She shifts her weight to a walking cane,
Toasts the last day her siblings wore work shoes

We are a family darned and patched;
Like hearty hand-me-downs

This grand house, between Beautancus and Faison at 422 Taylor Town Road, was the setting used in the film version of the novel Divine Secrets of the Ya-Ya Sisterhood, *by Rebecca Wells.*

From Mr. Julius to his son Lanny,
We made for sturdy work clothes
In the ceremonial South
The living bequeath the living
Over secret handshakes at the coolin board
—From *Matching Skin*, by Shirlette Ammons
  (Durham: Carolina Wren Press, 2008), 3.

At the intersection of Beautancus Road and NC 403, turn right to reach the next destination.

■ FAISON

"Throwed away" is an expression peculiar to eastern North Carolina. If a piece of land or a person or a stretch along the highway looks "throwed away," it can be in no worse shape. Fields left unattended and overcome with cockleburs are "throwed away." Ramshackle houses with boarded-up windows and rotten porches, or country stores that have bitten the dust are "throwed away."

But these are proud people. Throwed away they may be, but it won't do

In Throwed Away, *Faison writer Linda Flowers described the slow transition from agriculture to industry to technology that has left so many historic barns and houses leaning toward ruin.*

to count them out. Men and women who have seen how, in the 1960s, machines pushed up the demand for land, even as they made farm laborers increasingly obsolescent, who have experienced the breakup of smalltime agriculture, yet who have kept going nonetheless, kept looking ahead— they know they're up against a hard time, but they know, too, they'll make it somehow: they always have. Business is business, and if people still matter less than profits, why they've always known *that.*

—From *Throwed Away: Failures of Progress in Eastern North Carolina,* by
  Linda Flowers (Knoxville: University of Tennessee Press, 1990), xi, 209.

Linda Flowers, a brilliant scholar and gifted writer, was raised in a tenant-farming family in Faison, a background she held dear even as she left the state to earn graduate degrees from Ohio State University and the University of Rochester. She came back to serve as head of the English department at North Carolina Wesleyan College, in Rocky Mount. Cancer cut her life grievously short, and a literary prize for creative nonfiction, administered by the North Carolina Humanities Council, commemorates her life and work.

Follow NC 403 through Faison. In fifteen miles, the road reaches Clinton, where 403 becomes College Street. Don't be surprised if along the roadside you encounter a littering of feathers. Great numbers of chickens and turkeys are raised in the vicinity and exported by open-air truck.

■ CLINTON

> At first I thought about asking all the poets in North Carolina—there are approximately 37.5 poets per square mile in The State of the Arts—to contribute their favorite grits recipes to a special literary edition of breakfast recipes. Then I thought better of it and decided that, since I have never known a poet who could cook any food that is served in a solid state, I dared not risk it. So I am going to dream up my own recipes for southern living, Sampson County style, and publish them with mouth-watering Polaroids of meals I have made for special occasions like the Sunday after the Super Bowl.—From "Kathryn Gurkin's Collard Brunch," in *Zen Ironing*, by Kathryn Bright Gurkin (Charlotte: Main Street Rag, 2003), 35.

"Kathryn Gurkin's Collard Brunch" celebrates local traditions, the writer's tongue firmly in cheek. The essay is a departure for Gurkin, a gifted poet who has written four collections. *Terra Amata* won the Zoe Kincaid Brockman Book Award from the North Carolina Poetry Society, in 1980.

Clinton was also the boyhood home of novelist Michael Parker, whose work is represented in Tour 17. Parker's father was editor of the town's weekly newspaper. The rhythms and images Parker weaves through his fiction bear the lasting stamp of his years in Clinton.

Victor Small, a Clinton physician who was known for his generosity in serving patients who could not pay for his services, was an avid reader and sometime poet. Before his death, in 1971, he stipulated that the large Classic Revival–style house he owned at 709 College Street should be used to promote music, literature, and art. He further required that the furnishings remain intact, citing in particular the claw-foot bathtub where he often wrote his poems. The house is now the headquarters of the Sampson County Arts Council.

From the Victor Small House, take the next left on Warsaw Road (NC 24), which is also known as the Turkey Highway. In thirteen miles, you'll pass through Warsaw, the hometown of Sandra Carlton-Alexander—a place described in the excerpt that begins the introduction to this trail. Hillsborough novelist Michael Malone says he had this area in mind when he created the fictional town of Emerald in his 2009 novel, *The Four Corners of the Sky*.

On the east side of Warsaw, NC 24 joins up with NC 50 and reaches Kenans-

Eccentric physician and poet Victor Small willed his Clinton residence to the community for cultural events. It is now the headquarters of the Sampson County Arts Council.

ville—our next destination—in another 8.3 miles. Turn left on South Main Street (NC 24 Business) and look for Liberty Hall, a dignified white house on the right.

■ KENANSVILLE

This village is named for the Kenans—an energetic Scots-Irish family that came to this area in the early 1700s and has made many important philanthropic gifts to North Carolina, notably in higher education. Liberty Hall, one of the area's oldest and most elegant houses, belonged to them. Built in the late 1700s, the house served several generations and was the site of the internationally publicized wedding of Mary Lily Kenan to Standard Oil tycoon Henry Flagler, in August 1901. The bride was thirty-four, and the groom—then enter-

Dating from the 1700s, Liberty Hall belonged to the prosperous Kenan family of Duplin County. One of the family's major philanthropic efforts in recent decades has been to bring undereducated parents and their young children together to learn how to read.

ing his third marriage—was seventy-one. The couple immediately moved to Palm Beach, Florida, where Flagler built Whitehall, a fifty-five-room marble mansion, now a popular museum.

Becke Roughton, a longtime instructor of fine arts and creative writing at James Sprunt Community College in Kenansville alludes to the Kenan family's story in this poem:

VISIONS
Across the wide span of green-tinged fields
white-laced dogwoods
like a vision of brides
gathered at wood's edge,
nod with sporadic fans
at what will be.

In sweltering summer
tall, stately, so formal,
so sure in leatherly leaves
the proud magnolia

displays her finest white,
lovely, large as dinner plates,
heirloom of the South
intoxicating, heady,
the air belongs to her.

On certain days sunlight
slants through Spanish moss
draped low from branches of cedar
and cypress, transforms
in backlit silvery glow,
a glimpse of something
divine, aura of splendor,
antonym of eclipse.

Early morning mist hovers
over the lower places of this low land
and spreads out like a whisper . . .
white-tail, be safe . . .
then overtakes the road, the ditches, grasses,
and in the middle of the field
the oak.

Not mist but like snow,
blanketing far back
across distant fields,
rows and rows of cotton,
coppery leaves now dropped,
bolls bursting in brilliant white
as far as the willing eye
can see, this, our snow.

Crows cawl-calling
raid the tops of pecan trees,
swoop in and out, drop
like stones in stubble fields.

Day turns to dark without pause
or apology. At the edge of town
a lone farmer
behind the unsteady beams

of his tractor ploughs
far into the night.

Right on cue one by one, street by street
solstice windows show up show off
in classic white candles
while the fence bounding Liberty Hall
remembers fondly
a pre-electric time
and a clomp-thump
stick on the pickets,
click of the gate, the garlanded door.
Faces of guests, now tourists,
float in the wavy glass, and perhaps
a face of long ago, visage
come home.
—Used by permission of Becke Roughton

From Liberty Hall, proceed on NC 24 Business into Kenansville and turn right onto Front Street. Turn right onto North Main (NC 24 Business) and then turn left onto NC 50 South. In twelve miles, NC 50 meets NC 41. Turn left and cross the Northeast Cape Fear River. If you'd like to see the river up close, take the first left after the bridge and follow the signs to the public boat launch. Otherwise, continue on NC 41 to reach the tiny village of Chinquapin.

■ CHINQUAPIN

Novelist Randall Kenan was born in 1963, the year James Baldwin's collection of essays *The Fire Next Time*, about race relations in America, was issued by Dial Press. Kenan, who would become a devotee of Baldwin's, was raised in this town by his extended family. He left for college to study at the University of North Carolina at Chapel Hill with creative writing professor Doris Betts, who introduced him to novelist and editor Toni Morrison, in 1985. Through this connection, Kenan was hired at Random House, later working at Alfred A. Knopf.

Following the publication of his first novel, in 1989, Kenan left publishing to teach, first at Sarah Lawrence College and then at Columbia University. He is now on the creative writing faculty of his alma mater in Chapel Hill.

Kenan's fiction takes place mostly in and around Chinquapin, which he dubs Tim's Creek—a sometimes claustrophobic community where church and school are held in highest esteem and where everyone's business is common knowledge. The situation is tough for Kenan's protagonist, Horace Thomas Cross, whose coming-of-age also involves coming out as a homosexual.

> The congregation sat in their finery, their pastel pinks and greens and reds and blues absorbing and reflecting the early-morning light against the pristine white walls of the sanctuary. Expressions on their faces ran the gamut of all the feelings Horace had felt while sitting in those pews: boredom; anticipation of meals to come, the sermon, a ball game, seeing a friend after a long spell; tiredness; worry; restfulness; contentment. They were fat and thin, light and dark, tall and short, farmers, schoolteachers, plumbers, bus drivers, butchers, carpenters, salesmen, mechanics, barbers, nurses, mothers, fathers, aunts, uncles, cousins, lovers, friends. Here was community, not a word but a being. Horace felt it as though for the first time. Here, amid these singing, fanning, breathing beings were his folk, his kin. Did he know them? Had they known him? It was from them he was running. Why?—From *A Visitation of Spirits*, by Randall Kenan (New York: Vintage Books, 1989), 73.

Kenan's second book, *Let the Dead Bury Their Dead*, a collection of stories that also deals with what it means to be a gay African American man in southern culture, was a literary sensation, nominated for a slew of awards. Kenan has since published a biography of James Baldwin and an oral history of the lives of African Americans at the turn of the twenty-first century. *The Fire This Time* (2008) is a memoir and commentary on the contemporary status of African Americans across the United States, published as both homage and follow-up to Baldwin's *The Fire Next Time*.

Backtrack across the river on NC 41 and continue for 12.6 miles toward Wallace. Humor writer Celia Rivenbark hails from this neck of the woods. Now in Wilmington, the irreverent Rivenbark writes a weekly newspaper column that draws on her rural Duplin County roots to send up the world of southern womanhood.

As NC 41 weaves through Wallace, it becomes East Main Street. Turn left on Southeast Railroad Street, which will become Willard Railroad Street, and follow it for three miles. At the intersection with NC 11, turn right and proceed 4.4 miles to Garden Road and turn left.

The Penderlea Homestead Museum, in northwest Pender County, presents the story and a collection of artifacts from the first of 152 homestead projects that began in 1934 during the New Deal to put bankrupt farmers back to work. Carolyn Rawls Booth's novel A Chosen Few *is set at the homestead.*

■ PENDERLEA HOMESTEAD MUSEUM

284 Garden Road, Willard

The house itself had green and white striped awnings over the front windows and the side entry to the screened-in porch. Len had never seen awnings used in the country, but he'd been told that the house would be much cooler inside because of them. A pale green shingled roof would have the same effect. Awnings and dark green painted shutters set against the white siding of the house completed the little cottage that looked to have been taken right out of a picture book.—From *A Chosen Few*, by Carolyn Rawls Booth (Chapel Hill: Chapel Hill Press, 2008), 257.

This museum's hours are limited—but the house described here and its story are fascinating relics of an ambitious and radical development program conceived by Wilmington businessman Hugh McCrae and funded by the federal government to help bankrupt farm owners and tenant farmers get back on their feet during the Depression. Only a chosen few, as Carolyn Booth's title suggests, were allowed to occupy Penderlea Homestead Farms. The community was restricted to able-bodied white families with children who signed leases on the uniform houses built by the Department of the Interior. The government also loaned them feed, seed, livestock, and fertilizer as they began a new truck-farming enterprise. At the hub of the development, the government built a school and community center—buildings that are still standing.

The project excited the White House, and the president's wife, Eleanor Roosevelt, paid a visit to Penderlea in 1937. For the occasion, the homesteaders renamed a local variety of strawberry in her honor and performed a play they had written.

Booth, who lives in Cary, effectively renders the full story of Penderlea in the novel just quoted—the third in a trilogy set in eastern North Carolina. She was born the year her parents were selected to be part of the social experiment.

Continue beyond the museum on Garden Road and take the first left on Penderlea Highway. In ten miles, take a slight left onto West Wallace Street, and in a half mile, turn left on North Wright Street to reach this tour's final destination.

■ **BURGAW ELEMENTARY SCHOOL**

400 North Wright Street, Burgaw

In addition to its well-preserved train station, which is one of only two antebellum depots left in the state, Burgaw is the hometown of award-winning playwright and actor Samm-Art Williams. The school ahead on the right was once the C. F. Pope High School, where Williams graduated in 1964 and where his mother was a revered teacher. In an interview at the Signature Theatre in New York City, given during the 2008 revival of Williams's 1979 Broadway hit, *Home*, the writer explained a bit about his upbringing in Burgaw and how his mother steered him from mischief and toward literature:

She had me read the poetry of Langston Hughes and Edgar Allan Poe, and that was really what changed me. I must have been about fifteen years old when I read "The Raven." I did not know what a raven was! When I finished that poem, I was so scared of that bird. I said, "Wait a minute, how can I be afraid of something when I don't even know what the hell it is?" Which led me to believe that he was a wonderful writer. I said, "Hmm, I would like to do something like that!" — From an interview with Samm-Art Williams, reprinted at http://www.courttheatre.org/season/article/samm-art_williams_on_coming_home.

After a long stint in Los Angeles, where he wrote for television, Williams returned to Burgaw to care for his ailing mother. He lives in the neighborhood adjacent to his old high school and teaches several days a week at North Carolina Central University. He was inducted into the North Carolina Literary Hall of Fame in 2011.

■ LITERARY LANDSCAPE

Goldsboro Writers Group

c/o Arts Council of Wayne County
919-736-3300
Founded in the 1980s, this collective operates as a critique group for poetry and fiction writers. It meets at Wayne Community College, monthly during the academic year and weekly during the summer.

Wilson : Stantonsburg : Snow Hill : Kinston :
New Bern : Pollocksville : Jacksonville :
Topsail Beach

Green leaves of tobacco, collards, and common weeds popu-
late the fields where these writers found inspiration. White-
hot summers and busy country stores pepper tales of family
and duty, of survival and celebration.

*Writers with a connection to this area: Betty Adcock, James
Applewhite, Michael Beadle, Jim Clark, Needham Bryan Cobb,
Jerry W. Cotten, Edison Dupree, Jim Grimsley, John Lawson, V. S.
Naipaul, Louise Shivers, Nicholas Sparks, William Styron, Mark
Twain, Phyllis A. Whitney*

■ WILSON

In the early twentieth century, Wilson was the world's
largest bright leaf tobacco market. Today, the town is better
known for its barbecue and growing arts scene.

The Arts Council of Wilson, located in a beautifully restored
theater at 125 Nash Street SW, offers occasional writing workshops. It's also a sponsor of Theater of the American South,
which presents each spring two plays in repertory by celebrated southern writers such as Tennessee Williams, Carson
McCullers, and Horton Foote. It occupies two stages—one a
short walk from the arts council at 108 West Nash Street and
the other on the campus of Barton College.

Another Wilson standout is Vollis Simpson, from the nearby
village of Lucama. Simpson has spent years building colorful,
whimsical whirligigs that have been collected by the High
Museum of Art, in Atlanta, the North Carolina Museum of Art,
and the American Visionary Museum, in Baltimore. (Some of
his smaller pieces are available for purchase in the local arts
council's gallery shop.) Wilson's Downtown Development Cor-

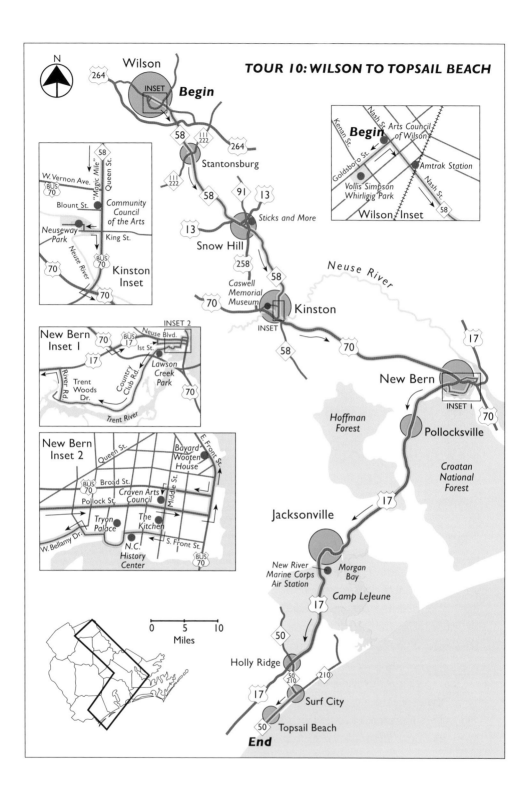

TOUR 10: WILSON TO TOPSAIL BEACH

N

Wilson
Begin
264
264
58
111
222
Stantonsburg
58
111
222
58
91
13
Sticks and More
13
Snow Hill
258
Neuse River
58
Caswell
Memorial
Museum
70
Kinston
INSET
58
70
17

Wilson Inset

Begin
Nash St.
Arts Council
of Wilson
Kenan St.
Goldsboro St.
Amtrak Station
Vollis Simpson
Whirligig Park
Nash St.
Wilson Inset
58

Kinston Inset

58
Queen St.
W. Vernon Ave.
"Magic Mile"
BUS
70
Blount St.
Community
Council
of the Arts
Neuseway
Park
King St.
Neuse River
BUS
70
70
Kinston
Inset
70

New Bern Inset 1

New Bern
Inset 1
70
BUS
17
Neuse Blvd.
INSET 2
1st St.
17
River Rd.
Country Club Rd.
Lawson
Creek
Park
Trent
Woods
Dr.
70
Trent River

New Bern Inset 2

New Bern
Inset 2
Queen St.
E. Front St.
Bayard
Wooten
House
BUS
70
Broad St.
Craven Arts
Council
Middle St.
Pollock St.
Tryon
Palace
The
Kitchen
W. Bellamy Dr.
S. Front St.
N.C.
History
Center
BUS
70

New Bern
INSET 1
70
Pollocksville
Hoffman
Forest
Croatan
National
Forest
17
Jacksonville
New River
Marine Corps
Air Station
Morgan
Bay
Camp LeJeune
17
50
Holly Ridge
50
210
210
17
Surf City
50
Topsail Beach
End

0   5   10
Miles

Working out of a repair shop on his Lucama farm near Wilson, artist Vollis Simpson has made enormous whirligigs, which are now exhibited in museums up and down the East Coast of the United States. A song written by Barton College creative writing professor Jim Clark celebrates the artist. Courtesy of the North Carolina Arts Council, North Carolina Department of Cultural Resources, © Burke Uzzle, photographer.

poration bought thirty large examples of Simpson's work for a public park and outdoor museum, which is scheduled to open in late 2013. The Vollis Simpson Whirligig Park will be two blocks southwest of the Amtrak train station on Goldsboro Street, at the intersection with Kenan Street in the heart of downtown. A Whirligig Festival celebrating Simpson's vision is held downtown on the first weekend in November.

Jim Clark, poet, singer, and songwriter, is writer-in-residence at Barton College, where he teaches southern literature. He composed these lyrics to commemorate the years Vollis Simpson spent in quiet labor in a workshop on his farm.

OLD MILL ROAD (EXCERPT)
Cold frosty night with a halo 'round the moon
There's an old man walking past a crooked stop sign
He's staring up ahead at a burnt patch of pine
In the light spilling from the circle 'round the cold frosty moon

Walking at night down the old mill road
My footsteps echoing in your dreams
Round the bend in the light of the pale moon beams
There's a wheel spinning by the ditch of the old mill road

Willing worker welding on a windmill frame
He sees her face in the arc of the flame

Wheel sparkle in the cold black night
Angel rising into the light
Crossroads burning like a thousand suns
Stamp my ticket to Kingdom Come
—Used by permission of Jim Clark

From Whirligig Park, head northeast on Goldsboro Street and take the third right onto South Nash Street (NC 58). Stay on NC 58 for nearly ten miles to our next destination.

■ STANTONSBURG

Within seven years of each other, two important North Carolina writers — poet James Applewhite and novelist Louise Shivers — were born and raised near this town of fewer than a thousand people. Applewhite, winner of the 1995 North Carolina Award for Literature, was inducted into the North Carolina Literary Hall of Fame in 2008. In his work, he often reflects on how life for those in his grandfather's generation revolved around the cycle of tobacco — planting, growing, picking, curing, grading, and selling. Applewhite's father sold appliances and ran a gas station on Main Street in Stantonsburg. The family attended the Methodist church, which you'll see coming into town.

Applewhite left the family farm to attend Duke University, where he eventually earned a doctorate and then joined the faculty of the English department. Winner of the Jean Stein Award in Poetry from the American Academy of Arts and Letters, Applewhite has written poems based on his travels around

Poet James Applewhite's father sold appliances on this street in Stantonsburg.
His grandfather grew tobacco on a farmstead outside of town.

the world, but again and again he has returned to his home place and people,
to their rituals and traditions, writing in language by turns elegant and simple.

COLLARDS

Green hens perching the pole
  Of a row, concentric wings
Fly you down into soil.

You catch the rain like rings
  Where pine stump tunnels
Time backward down roots' seasonings.

Beside roots' dark channels
  Mining the forest, your fiber
Threads grease in the entrails

A poem by James Applewhite speaks of "Green hens perching the pole / Of a row, concentric wings / Fly you down into soil." On the road to Snow Hill in winter, collards, a staple for New Year's dinner, fill the fields.

Of families, whose bodies harbor
    Scars like rain on a hillslope,
Whose skin takes the sheen of lumber

Left out in the weather. Old folk
    Seem sewed together by pulp
Of your green rope and smoke

From the cook fires boys gulp
    For dinner along roads in winter.
Collards and the ham grease they drop

In a pot come back as we enter
    The house with porch and a pumpkin.
This steam holds all we remember.

Sweet potatoes clot in a bin,
    Common flesh beneath this skin
Like collards. Grainy-sweet, kin.
—From *James Applewhite: Selected Poems*, by James Applewhite (Durham:
    Duke University Press, 2001), 78.

Louise Shivers left Stantonsburg at eighteen to study at Meredith College, dropping out after a year to marry. She had three children in rapid succession and moved with her family to Augusta, Georgia. She did not begin writing in earnest until the age of forty. Like Applewhite's, her work draws on memories of growing up in Wilson County. *USA Today* named Shivers's Depression-era novel, *Here to Get My Baby Out of Jail*, the "Best First Novel of the Year" in 1983. It was adapted for the screen as *Summer Heat*, which was filmed in the nearby towns of Nashville, Robersonville, Tarboro, and Wilson.

Shivers's second novel, *A Whistling Woman*, imagines life in and around Stantonsburg just after the Civil War and describes the tent meetings, foot washings, hog killings, and barbecue cook-offs that residents so relished in the midst of their hardscrabble lives.

In a long interview with writer V. S. Naipaul, James Applewhite talked about the same theme Shivers takes up in *A Whistling Woman*—how the pre-automobile isolation of farming communities made common ritual so crucial. "People did feel lost here," Applewhite told Naipaul. "The sense of needing to form a life that had its own regularities, its own formalities—that was a reason that religion had the contour it had. That's why the formalities of tobacco growing were so important" (*A Turn in the South*, by V. S. Naipaul [New York: Alfred A. Knopf, 1989], 271).

In her novels, Shivers uses actual place-names, such as Sand Pit Road, off NC 58 just south of town on the way to Snow Hill.

■ SNOW HILL

Mama let me go into Snow Hill by myself for the first time that day. I think it was her way of accepting that I was getting older. Slender had come back and rigged me up a little pony cart.

I was high with a free feeling all the way into town. When I got there I tied the pony in front of the store, then stopped to look into the window. I saw myself reflected in the glass in my pinafore.

The store was a house of treasures . . . to the farmers and their families all over Tar County. People didn't just jump on a train and go off to Raleigh or Richmond then. Eastern North Carolina was made up of little towns and crossroads with just the right distance between them for a horse ride and back in a day. People from the farms didn't just come to Willy's store to get flour and salt and sugar; they came to see new things and to visit. And Willy knew how to give them a show.

—From *A Whistling Woman*, by Louise Shivers (Atlanta: Longstreet Press, 1986), 26, 93.

Though the general store Louise Shivers writes about is no longer to be found in Snow Hill, visitors might enjoy a stop at Sticks and More, at 216 SE Second Street. There, store owners Donna Haggerty and Mollie Murphrey, both raised on tobacco farms, sell crafts they make from tobacco sticks and other farm odds and ends. They also sell children's books.

As you come into town, NC 58 joins US 13. Take the fourth right onto Greene Street (US 258) and then turn right on SE Second Street, where US 258 turns south. The store is on the left in a converted gas station.

From Snow Hill, head south on US 258 and bear left onto NC 58 to continue another fifteen miles to Kinston.

■ KINSTON

Arriving in town on NC 58, you come straight down Queen Street, which was known as the "Magic Mile" when tobacco was Kinston's mainstay. Today, Kinston is recognized for its importance in the history of North Carolina roots music. A number of important regional musicians got their start here, including James Brown's drummer, Melvin Parker, and his brother, saxophonist Maceo Parker. On South Queen Street, a public park featuring sculpture, spaces for informal musical performances, and site-specific displays by artists and landscape architects will provide a visual interpretation of the musical heritage of the area. Information about the African American Music Trail, which winds through Lenoir and seven other eastern North Carolina counties, is available at the Community Arts Council, at 400 North Queen Street, or by visiting http://www.ncartstrails.org.

Kinston's arts council focuses chiefly on visual art and music these days, but in the 1980s and early 1990s the council published an ambitious literary journal. A story by a young Ron Rash—"The Night the New Jesus Fell to Earth"—that appeared in *A Carolina Literary Companion* in 1987 won the prestigious General Electric Younger Writers Award for that year: a triumph for the arts council and the start of a distinguished career for Rash. (His work is discussed in detail in *Literary Trails of the North Carolina Mountains*.)

Kinston's Civil War history is celebrated at the Governor Richard Caswell Memorial Museum, at 2612 West Vernon Avenue, which houses the hull of the Confederate ironclad the CSS *Neuse*. A replica of the ship also sits on the banks of the Neuse, which flows through Neuseway Park at 401 West Caswell Street, on the edge of downtown. The Neuseway Nature Center (in the park) is the place to register for camping and canoe rentals if you want to explore the river up close.

Poet Edison Dupree, now a librarian at Harvard University, was raised in Kinston. In this whimsical poem, he remembers a dazzling summer day:

RECORD
Kinston, N.C.
The sun climbed higher. The air
thickened among the buildings
like a rich batter, and set.
Then the humped cars came tunneling,
eating their way like beetles.
One burst, and its white kernel
ghosted out from the grille,
labored high over the town,
and vanished, unnoticed.

Asphalt of streets softened.
On her high porch, a lady's face
trickled its thin whey. Her neighbor,
passing by on the sidewalk, dropped
an egg from his grocery bag. It splashed
to a black star of carbon.
Beside it, somebody's lost dime
blazed, and could not be touched.
—From *Prosthesis: Poems*, by Edison Dupree
      (Emporia, Kans.: Bluestem Press, 1994), 37.

Michael Beadle, a popular poet who performs his work in classrooms across North Carolina, spent his childhood in Kinston and the nearby village of Eureka. Beadle recalls the backbreaking task of harvesting tobacco. It's a memory shared by many in Kinston, though less and less of the leaf is grown around here.

A TOWN TOO SMALL FOR MAPS (EXCERPT)
Outside town long rows of tobacco
lined the highways. How I'd pray
the harvester would get to the end.

Reach down, curl a hand around the stalk,
break off three, four leaves, dump it
in the tray again and again.

Hands and forearms turned gummy black.
'Baccer dew wet our shirts, dried stiff as blood.
Early mornings we'd top and sucker,

flick fat, green worms from the leaves.
We'd stop mid-morning when the boss man
or the boss man's son brought us

Little Debbies and a bottle of coke
I'd tilt sideways to chug faster, feel the burn
in my cheeks. By August we'd be at the bulk barns,

sifting through crispy, golden leaf,
toss out what's burnt. Burlap bundled,
knotted, bound for market.

Stack 'em high in the big trucks, boys!
Leaves littered the sides of highways
like money spilled from a stolen bank truck.

The best brand of flue-cured that season
paid for school clothes and car payments.
—Used by permission of Michael Beadle

Cross the Neuse River west of town to pick up US 70 East to New Bern, thirty miles away. As you get close to New Bern, watch for US 17B North and exit toward downtown on Neuse Boulevard. When the road is no longer divided by a median, take the first right on First Street, then left on Pollock Street, to reach the waterfront.

■ NEW BERN

As a setting for literature, New Bern made its national debut in the work of Mark Twain, through a story that the writer heard in 1874 at his sister-in-law's house, in Elmira, New York. "A True Story, Repeated Word for Word as I Heard It" was based on an experience revealed to Twain by a family servant, Mary Ann Cord, who tells how, as a young enslaved woman, her children were sold away from her. Years later and still grieving, Cord was working in New Bern as a cook and had a chance encounter with a group of black Union soldiers who were occupying the town in the aftermath of the Civil War. As she was making the group's breakfast one morning, Cord noticed telltale marks on the wrist and forehead of one of the soldiers and realized he was her youngest child. Mother and son embraced with tears and thanksgiving.

Twain's original handwritten manuscript, available online, suggests that the writer worked hard to capture Cord's diction and tone, and the result was the first piece he ever published in the *Atlantic Monthly*. According to scholar Stephen Railton, it was also Twain's "first sustained attempt to represent the experience of slavery and to employ an African American voice." When Twain sent the piece to the magazine's editor, William Dean Howells, he admitted his concern that the essay was unusual for him: it had no humor. The full text along with Stephen Railton's analysis is available at http://etext.virginia.edu /railton/huckfinn/truest1.html.

■ BAYARD WOOTTEN HOUSE

519 East Front Street, New Bern

Adventurous female photographer Bayard Wootten was born in New Bern in 1875. Her maternal grandmother was poet Mary Bayard Clarke, of Raleigh. Wootten designed the first logo for Pepsi Cola, which was invented here in 1898. Her extraordinary photos illustrated works by North Carolina writers, including *From My Highest Hill*, by Olive Tilford Dargan, and *Cabins in the Laurel*, by Muriel Earley Sheppard. (See *Literary Trails of the North Carolina Mountains*.) Though she worked most of her life out of a studio in Chapel Hill, where she photographed Thomas Wolfe as a student and befriended his professor Frederick Koch, Wootten came home to New Bern to retire. The University of North Carolina Press published a biography and collection of Wootten's photos, *Light and Air*, by Jerry W. Cotten, in 1998.

Novelist Nicholas Sparks calls New Bern home. Though not a North Carolina native, the writer has set many of his books in the eastern part of the state. *The Best of Me* is set in Oriental; *A Walk to Remember*, in Beaufort; *Safe Haven*, in Southport; and *The Notebook*, in New Bern. In addition to his contributions to eastern North Carolina's film industry whenever his novels are made into films shot on location in the region, Sparks has also invested generously in his local community. He gave the funds to build track and field facilities at New Bern High School.

Local fans revealed that Baker's Kitchen, at 227 Middle Street, in the heart of downtown, is a Sparks family favorite—try the French toast! And while you're in the neighborhood, the Craven Arts Council, in a former bank building now

New Bern photographer Bayard Wootten took this image of her half-sister, Celia Moulton, on a dune near Beaufort. Celia, her brother George Moulton, and Wootten worked together and were the official photographers of the Carolina Playmakers. Courtesy of the North Carolina Collection Photographic Archives, Wilson Library, UNC–Chapel Hill.

Eastern North Carolina writers David Rigsbee, Marjorie Hudson, Gerald Barrax, and Margaret Maron share a moment at the 2012 North Carolina Writers Conference, held in New Bern.

called "The Bank of the Arts" at 317 Middle Street, has a fine gift shop stocked by local and regional arts; stop there for a souvenir of this tour.

Continue around Front Street to the North Carolina History Center, next door to Tryon Palace—both are worthy stops for a lesson in the state's colonial history. Beyond the palace, turn left on Walt Bellamy Drive and follow it to Country Club Road and turn left. The next left will take you to Lawson Creek Park, a great place to picnic or bird-watch with a view back toward town. Lawson Creek is named for explorer and writer John Lawson who built his first house in the New World high above this stream and set about gathering his journals and notes to write *A New Voyage to Carolina*, published in 1709, the only book to come out of the era when the colony was governed by the English Lords Proprietors. Lawson eventually helped establish the town of New Bern but met an untimely end at the hands of the Tuscarora Indians.

Country Club continues from here all the way to Trent Woods Drive, where Nicholas Sparks's house is among several large estates that overlook the Trent River. When you come to River Road, turn right and follow it to US 17. Turn left to reach our next destination.

You named this place the Fish House, because before you lived in it the owner Mrs. Edna Crenshaw had run a fish store in the building, and the smell of the fish had soaked every board. Mrs. Crenshaw, a large, powder-fleshed woman, had been in the fish market business many years, buying fresh seafood off trucks that drove straight up the highway from the coast. Her customers were the local farmers and merchants, who got tired of their wives' fried chicken and fatback and greasy pork chops. Over the years Mrs. Crenshaw had done well enough to lay aside money to build herself a brand-new brick fish store across the highway from the old one. You could see it from the window of your house, a small, square brick building with a multicolored sign in front, that Mrs. Crenshaw's husband retouched lovingly every week from the same four cans of paint. Amy Kay called him Mr. Fish Face because of the way his eyelids drew back from his eyeballs, exposing the whites all around.—From *Winter Birds*, by Jim Grimsley (Chapel Hill: Algonquin Books of Chapel Hill, 1984), 24.

Novelist Jim Grimsley spent his first eighteen years in this village on the Trent River in Jones County, which became the setting for his first novel, *Winter Birds*. Written in the second person, perhaps to preserve the narrator's distance from the trauma of his childhood, the novel was initially rejected by U.S. publishers for its dark themes. A German publisher finally took it, however, and two years later, Algonquin Books of Chapel Hill brought out an English edition. The American Academy of Arts and Letters awarded it the 1995 Sue Kaufman Prize for First Fiction.

Grimsley—who by then had worked as a secretary in an Atlanta hospital for twenty years and had written fourteen plays that had been produced around the country—was invited to join the creative writing faculty at Emory University. His second novel, *Dream Boy*, won the American Library Association's Stonewall Book Award. His third book, *My Drowning* (1997), won the Lila Wallace Readers' Digest Award.

Jones County was also home in the late 1800s to poet and schoolteacher Needham Bryan Cobb, whose sole claim to literary fame was the charming doggerel he wrote to help his students memorize the names of rivers, mountains, and other geographical features of North Carolina:

SOUNDS
Just eleven shallow sounds
Slumber on our shore

Albemarle and Pamlico
Topsail, Stump, and Core

Currituck and Croatan
Where the wild geese soar

Wrightsville, Masonboro
Bogue, Roanoke—and no more.
—From *Poetical Geography of North Carolina*, by Needham Bryan Cobb
   (Cambridge, Mass.: Riverside Press, 1887), 23.

Continue south on US 17 to Jacksonville.

■ JACKSONVILLE

The seat of Onslow County, on the New River, Jacksonville was forever changed when the U.S. Marine Corps decided to build "The World's Most Complete Amphibious Base" here, in 1941.

The creation of the base and air station required moving hundreds of local residents out of the swamplands surrounding Morgan Bay. Among the early troops trained here was future novelist William Styron, who wrote powerfully of his first encounter with the vestiges of those who had been displaced:

Behind them they left scattered along dusty tracks through the pine-woods a dilapidated hodgepodge of tobacco barns, sheds, privies, cabins, and a handful of crossroads stores plastered with signs advertising RC Cola and Dr. Pepper and Copenhagen snuff. Windowless and abandoned, with porches rotting and tar-paper roofs in tatters, they sagged amid overgrown plots of sunflowers and weeds, or became carapaced in sweet jungles of honey suckle where the drowsy hum of bees only made more pronounced the sense of a final silence of bereavement, of life stilled. . . . On a hot summer day in 1944 my own platoon had laid down round after round of mortar fire upon one of these derelict shanties, firing for effect until our barrage had turned the place to splinters and nothingness save for a single crudely painted metal signboard that we discovered amid the wreckage, which read, WHITEHURST'S STORE. And I recalled feeling then a small tug at my heart, not for any damage done to an already ruined hulk, nor even out of conscience, but because Whitehurst was the name of my father's mother, whose family had lived here on this Carolina coast for two centuries and had owned Negroes who bore the Whitehurst name. Thus this storekeeper had most certainly descended from slaves owned by my ancestors—could it be that he was one of those who had sought suicide in his grief? I never found out—and as I stood on that smoking ruin with its intermingled fragrance of gunpowder and honey suckle I could not help but feel a pang of morbid regret over the fact that it was I who had presided so efficiently at the obliteration of a place one Whitehurst must have once cherished dearly.—From *The Suicide Run: Five Tales of the Marine Corps*, by William Styron, edited by James L. W. West (New York: Random House Digital, 2009), 45–46.

Continue south on US 17 for twenty-one miles to Holly Ridge and take NC 50 across the Intracoastal Waterway from Surf City to Topsail Island.

■ TOPSAIL ISLAND

North Carolina's twentieth-century military history has another chapter on this island that was adopted by the navy as the site for a top-secret mission, as described by Phyllis A. Whitney in her thirty-eighth novel of romantic suspense:

Ahead on the right an odd-looking structure came into view—a sturdy concrete tower three stories high, with square corners. There were centered windows and what appeared to be a door at the bottom.

"What's that?" I asked as we drove past. "Those towers were built after World War II, when there wasn't much else on the island except fishing communities—mostly shacks. There were nine towers originally, but one of them is gone so now there are eight. They were part of what was called Operation Bumblebee."

—From *Amethyst Dreams*, by Phyllis A. Whitney (New York: Crown, 1997), 14.

Operation Bumblebee's towers were used to track and film the path of experimental rockets launched from the beach. Several of those still standing have been turned into residences among the agreeable vacation houses and rentals available on this quiet island.

Our tour ends with a poem by Betty Adcock. Originally from Texas, Adcock has spent her entire writing life in North Carolina. As one of the state's most celebrated poets, her work has been compared to that of James Dickey and Elizabeth Bishop. Here, Adcock aptly describes the charms of Topsail in the off-season:

TOPSAIL ISLAND
January absolves the village.
Summer left no flags. I'm living
just now alone in a room on stilts:
whatever silts this way
is what I've got.

It's clean. Even the fake flowers
somebody left outside are stripped
of pretensions. They bloom
nocolor, original plastic.

Perhaps I am here to practice.

Every night I sleep like the drowned,
and dream these houses break and sail
on perfect silence into the world's
dreams of vacant houses.
Every morning's drydock light
establishes them again on their bad knees.

Miles under a blue sun,
sand in my shoes, a heavy parka on:
these are the times the child whispered
I'm the only one.
Swimmers went out once, so many,
and never reached back.
I'm learning the stroke, stroke,
afloat and purposeful along the paths
following a wind full of gulls and grackles.

This is my sandfinger, my blue light with birds.
We talk a cold tongue, and the tide's
good to us all: here's that plain
stretch I never believed, all bone
and shell, lost gull feathers,
old, washed empty claws:
this perfect weather.
—From *White Trash: An Anthology of Contemporary
    Southern Poets*, edited by Nancy C. McAllister and
    Robert Waters Grey (Raleigh: Boson Books, 1996), 4.

■ LITERARY LANDSCAPE

The Sam and Marjorie Ragan Creative Writing Center
Barton College
700 Vance Street NE, Wilson
800-345-4973
http://www.barton.edu/writing-center
This facility, named for the late Sandhills poet (an alumnus) and his wife, is
the site of the college's annual Creative Writing Symposium, which features a
day of readings and discussions of North Carolina literature. The center is also
the headquarters of *Crucible*, a long-running literary journal published by the
college's English department, which also sponsors several annual writing competitions, including the Sam Ragan Poetry Prize.

Arts Council of Wilson
124 Nash Street SW, Wilson
252-291-4329
http://www.wilsonarts.com

In addition to a gallery with rotating exhibitions, the Arts Council offers workshops in fiction writing.

The Next Chapter Bookstore
320 South Front Street, New Bern
252-633-5774
http://www.thenextchapternc.com
Though this cozy store primarily sells used books, it also hosts writers and exhibits the work of New Bern artists.

Quarter Moon Books
708 South Anderson Boulevard, Topsail Beach
910-328-4969
http://www.quartermoonattopsail.com
This shop is made for social gatherings of book lovers who like to sit, sip wine, and talk about what they've been reading. In addition to selling books and gifts, Quarter Moon regularly hosts lunches at area restaurants where writers are featured speakers.

Swansboro : Salter Path : Atlantic Beach : Morehead City : Beaufort : Harker's Island : Minnesott Beach

Tour the Core Banks with poets and environmental writers and discover why generations of North Carolinians have headed to the beaches that run between the mouths of the Neuse and the White Oak rivers.

Writers with a connection to this area: Rachel Carson, David Cecelski, Pamela Duncan, Carol Bessent Hayman, Pete Hendricks, Janet Lembke, Peter Makuck, Margaret Maron, Bill Morris, Florence Nash, Michael Parker, Susan Schmidt, Julia Montgomery Street

■ SWANSBORO

Originally an Algonquin Indian village and incorporated in 1783 as a colonial port town, Swansboro was the site of the construction of the first steamboat in North Carolina. Today, Hammocks Beach State Park provides camping, kayaking, fishing, and a popular ferry ride to unspoiled Bear Island. Swansboro's eclectic collection of shops and restaurants meanders along the mouth of the White Oak River.

Swansboro also figures in the fiction of western North Carolina writer Pamela Duncan. Duncan's characters come this way from Salter Path to eat seafood. They return, as does this tour, via NC 24 to reach NC 58 and the bridge to Bogue Banks, a barrier island with several distinct municipalities: Emerald Isle, Indian Beach, and then Salter Path, our next destination.

tour 11

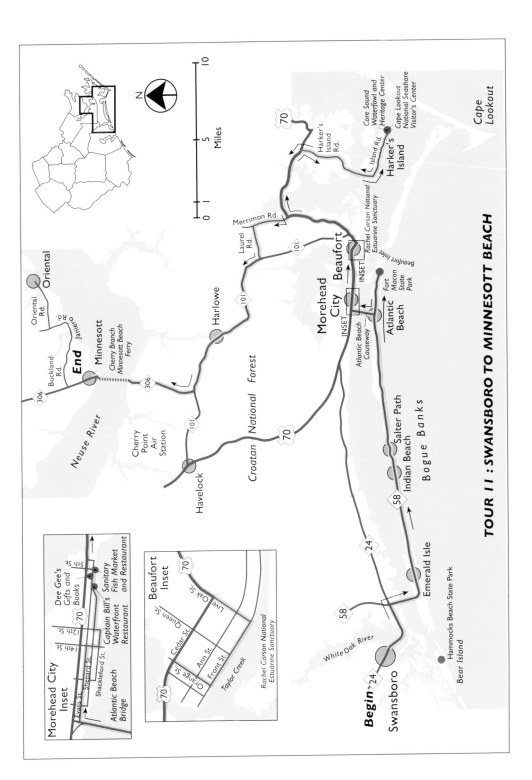

Morehead City Inset

Dee Gee's Gifts and Books
Captain Bill's Waterfront Restaurant
Sanitary Fish Market and Restaurant
4th St.
5th St.
70
12th St.
14th St.
Shepard St.
Shackleford St.
Evans St.
Atlantic Beach Bridge

Beaufort Inset

70
Live Oak St.
Queen St.
Cedar St.
Ann St.
Orange St.
Front St.
70
Taylor Creek
Rachel Carson National Estuarine Sanctuary

N

Miles
0   1   5   10

Oriental
Oriental Rd.
Janiero Rd.
Buckland Rd.
306
End Minnesott
Cherry Branch Minnesott Beach Ferry
306
Neuse River
Cherry Point Air Station
101
Havelock
Harlowe
101
Croatan National Forest
70
Laurel Rd.
Merrimon Rd.
101
70
Harker's Island Rd.
Island Rd.
Harker's Island
Core Sound Waterfowl and Heritage Center
Cape Lookout National Seashore Visitor's Center
Cape Lookout
Morehead City
Beaufort
INSET
INSET
Rachel Carson National Estuarine Sanctuary
Beaufort Inlet
Fort Macon State Park
Atlantic Beach
Atlantic Beach Causeway
Salter Path
Indian Beach
Bogue Banks
58
24
Emerald Isle
58
White Oak River
Hammocks Beach State Park
Bear Island
Begin 24
Swansboro

TOUR 11 : SWANSBORO TO MINNESOTT BEACH

■ SALTER PATH

Pamela Duncan describes this popular beachfront area in her irresistibly funny first novel, *Moon Women*, and in its sequel, her fourth novel, *The Big Beautiful*.

It is a happy ritual for Duncan's protagonist, Cassandra Moon, to come down from the mountains to visit her relatives on the coast. In this passage, Cassandra walks the beach at night, remembering an earlier visit here with her brother-in-law A.J. and his son:

> The first touch was cold, but she got used to it and walked in the shallow water toward Salter Path. She was in no shape to walk that far, but it felt good to move against the wind and have it blow the hair off her face.
>
> The three-quarter moon made a bright white path on the calm water and lit up the beach enough that Cassandra could see if there were jellyfish ahead. She'd stepped on one and been stung once, and A.J. got Alex to pee on the stung place to take away the pain. Alex was only five then, and nobody thought a thing about him whipping it out right there in the middle of the day. So he peed on her leg, with people they didn't even know standing around watching because she was carrying on so. It embarrassed the life out of her. But A.J. was right. It did quit hurting after that. She never did find out how he knew that, but ever since then she kept a lookout for jellyfish, especially at night when they was just about invisible.
>
> —From *Moon Women*, by Pamela Duncan (New York: Delacorte, 2001), 365.

■ ATLANTIC BEACH

Farther up the island, at Atlantic Beach, novelist Bill Morris begins his witty mystery, *Saltwater Cowboys*, which seamlessly manages to convey tidbits of local history and folklore while also offering a loving characterization of the native residents as seen from an outsider's perspective:

> People here do have their own way of talking. When you first hear them, they don't sound right. Or, soand roight. High tide comes out hoi toide, and when the wind drops and the water is flat, they say it's slick cam. Something that's screwed up is mommicked. Male blue crabs are jimmies, and a dark thundercloud is known as a gillyard head. Marsh has two meanings; soft ground, and the size of the holes (e.g., "two-inch marsh") in

a net.—From *Saltwater Cowboys*, by Bill Morris (Wilmington: Coastal Carolina Press, 2004), 52.

It's a pleasant drive (or bike ride) from Atlantic Beach to Fort Macon State Park, at the eastern end of Bogue Banks. In addition to an interpretation of the fort's history in the visitors' center, you can climb the dunes and look across Beaufort Inlet Channel toward the Rachel Carson National Estuarine Sanctuary, accessible only by boat. Historian David Cecelski, who grew up in the region, explains: "Long before she was famous, Rachel Carson visited Bird Shoal. Her bestselling books about the sea lay years ahead of her. She had not yet dreamed of changing history with *Silent Spring*, her trailblazing exposé on the dangers of DDT (dichloro-diphenyl-trichloroethane) and other pesticides. At Bird Shoal she was an obscure biologist discovering the mysteries of the sea" (*A Historian's Coast: Adventures into the Tidewater's Past*, by David Cecelski [Winston-Salem: John F. Blair, 2000], 143).

During her early years of study here, Carson was also developing a winning prose style that would draw readers into the salty swirl with her:

> To visit Bird Shoal, one goes out by boat through channels winding through the Town Marsh of Beaufort and comes ashore on a rim of sand held firm by the deep roots of beach grasses—the landward border of the shoal. The burrows of thousands of fiddler crabs riddle the muddy beach on the side facing the marshes. The crabs shuffle across the flats at the approach of an intruder, and the sound of many small chitinous feet is like the crackling of paper. Crossing the ridge of sand, one looks out over the shoal. If the tide still has an hour or two to fall to its ebb, one sees only a sheet of water shimmering in the sun.
>
> On the beach, as the tide falls, the border of wet sand gradually retreats toward the sea. Offshore, a dull velvet patch takes form on the shining silk of the water, like the back of an immense fish slowly rolling out of the sea, as a long streak of sand begins to rise into view.
> —From *The Edge of the Sea*, by Rachel Carson (Boston: Houghton Mifflin, 1956), 146.

■ **MOREHEAD CITY**

From Atlantic Beach, cross the bridge back to the mainland and take the first right on Evans Street, in Morehead City. In nine blocks, turn right on Fourteenth

One of the early cottages in Morehead City's "Promised Land" neighborhood has survived years of storms. Peter Makuck's poem tells the story.

Street. The private residence at 405 Fourteenth Street is one of the few remaining houses that originally belonged to refugees who abandoned the hurricane-ravaged Diamond City community at the westernmost tip of Shackleford Island across the sound. Diamond City folks began building this neighborhood in 1899 from lumber scraps and parts of whole houses ferried across the water. They called the area "The Promised Land."

Peter Makuck, distinguished professor emeritus of English at East Carolina University and founder of the literary journal *Tar River Poetry*, recounts their story:

PROMISED LAND
First sails of the season patch and color the bay.
My skiff tugs at its lines, antsy to be elsewhere

as I talk to the dock master, an old-timer
who knows the whole necklace of islands

like his right hand, rough as a barnacled hull.
He tells me how little by little on Shackleford,

the next island east, they cut down trees
for houses and boat wood, and how they

cut their own throats at the same time.
Sand traveled, barrier dunes came down,

and when the big blow hit, wash-over
killed all the gardens and wells. No going back.

In less than two years, wild horses
had the island all to themselves.

Some families dug up their dead
and took boxes of bones when they fled.

His granddaddy floated and sailed their house
to the mainland, Promised Land,

they call it, a few waterfront blocks in the city.
But look around, he says. It's happening here:

Down with the live oaks, up with the condos!
Years ago, out at the point—hell, what's the use?

Shakes his head, says he knows what I'm thinking:
The older you get, the better it was. But it *was*.

Now he sketches a map to the old burial ground,
and puts X's where sunken timbers mine the way,

explains how to find the old ferry channel
that every year travels with shoaling:

Tip up your lower unit and prop.
Ease ahead slow. Feel your way

and watch your depth—what you don't see
can take you straight to the bottom.
—From *Off-Season in the Promised Land*, by Peter Makuck
   (Rochester, N.Y.: BOA Editions, 2005), 19–20.

In Michael Parker's fourth novel, *If You Want Me to Stay*, "The Promise Land"—as the narrator Joel Dunn Jr. calls it—is a destination of hope in the midst of a family crisis. When his father suffers a violent mental breakdown, Joel Jr. escapes in the family pickup with the younger of his two brothers and drives illegally to Bottomsail (Topsail Island) where his sister, who has already run away from home, is a waitress. Joel Jr. leaves his baby brother in her care

Over the years, visiting writers have autographed a column in the regional books section of Dee Gee's Gifts and Books, on the waterfront in Morehead City.

and hitchhikes to Bulkhead (Morehead City) in search of his estranged mother's consolation and advice. On his quixotic journey, he is enticed by stories of the Promised Land and the reported virtues of the hushpuppies at the Sanitary Restaurant.

Julia Montgomery Street's popular children's book *Dulcie's Whale* recalls the year during World War II when the remaining shacks at Diamond City that had not been moved to the Promised Land were used as lookouts for German ships and submarines. Young Dulcie lived on the island with her family, and at the climax of the story the "whale" that she spots off the shore turns out to be a German sub:

> She tried to think of all the exciting things Papa had told her of his boyhood here at Diamond City—this place that wasn't a city at all, only a cluster of old, dilapidated shacks. When he had talked of it, his eyes shining and his voice wistful, telling of the long stretches of golden beach strewn with

shells, driftwood, and all sorts of treasures washed up by the tides, she had envisioned Cape Lookout as a place of magic.

In reality it was bleak and dreadful. Nothing but storms, wind and rain that kept them shut up in this bare little shack that was hardly fit for a chicken coop. She had never dreamed a place could be so scary and terrible. Papa had laughed at her anxiety over the storms they'd been having, calling them "little blows," but this one this morning was certainly no little blow. It was the most frightening thing she had ever heard.

—From *Dulcie's Whale*, by Julia Montgomery Street (New York: Bobbs-
   Merrill, 1963), 12–13.

Continue ahead on Shepard Street to the Morehead City waterfront, where generations of vacationing North Carolinians have taken meals at Captain Bill's Waterfront Restaurant and the reassuringly named Sanitary Fish Market and Restaurant. Across from the docks, duck into Dee Gee's Gifts and Books at 508 Evans Street to see the post in the regional books section inscribed with autographs from visiting writers who've stopped in over the years.

One block north, pick up US 70 again and head east. After you cross two bridges and arrive in Beaufort, US 70 becomes Cedar Street. Watch for Orange Street and turn right, which ends at Front Street by the water.

■ BEAUFORT

THE OLD HOMES OF BEAUFORT
Old houses with high peaked roofs,
balconied porches, banistered stairs and fences
seem alive
as if they are the enduring defenses
of this town with the sea at its door,
the wind in its face . . .
—Used by permission of Carol Bessent Hayman

So begins the Town of Beaufort's official poem, written by the poet laureate of both Beaufort and Carteret County, Carol Bessent Hayman. Downtown Beaufort is easily explored on foot, so park and stroll around according to your fancies. Many writers have been charmed here, including Johnston County mystery novelist Margaret Maron, who writes nostalgically in *Shooting at Loons* of the Beaufort and Harker's Island she remembers from family trips in her childhood.

Susan Schmidt is a scientist and poet who lives in Beaufort. In the spirit of Rachel Carson, she often writes about marine life, sea birds, and the importance of environmental protection.

GREEN THOUGHT IN GREEN SHADE

annihilating all that's made
—Andrew Marvell's "The Garden"

We have lost their laughing color in the sky,
the only tropical bird this far north,
lost because honeybees filled their nests,
because we chopped down cypress swamps.

I count seven askew in Audubon's print above my bed:
life size, a foot long, leaf-green tail and wings,
yellow neck and scarlet cheeks, big black eyes
and curved beaks biting cockleburs.

When one bright parrot was shot:
the loud emerald flock would sink
and surround her, bewildered.
We humans rarely see such devotion.

Was it love? fearlessness or folly, for a hunter
could shoot a hundred more on the ground
and fill a burlap sack for the milliner
to adorn preening ladies' bonnets.

One gunman said, "Several shots fill a basket."
After shooting these seven to paint, Audubon wrote:
"The flesh is tolerable food. But,
kept as pets, they never learn to talk."

Shot for green fashion-feathers
Shot because hundreds picked an orchard clean
in fact bit to the core for the seeds
and spit out whole the white apple fruit.

The last died in the wild a hundred years ago
The last one in a zoo soon after—What fun
would one have alone who
frolicked with raucous company?

Women no longer wear hats but
Carolina Parakeets are long gone
like the Ivory-Bill despite uncertain
flashes of vivid green through the trees
—Used by permission of Susan Schmidt

Return to US 70 and continue east for approximately eight miles. Watch for Harker's Island Road, on the right.

■ HARKER'S ISLAND

This long-settled island of skilled boatbuilders and dedicated fishermen is holding fast to its customs and making its storied past accessible through the Cape Lookout National Seashore Visitor's Center and the Core Sound Waterfowl Museum and Heritage Center (252-728-1500). Both centers are at the end of Harker's Island Road and give visitors a chance to learn the history of Harker's artisans and to witness the constant bird traffic overhead as ducks and egrets stream in and out of the maritime forest. If you're on the island in December, catch the storytelling at the annual Waterfowl Weekend while you chow down on Core Sound seafood. (The festival also features music and displays of woodcarvings.)

Tarboro-born poet Florence Nash describes her family's tradition of coming to Cape Lookout, just across the sound from this island:

GETTING TO CAPE LOOKOUT
This old road and I run
right to the continent's edge
and then some, bearing east and south
down the flat counties at first light
past huddled crossroad buildings
that flash the fundamental comforts,
    Cold Beer
    Live Bait
    Video Rentals
    Jesus Saves.
Half of me is always running away,
half aching to come home.

From Havelock to Harlowe, Bettie to Otway,
the roadbed of crushed oyster shells

spins past ditchbank houses
in whitewashed chinaberry yards,
big-hipped laughing women, whip-thin men
along the highway shoulder,
past the Full Pentecostal Holiness Church
where split pig in a rusty oil drum
already smokes and drips toward Sunday evening.

At the Harker's Island dock the waiting outboard
throttles up, noses out. Leaning into open sound
and spray, we buck and slam spring-kneed past
channel markers, marsh and shoal, weave across
the wide-stretched silver water, past the lighthouse
to the Cape's calm bight where boats
nod upwind on their anchor lines like birds.

Easing into the shallows
we slip over the gunwales,

holding our gear overhead, and wade ashore.
My brother stoops and plucks a shell
from the water's edge, twists
his knife blade in a seam I cannot see.
I lift my chin, squinting against the sun, and feel
the shell's gritty rim tilt to my lips as,
cold and briny, the oyster slips
onto my tongue, the whole ocean
in one mouthful.
—From *Crossing Water*, by Florence Nash (Durham: Gravity Press, 1996),
14–15.

From here we head to the ferry at Cherry Branch and cross into Pamlico County at Minnesott Beach, once the site of a large American Indian trading center. Retrace your route on Harker's Island Road to US 70 and turn left. Once you cross back over the second bridge, watch for Merrimon Road and turn right. In 2.4 miles, turn left on Laurel Road, which will take you to NC 101, the route Florence Nash described. Head north (right) toward Harlowe through the Croatan National Forest. Turn right onto NC 306 and follow the signs to the ferry.

■ MINNESOTT BEACH

Leisurely crossing the wide Neuse River brings us to the work of two writers worth reading on your passage to Minnesott: Janet Lembke, who lived for eighteen years downriver at Great Neck Point, and G. C. "Pete" Hendricks, who served in the Marine Corps at Cherry Point Air Station, which is upriver. Both sites are on the Cherry Branch side of the Neuse.

In his novel *The Second War*, set in the Vietnam era, Hendricks's first-person narrator, Truck Hardy, describes his stint as a Marine test pilot over these waters:

The bird had just been overhauled. They needed somebody to fly it before somebody could fly it. That was my job. Fly those birds before the new guys get in them. Make sure they are safe.

I took my usual shots of Jack Daniel's and suited up for the test. The one thing I always loved to do was fly those airplanes the way they were designed to be flown. I always wanted to make them do all they could do.

I leveled at twenty thousand feet over the ocean and went through the engine tests. Slow flight. Stalls. High G turns. Negative Gs. Then I pushed

A Marine Corps jet from Cherry Point Air Station flies low over the Neuse River, thrilling passengers on the Minnesott Ferry. This historic river setting is taken up from different angles in naturalist essays by Janet Lembke and a post–Vietnam War novel by G. C. Hendricks.

the nose into a thirty-degree dive toward the ocean, picked up point-eight-five Mach and executed an Immelmann, a split S from thirty thousand feet into a loop, then a full cloverleaf to a Chinese Immelmann. Seven minutes of constant Gs. That left me at twenty-eight thousand feet sitting almost still. I could see my reflection in the canopy mirror against the brilliant clear sky. All the colors were pure. There were no shadows. I could have been anybody there in the cockpit. I could have been nobody, just a pile of flight equipment, helmet with visor down, gloves and survival gear and speed jeans. There was no skin showing. The pile of flight equipment that was me was not moving.

—From *The Second War*, by G. C. Hendricks (New York: Penguin, 1990), 132.

Janet Lembke, a literary translator and naturalist, spent her days along these waters in a reverie of observation, which, she admitted, was sometimes abruptly interrupted by the sound of a low-flying jet from the Marine Air Station. Her stories are of wildlife and weather and the adventure of living according to the rhythms of nature.

On the River Neuse in coastal North Carolina, days and nights tick for us the way they must have for the people here long before we arrived in our automobiles and blue jeans—colonists who did have clocks, the Indians who didn't. River time depends upon the circlings of sun and moon and the sweep of the constellations. The seasons make their rounds, directing the migrations of fish and birds, orchestrating the birth, death, and resurrection of the green world.—From *River Time*, by Janet Lembke (New York: Lyons and Burford, 1989), 1.

From Minnesott, you may want to end this tour by traveling a bit farther along the coastline, east to the sailing village of Oriental, for a meal and a visit to the town's Old Theater, where musical entertainment and theatrical productions are held monthly.

■ LITERARY LANDSCAPE

The Rocking Chair Bookstore
400 Front Street, Beaufort
252-728-2671
http://www.rockingchairbookstore.com
With a view of the water, this shop is chock-a-block with local titles and good beach reads.

Pamlico County Arts Council
http://pamlicoarts.org/index.html
This all-volunteer arts council hosts writing workshops. Check the website to see what's coming up.

trail three

The Northeastern Corridor: Lost and Found

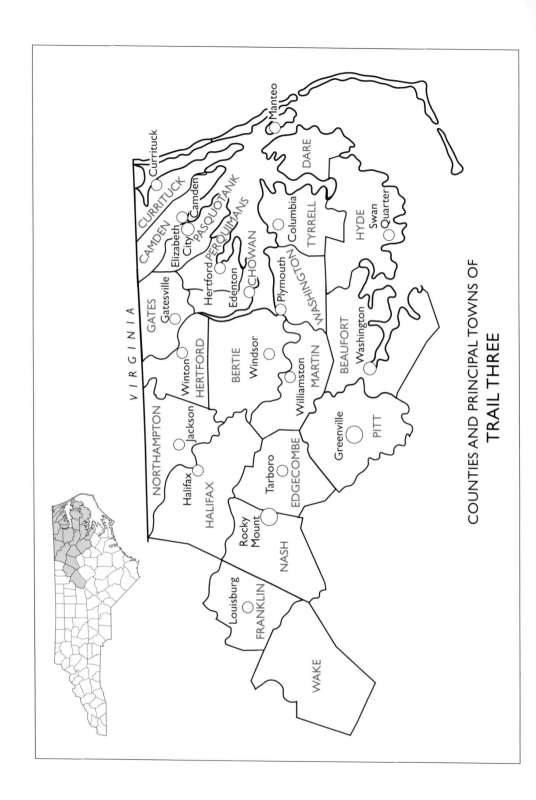

COUNTIES AND PRINCIPAL TOWNS OF

TRAIL THREE

Give me my scallop-shell of quiet,

My staff of faith to walk upon,

My scrip of joy, immortal diet,

My bottle of salvation,

My gown of glory, hope's true gage;

And thus I'll take

my pilgrimage.

—From *Daiphantus*, attributed to Sir Walter Raleigh,
    written ca. 1603, drawn from *A Book of Elizabethan Lyrics*,
    edited by Felix E. Schelling (Boston: Ginn, 1895), 129.

Raleigh's "gown of glory" and his "hope's true gage" are forevermore linked to the Outer Banks of North Carolina. Though Raleigh never set foot here—he only helped to plan and raise funds for the voyages—his vicarious pilgrimage to the New World has become one of the state's oldest and most famous stories. The unsolved mystery of the disappearance of that first English settlement, the Lost Colony, led to the creation of a new genre in playwriting—the symphonic drama, our first instance of "lost and found."

Paul Green's masterwork is still playing at the location of the colony's disappearance. Every summer, hundreds of visitors sit each evening in the amphitheater at the site of Fort Raleigh City, now a national park, with the Albemarle Sound lapping quietly nearby, and surely they wonder what really happened.

What really happened is one of the perpetual questions that creative writers tackle—whether in fiction or poetry, playwriting or memoir. It is a question that echoes throughout this section of the state. It was surely on the lips of kidnapped Africans brought in bondage to these shores and years later on the minds of young soldiers doing battle in the chaos of the Civil War. It is a question that comes up when the runaways who hid and died in the Great Dismal Swamp are discussed, and it is the question that must inevitably haunt the families left behind when sailors and fishermen are lost in eastern waters. It was a question during the Depression when farm families lost everything they'd worked to build. And it's a question that always arises when hurricanes pound the earth, topple trees, and flood roads.

In the long expanse of real estate on this trail, the land is interrupted by meandering rivers and sounds. It's easy to get lost or reach a dead end at a large body of water. Lost and found live side by side on farms where family headstones rise up in the midst of fields lovingly tended. It is not an easy condition to sum up, but this poem by Shelby Stephenson, who lives on the farm where he was raised, near Benson, speaks of it in metaphor:

BLUE COUNTRY RISING

In the powder-dry dust of August,
A clatter of trace-chains secured his mule
In the five-acre field.

He'd look over at the Family Graveyard
Where seventeen slaves lay, unmarked,
And wonder where he came from.

The furrows beach up rolls of clods,
Ridged hate, ridged forget,
The years brought relief.

Nodding in the slow and steady switch
Of the lines on the mule's back,
He learned not to break down.

Identity wrenched from his soul.
The end and beginning were the rows
He turned around.
—From *Greatest Hits, 1978–2000,* by Shelby Stephenson
(Johnstown, Ohio: Pudding House, 1990, 2002), 21.

Greensboro novelist Lee Zacharias, writing of her annual pilgrimage to Ocracoke Island, also addresses it:

An island is not meant to progress. To watch an island develop is to know your own diminishment, to mark the years off your life like days off a calendar, to count not what has been added but what has been lost.—From "Morning Light," by Lee Zacharias, in *Crab Orchard Review* (Winter/Spring 2007): 249.

This trail ponders what really happened, what is lost and what is found, questions that echo along the route to the very end.

Zebulon : Wake Forest : Louisburg : Littleton : Thelma : Roanoke Rapids : Weldon

Deep literary roots run through this tour fed by Civil War memories, the influence of religion on higher education, and small-town pride.

Writers with a connection to this area: Russell Brantley, Clifton Daniel, Edwin Wiley Fuller, G. C. "Pete" Hendricks, R. B. House, Cherryl Floyd-Miller, E. T. Malone, Ovid Williams Pierce, Leon Rooke, Gibbons Ruark, Laurence Stallings, Helen Tucker, Plummer Bernard Young

■ ZEBULON

PLAY BALL
1936 (EXCERPT)
"Play ball," his father yells, having become
Sunday's sole high priest when the real umpire
didn't show up; ambling to sweet home plate
so as to signal neither limp nor delight,
empowered to call the game he loves,
to become baseball's villain for a day
in this North Carolina country town
which has one street for stores and one street for the
    granite courthouse and public school.
Both have big oaks and will last forever.
—From *Fetch Life*, by Russell Brantley
    (Winston-Salem: Stratford Books, 2000), 7.

Poet and novelist Russell Brantley aptly describes the scale of life in his hometown in the 1930s. Zebulon, just off US 64, some twenty miles east of Raleigh, was named for North Carolina's Civil War governor, Zebulon Vance. The town was incorporated in 1907—late by eastern North Carolina standards—

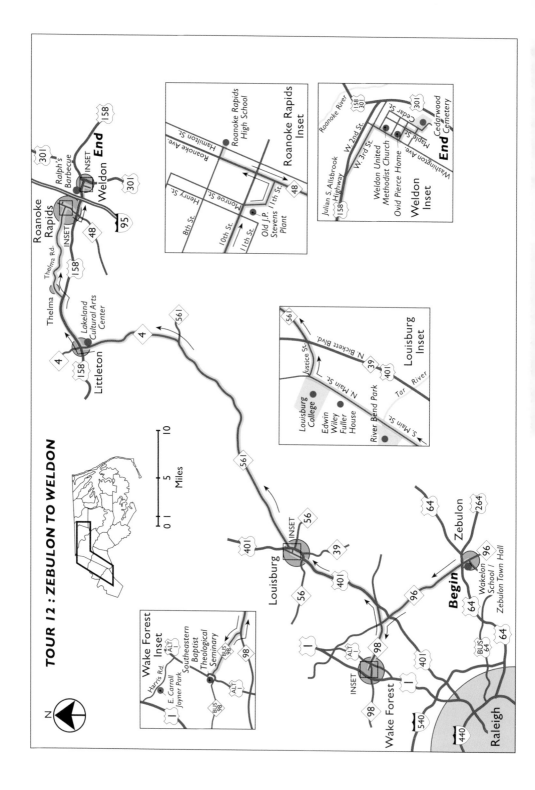

TOUR 12 : ZEBULON TO WELDON

N

0 1   5   10
        Miles

Roanoke Rapids Inset

Roanoke Ave.
Hamilton St.
Roanoke Rapids High School
Henry St.
8th St.
10th St.
11th St.
Monroe St.
48
Old J.P. Stevens Plant

Weldon Inset

Roanoke River
158 301
Julian S. Allsbrook Highway
158
W. 3rd St.
W. 2nd St.
Weldon United Methodist Church
Ovid Pierce Home
Washington Ave.
Maple St.
Cedar St.
301
End Cedarwood Cemetery

Roanoke Rapids
301
Ralph's Barbecue
INSET
Weldon End
158
301
95
48
INSET
158
Thelma Rd.
Thelma
Lakeland Cultural Arts Center
158
4
Littleton
4
561

Louisburg Inset

56
Justice St.
N. Bickett Blvd.
39
401
N. Main St.
Louisburg College
Edwin Wiley Fuller House
River Bend Park
S. Main St.
Tar River
Louisburg Inset

Wake Forest Inset

Harris Rd.
ALT 1
E. Carroll Joyner Park
1
Southeastern Baptist Theological Seminary
BUS 98
ALT
98
98
1

561
40
INSET
56
Louisburg
39
401
56
I
ALT 1
98
98
INSET
Wake Forest
98
I
401
I
540
440
Raleigh

64
Zebulon
264
96
Begin
64
96
Wakelon School / Zebulon Town Hall
BUS 64
64
401

Once serving Zebulon students from first through twelfth grade, including future
journalists Clifton Daniel Jr. and Russell Brantley, the Wakelon School, built in 1908,
is now the town hall.

when the Raleigh–Pamlico Sound Railroad was routed through the area, creating a boom in the local timber business. A tobacco market was established here a decade later and lasted until the stock market crash of 1929.

In *Fetch Life*, the poetry collection Russell Brantley published only five years before his death at the age of eighty, the author describes a childhood of imagined heroics inspired by the pulp characters of his era: Bomba the Jungle Boy, Doc Savage, and the Hardy Boys. Brantley, a lifelong journalist who began his career at the *Durham Herald*, also wrangles in verse with the hard-shell Baptist doctrines that he bridled against as a youth and that he later confronted head-on in his only novel, *The Education of Jonathan Beam*. The book—a statewide sensation when it appeared in 1962—parodied student life at Brantley's alma mater, Wake Forest College, where he worked as communications director for most of his career.

Russell Brantley's father was a drug salesman, and his mother was an operator for the Zebulon telephone company. Undoubtedly, the Brantley family was familiar with another budding journalist in town—Elbert Clifton Daniel Jr. Daniel was born a generation ahead of Brantley in 1912. His father, William, owned Zebulon City Drugs and was the first in town to have telephone service. Daniel's father was elected mayor twice, and he went on to become head of the North Carolina Pharmaceutical Association.

At the age of fourteen, Clifton Daniel began his writing career with a story about his Boy Scout troop, published in the *Zebulon Record*. Daniel often said his nose for the news came as a natural consequence of working part-time in his father's drugstore, which was a hub for community gossip and storytelling.

"In fact, nearly everybody in town went down to the drugstore for one reason or another during the week," Daniel explained years later in a speech in Chapel Hill. "I can still remember one night when a fellow walked in, apparently holding his head on with his hands. His throat was cut from ear to ear. I got a doctor for him—and a story for the *Record*."

As an undergraduate at the University of North Carolina at Chapel Hill, Daniels was editor of the campus literary magazine and became a reporter for the *Dunn Daily Bulletin* after college. He worked for the *Raleigh News and Observer* from 1934 to 1937 and then for the Associated Press as an international correspondent. The *New York Times* hired him in 1943, where he enjoyed a distinguished career—ultimately, from 1964 to 1969, as the paper's managing editor.

After many years as an eligible bachelor known internationally for his sartorial flair, Daniel married Margaret Truman, the only child of the former haberdasher and U.S. president, Harry S. Truman, in 1956. In his lighthearted 1984 memoir, *Lords, Ladies, and Gentlemen*, Daniel explained that he and Margaret were cut from the same cloth—"a couple of citified small towners, puritans among the fleshpots." Daniel laces the book with colorful anecdotes about his globe-trotting for interviews with dignitaries and his experiences as a dignitary himself—the son-in-law of an American president.

Daniel enthusiastically supported his wife's literary ambitions. Margaret Truman Daniel earned best-seller status in 1980 for her first mystery novel, *Murder in the White House*.

In an obituary published in February 2000, the *New York Times* praised Daniel for his distinctive contributions to the paper: "Society news, which had been mainly dry wedding and engagement announcements, began to burst with spicy detail, human interest and social insights. Cultural coverage studied the flaws as well as the fame of important artists. Obituaries became less reverent." Daniel was further credited with the now-common practice of sending reporters to interview leaders and celebrities and draft obituaries, keeping the narratives on file until needed.

Both Russell Brantley and Clifton Daniel attended historic Wakelon School, now Zebulon Town Hall, at 1101 North Arendell Avenue near the Zebulon exit (NC 96) off US 64.

From Zebulon, head north on NC 96, follow it twelve miles to NC 98 (Wait Avenue), and turn left. Continue three miles and bear right onto NC 98 Business, which leads to Wake Forest and the campus of what is now Southeastern Baptist Theological Seminary, formerly Wake Forest College.

■ WAKE FOREST

> Silently, August surveyed the surroundings. A low stone wall, waist high, extended from each side of the arch around the campus as far as the eye could see. The campus itself resembled a forest, a well-cultivated thicket of giant oak, elm and magnolia trees. Through the trees August could see traces of dull red, the brick buildings of the college. The nearest was a shade lighter than the others—probably newer, August thought—and from the top of this building a white spire appeared to be climbing toward heaven, towering over the campus and the tops of the tall trees.—From *The Guilt of August Fielding*, by Helen Tucker (New York: Stein and Day, 1971), 8.

Louisburg novelist Helen Tucker is among several writers who have set novels in Wake Forest, describing its picturesque qualities and noteworthy architecture while also capturing the proscriptive culture of the college, which Baptist Brahmins founded in 1834. *The Guilt of August Fielding*, Tucker's second historical novel, traces eighty years in the life of a man deeply torn between worldly temptations and his calling to the ministry at the turn of the nineteenth century.

Tucker was among the first women to be admitted to Wake Forest College, graduating in 1946, a year after Russell Brantley and two years after Brantley's wife, Elizabeth Jones, daughter of Wake Forest English teacher Broadus Jones, under whom Tucker studied. Tucker graduated with a degree in English and went on to do graduate work at Columbia University. She eventually turned to writing romance novels.

In Russell Brantley's farcical novel *The Education of Jonathan Beam*, set in the 1950s, Wake Forest is called Convention College. The book centers on the coming-of-age of a naive young man, not unlike Tucker's protagonist. Jonathan

The former gateway to Wake Forest College, now Southeastern Baptist Theological Seminary, is across the railroad tracks from the village of Wake Forest. The seminary appears in Randall Kenan's novel A Visitation of Spirits.

Beam has been sent to college with the warning that he must study hard but also report back to his mother and his preacher whether rumors of sinful practices on the Baptist campus are true. Beam is horrified by what he discovers:

> I found out that the professor who taught me Religion and the professor who taught me Biology and the professor who taught me Latin didn't believe the Bible. . . . The Latin professor even said it didn't make any difference to him whether Jesus was born of a virgin or not. . . . "But it's in the Bible," I said. "It's right there in the Bible." —From *The Education of Jonathan Beam*, by Russell Brantley (New York: Macmillan, 1962), 65.

Initially disillusioned, Beam begins to think for himself. When a controversy erupts because the college has decided to allow dancing on campus, Beam vows to keep dancing off campus, even in public, but only with his sweetheart.

The controversy in Brantley's novel was not fiction. In 1957, Wake Forest trustees voted to allow dancing on campus as a means to chaperone student activities, rather than forcing students to go off campus where their socializing might get them into trouble. The trustees' decision scandalized Baptist leaders nationwide because dancing was viewed as lascivious, regardless of the setting. The furor caught the attention of *Time* magazine.

Russell Brantley was right in the middle of the hullabaloo as the college's news bureau chief, and he once joked with reporters that someone should write it up as fiction. Only a year before, Brantley had been in the line of fire managing the controversy that erupted when the college decided to move to a new campus in Winston-Salem. When Brantley's mischievous novel about the whole dancing affair was published in 1962, friction between the college and the Baptist State Convention of North Carolina flared up again, and some people called for Brantley's resignation from the news service. Free speech prevailed, however, and Brantley kept his job. He would go on to become one of the architects of the formal disengagement of Wake Forest University from the state Baptist convention in 1986.

Brantley passed his critical eye and pugnacious skills as a wordsmith along to his son, Benjamin Brantley, who became chief theater critic at the *New York Times* in 1996. Benjamin's mother, Lib, was a features writer for the *Winston-Salem Journal* and contributed to such national magazines as *Redbook* and *Jack and Jill*.

Another important literary figure had connections to the Wake Forest College faculty and administration on the original campus. Laurence Tucker Stallings, who enrolled here in 1912, married Helen Poteat, daughter of college president William Louis Poteat. Stallings, who would eventually join the literary elite as a member of the Algonquin Round Table, served in France during World War I and lost a leg. While working as a reporter and critic in New York, he wrote *Plumes*, a best-selling novel about the war. It was published in 1924 and adapted for film as *The Big Parade*. Meanwhile, Stallings took up playwriting and wrote three notable works with Maxwell Anderson: *What Price Glory*, *The First Flight*, and *The Buccaneer*. He then wrote the book and lyrics for the musical *Deep River* and adapted Hemingway's *A Farewell to Arms* for the stage. He spent his last years in Hollywood as a screenwriter.

G. C. "Pete" Hendricks is another writer with a military background who has a close connection to Wake Forest. His father was a Baptist minister who had deep ties to the college. Hendricks's novel *The Second War* deals with the coming-of-age in the mid-1960s of Truck Hardy, a preacher's kid raised in a rural church community outside Wake Forest named Hepzebiah. (See Tour 11.)

Hendricks, who is also a master builder, had a hand in restoring and documenting the tobacco homestead buildings on exhibition at E. Carroll Joyner Park. The park, at 701 Harris Road on the outskirts of Wake Forest, is worth a visit if you want to know more about the area's early history.

To continue northeast to Louisburg, the seat of Franklin County, backtrack on NC 98. Cross NC 96 and then bear left on US 401 North for approximately eighteen miles. As you come into the outskirts of Louisburg, look for the intersection with NC 56 on the left and turn left. Then immediately turn right on South Main Street.

■ LOUISBURG

The Tar River flows under a long bridge about a mile ahead at the entrance to Louisburg's historic commercial district. The city park along the riverbank on the left side of the road offers a pleasant picnic stop.

Louisburg is the setting of Helen Tucker's popular first novel, *The Sound of Summer Voices* (1969). The protagonist, Patrick Quincannon Tolson, is a twelve-year-old boy who comes to believe that one of his aunts must actually be his mother (supposedly dead), and he spends the summer in the small town of "Laurelton" spying on the members of his rather privileged family and trying to figure out the secrets his relatives have kept from him. Critics compared the novel favorably to *To Kill a Mockingbird*.

A member of a prominent North Carolina family, Helen Tucker was a niece of the founder of the Welch Company, the manufacturer of Junior Mints and Milk Duds candies, which some local residents still remember as always plentiful in the Tucker household. Tucker's other uncle, Robert H. W. Welch Jr., founded the John Birch Society in 1958. Vehemently anticommunist, the group alleged that communists were behind the civil rights movement of the 1960s. It is easy to speculate that Tucker's relative might be reflected in the character of Uncle Darius in the novel.

> There were a lot of things in the world which Uncle Darius refused "to tolerate." This was, Patrick knew, his way of saying he hated all liars, Yankees, casseroles and pastry, Catholics, women who giggled, and Laurelton businessmen who wanted to bring Yankee industry into town. — From *The Sound of Summer Voices* (New York: Stein and Day, 1969), 15.

Though the Tucker family home in Louisburg has been razed, another writer's home, dating from 1856, still stands on Main Street, north of the business district. Situated in the middle of the 300 block, the Edwin Wiley Fuller House is the only structure set back from the street and is fronted by a circular drive.

Fuller began his literary career modeling himself on his favorite writers—

Edwin Wiley Fuller lived in this house in Louisburg. He was a poet, novelist, Louisburg mayor, and Franklin County commissioner. He dictated his last poem moments before his death, from consumption, in 1876.

Poe, Tennyson, and Dickens. His poems were widely published, but his greatest success came with his melodramatic novel *The Sea Gift*, which was especially popular with University of North Carolina students. According to literary scholar E. T. Malone, writing in the *Dictionary of North Carolina Biography*, "Elements of *The Sea-Gift* plot involving, first, a long train ride to enter college, and second, the burning of a plantation house by Yankee soldiers, may have influenced Thomas Wolfe and Margaret Mitchell in the writing of their later novels, *Look Homeward, Angel*, and *Gone with the Wind*, respectively."

Continue north on Main Street to Louisburg College, a private two-year institution. Turn right on Justice Street and cross North Bickett Boulevard, continuing east on NC 561 through twenty miles of rolling farmland to pick up NC 4 near the homelands of North Carolina's Haliwa Saponi Indian Tribe and its historic school.

This haunting corridor leading toward the Virginia state line is flanked by antebellum mansions and farmsteads in various states of disrepair, aptly described by Weldon native Ovid Pierce in his last novel:

An air of desertion lingered over the land. I can see the landscape: leaning barns in old fields, crossroad stores, all covered with fading, peeling signs—

Lydia E. Pinkham's Vegetable Compound, Carter's Little Liver Pills, Groves Chill Tonic, hanging helter-skelter as if plastered there during a wild antic night in a forgotten time. Two forlorn gas pumps looked like sentinels in front of the little stores. —From *Judge Buell's Legacy*, by Ovid Pierce (Greenville, N.C.: Morgan Printers, 1985), 16.

■ LITTLETON

As you come into the town of Littleton on NC 4 (Mosby Avenue), watch on your right for the Lakeland Cultural Arts Center, a thriving hub of local theater since 1978. After restoring the former Littleton High School auditorium, this plucky community theater group has produced scores of popular musicals and dramas, all cast with local talent.

In the heart of Littleton, turn right on US 158, which is East South Main Street. Watch for the historical marker on the right that commemorates the life of native son Plummer Bernard Young. Young's father ran a newspaper here, and he taught his son the trade. Young went on to study at St. Augustine's College in Raleigh, and from there he moved to Norfolk, Virginia, taking over a small publication, the *Norfolk Journal and Guide*. Young sent his reporters out to cover stories of racial conflicts, lynchings, and voter registration scandals. Soon his publication became the only African American–owned newspaper in the South that produced a national edition. Young died in 1962, just as the civil rights movement was gaining ground.

■ THELMA

Some seven miles beyond Littleton, turn right on Thelma Road, a route that parallels the Roanoke River and leads into Roanoke Rapids. Robert B. House, who served as the first chancellor of UNC–Chapel Hill from 1945 to 1957, was raised here. House, for whom the undergraduate library at the university is named, wrote a memoir, *The Light That Shines*, about his beloved university. Less well known is his book *Miss Sue and the Sheriff*, a delightful memorial to his parents rendered through vivid scenes of his upbringing among his Thelma neighbors:

Hunting was their passion in fall and winter. Not fox-hunting or 'possum hunting, and only occasionally a turkey or a goose. It was bird-hunting— the swish of corduroy or duck pants through the bushes and the broom straw, the dogs circling and quartering. The point, with dogs and men frozen like statues in the fields. The boom of wings, the bang of guns, the pant and snuffle of retrievers, the leisurely round-up of single birds. No day was too unseasonable for them to go out. It was their dream when they worked, their talk till bed-time. And they were masters of it. —From *Miss Sue and the Sheriff*, by R. B. House (Chapel Hill: University of North Carolina Press, 1941), 71.

■ ROANOKE RAPIDS

In House's time, many of Thelma's citizens worked in textiles, and Roanoke Rapids was their daily destination. Generations labored in these mills, enduring low wages and harsh working conditions. Then, in 1973, Roanoke Rapids made headlines when one small woman ignited a movement. Crystal Lee Sutton, better known as Norma Rae in the movie version of her story, created a work stoppage by holding up a sign in the J. P. Stevens weave room with a single word printed on it: UNION. Though the film, starring Sally Field, was shot in Alabama, the plant in the movie closely resembles what is left of the Stevens facility—the first textile mill to be unionized in the South. Sutton, who became a lifelong labor activist, eventually moved to Burlington. She died in 2009 and left her papers to Alamance Community College.

Louise Rooke, the mother of writer Leon Rooke, also worked as a weaver at the Stevens plant. She encouraged her son's early interest in reading and writing. Rooke, who was born in 1934, says that his earliest longing was for books, and his mother obliged to the extent her paycheck allowed. He published his first poems as a high school student in the *Raleigh News and Observer*. Rooke left to study at Mars Hill College, where his first plays were produced, and he finished his undergraduate degree at UNC–Chapel Hill, where he studied with writers Jesse Rehder, Max Steele, and Paul Green. Rooke then took up graduate work in the Radio, Television, and Motion Pictures program at Chapel Hill, followed by a stint in the army. He returned to North Carolina to work as an actor and tech hand in *Unto These Hills*—the symphonic summer drama produced in Cherokee. In the 1960s, he made his way back to Chapel Hill to work as an assistant to his former teacher, novelist John Ehle, who was an "idea man" on the staff of Governor Terry Sanford, helping to stimulate several new state initiatives in the arts.

Rooke thrived in the company of other Chapel Hill writers of the 1960s era: Russell Banks, William Matthews, and Laurence Naumoff. (Naumoff once described his friend Rooke as "the most thoroughly bohemian and natural outsider I knew.")

Rooke cofounded *The Anvil*, a weekly newspaper considered radical by many in Chapel Hill for its antiwar and pro–civil rights opinions. In 1969, Louisiana State University Press published his first collection of short stories: *Last One Home Sleeps in the Yellow Bed*. Also in that year, he married Constance Raymond, an editor of the campus literary magazine, *Carolina Quarterly*. The couple then moved to Canada, where they have lived ever since. In the years following, Rooke has written another thirty-some books, many of which have been produced on radio and for the stage.

Rooke won the North Carolina Award for Literature in 1990. He has seldom written about North Carolina, but his upbringing is evident in his literary preoccupations.

To see the infamous J. P. Stevens plant, proceed into Roanoke Rapids on Thelma Road, which becomes West Tenth Street. Watch for Monroe Road and turn right. Monroe runs beside the old plant, which has been partly dismantled. From Monroe, turn left on Eleventh Street, and in two blocks, you will reach Roanoke Avenue (NC 48), a central artery downtown. Turn left (north) and take the third right onto East Eighth Street. Straight ahead is Roanoke Rapids High School, where Leon Rooke did his first serious writing. The main building, now on the National Register of Historic Places, dates from 1921 and is a striking marriage of Elizabethan Gothic and Tudor Revival styles.

From here, backtrack on Roanoke Avenue to US 158 and turn left. You will cross under I-95 at a busy interchange where travelers coming from north of the Mason-Dixon Line have their first chance at down-home North Carolina seafood and barbeque at Ralph's—an establishment operated by the same family for more than six decades.

Roanoke Rapids poet Cherryl Floyd-Miller offers this rhythmic appraisal of the beverage of choice at Ralph's and in her family's household:

THE WAY OF (CAROLINA) TEA
southern sake, pitcher-poured,
archipelago of ice.
sweet tea suppers, *praise the Lord!*

Tea—the juice we could afford.
Bags of caffeine, boiled 'em twice.
Southern sake, mama poured

tea into tupperware gourds.
porked the gut like beans and rice
Sweet tea suppers, *praise the Lord.*

"room" was kitchen, ice tea—board.
sugar, sugar, lemon slice.
southern sake, tumblers poured.

Reused gallon jugs engorged.
Between helpings, lips enticed
Sweet tea suppers . . . praise You, Lord!

Bellies smaller than our orbs,
kuppatay and burps on ice
southern sake, frothy, poured—
sweet tea suppers, *oh my Lord!*
—From *Utterance: A Museology of Kin*, by Cherryl Floyd-Miller
    (Durham: Sadorian Publications, 2003), 18.

In Weldon, US 158 becomes Third Street. An enormous replica of a bass signals the town's preoccupation with fishing and its designation as Rockfish Capital of the World.

Two important North Carolina writers have their roots here. Poet Gibbons Ruark, born in Raleigh, spent four years as a child in Weldon when his father was appointed minister at the Methodist Church at 415 Washington Avenue. Ruark, whose work has appeared in magazines such as the *New Yorker* and *Poetry*, recounts an event that was one of the most visceral and mysterious of his childhood:

QUARANTINE
Some things happened every year, no matter what:
The air cooled down a little after a storm,
The fireflies rose and fell in total silence,
Unlike those mournful gnats along the river
In that poem the lovelorn teacher read us
We were every one too young to understand.
The berries fell from the chinaberry tree
And left the backyard slithery underfoot.
But this was the year of Mama's polio,
The summer when the epidemic kept us
On the block, then under the trees, and then,
When she came down with it and went away,
Behind the head-high railings of the balustrade.

Next door was the church, high sunlight angling
Through the steeple's stained glass, unfolding then
Like a flickering board game on the floor.
I stood on the steps and hollered "Polio!"
Then came the parade of openhearted aunts,
Spelling each other, stern and sweet by turns,
One not caring if we saw her naked,
Since we were only children, after all.
Beautiful and young, an Army nurse in the war,
Milk-pale except for the dark touch here and there,
Did I dream she made us buttered toast and eggs
Before remembering to put her clothes on?
She died in childbirth, fifty years ago,
And I have wondered at her all my days.
When Mama came home, there was the wheelchair,
Strange, like a marvelous oversized toy,
And then the crutches and the metal braces.
Crutches I knew, big boys with football injuries,
But the braces were hinged and ominous,
Not Mama's legs, not anything like them.
Only late at night could you not hear her coming.
Then she lay down and they were taken off
And stood till first light in a bedroom corner
Like parts of a skeleton, and she slept
As we all did, swimmers floating in a salt pond.
In those hours nobody needed to walk,
Unless you had to pee or the house caught fire.
—From *Staying Blue*, by Gibbons Ruark
    (Duluth, Minn.: Lost Hills Books, 2008), 3–4.

In the next block, at 515 Washington, is the Classical Revival house where
Weldon novelist Ovid Pierce was raised. Pierce, longtime writer-in-residence
and founder of the literary magazine *The Rebel* at East Carolina University,
studied at Duke and Harvard and then began his academic career at Southern Methodist University. He was teaching at Tulane when his first novel, *The
Plantation*, was published, in 1953. Pierce eventually came back to North Carolina and continued writing short and long fiction that mirrored his fascination
with the Civil War and its aftermath. When he inherited a 350-acre farm south
of Weldon from his parents in 1951, he hired a Richmond architect to remodel

East Carolina College professor and novelist Ovid Pierce was raised in this house in Weldon. He often traveled on weekends from the campus in Greenville to Halifax County to write and look after his farm south of town.

the nineteenth-century residence and regularly came to the farm to write after his teaching duties in Greenville were ended for the week. The land and house served as inspiration for his five novels, which ponder the challenges of change in a society and economy so long built on subjugation.

A review of *The Plantation* in *Jet* (a magazine addressed to African American readers) said: "Unlike most books now being written about the South which describe bygone grandeur, present-day poverty or racial violence, *The Plantation* is a quiet little volume about one man's North Carolina family and what became of it. The story unravels rather than weaves together, the loose ends of the lives of those who once peopled Mr. Ed's plantation" (March 19, 1953, 54).

Pierce is buried nearby, in Weldon's Cedarwood Cemetery. On his grave is a line from a poem by his namesake, Ovid: "O lente, lente, currite noctis equi!" (Run slowly, o slowly, horses of the night!).

Storyteller's Bookstore

158 South White Street, Wake Forest

919-556-3903

http://www.storystorewf.com/

In addition to a wine shop, an art venue for kids, a crab house, a day spa, a violin shop, and a local artists' emporium, downtown Wake Forest has a charming bookstore to suit a wide range of tastes.

The Coffee Hound Bookshop

103 West Nash Street, Louisburg

919-496-6030

http://www.coffeehoundbooks.com

This downtown store has well-stocked bookshelves and also hand-crafted espresso drinks, pottery, and other work by local artists.

Seaboard : Jackson : Rich Square : Windsor : Murfreesboro

Small northeastern towns that once boomed with farming are reinventing themselves and celebrating their storied pasts. Women writers prevail here.

Writers with a connection to this tour: Sarah Sawyer Allen, Mebane Holoman Burgwyn, Julia Fields, Bernice Kelly Harris, Alice Eley Jones, Shelia P. Moses, George Higby Throop, Valerie Raleigh Yow

■ SEABOARD

It was the day of the excursion. The neighborhood turned out early in wagons, surreys, and top buggies. With loads of watermelons piled near the railroad to be shipped, Pate's Siding looked like a village market-place. Everybody, dressed in Sunday clothes, carried great boxes of food and fruit; a few mothers toted satchels. Uncle Israel was in charge of arrangements. He had engineered this trip to Morehead City through strenuous opposition. One faction had objected because the Sunday school had never been on an excursion before; another, because the ocean was dangerous; cost was mentioned; others spoke of train wrecks; Uncle Job thought it was too worldly.—From *Purslane*, by Bernice Kelly Harris (Chapel Hill: University of North Carolina Press, 1939), 30–31.

This short passage about a small-town church group heading by train for a day at the coast speaks volumes about the fears and preoccupations of rural people in early twentieth-century North Carolina. The village of Seaboard, where writer Bernice Kelly Harris made her home, is still small, quiet, and close-knit. When she moved to Seaboard as a young woman to

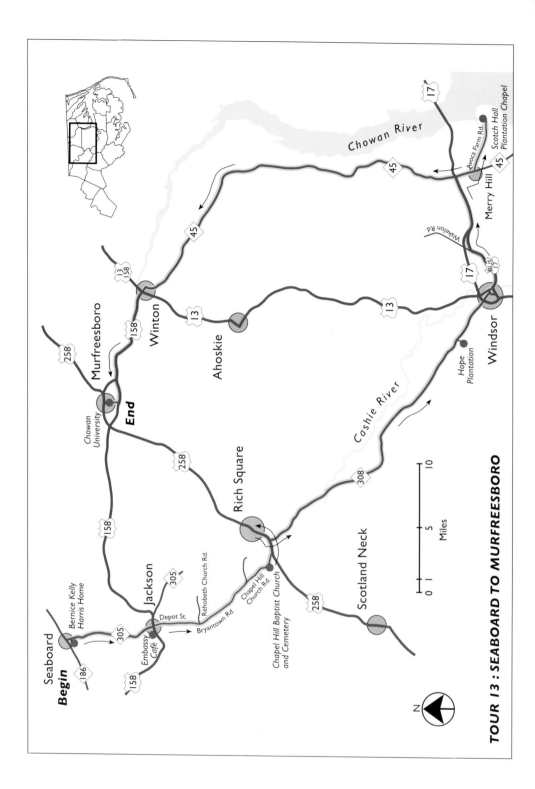

TOUR 13 : SEABOARD TO MURFREESBORO

teach high school, the rhythms of life here felt familiar, much like the community near present-day Clayton where she was raised.

Harris wrote plays, newspaper features, and novels and has been compared to Mississippi writer Eudora Welty for the keenness of her perceptions and her prose. Both writers also conducted oral history interviews for the Federal Writers Project and would eventually share the same literary agent and editor at Doubleday in New York.

Bernice Kelly began writing stories as a student at Meredith College. She then taught in Duplin and Catawba counties before taking a job in 1916 at the high school in Seaboard. She spent summers at the University of North Carolina in Chapel Hill under the tutelage of Playmakers founder Frederick Koch, who encouraged his students to study the customs, culture, and language of the people around them in order to create authentic plays about North Carolina life. Kelly brought this idea back to Seaboard and began producing her own locally based work and that of her students, for enthusiastic audiences.

In 1925, Kelly's drama troupe traveled to Chapel Hill to compete in Koch's first spring theater festival. They came away with first prize, for a play written by her student William Ivey Long. Long would later become a professor of theater studies. His son (who bears the same name) is a Tony Award–winning costume designer, who still keeps a residence in Seaboard.

The Seaboard Players continued to win statewide competitions even as Bernice Kelly was being courted by Herbert Harris, the owner of the local cotton gin and eight years her senior. They married in 1926, and though Bernice desperately wanted children, her husband refused, beginning a pattern of control that also confined and constricted her writing career in significant ways. As a married woman, Harris gave up teaching high school but continued producing original plays, expanding her reach to other communities in Northampton County. She also began offering adult classes in playwriting in her living room.

With the encouragement of Professors J. O. Bailey and Frederick Koch, in Chapel Hill, Harris tackled her first novel, *Purslane*. In 1939, it became the first work of fiction to be published by the University of North Carolina Press. Other editions followed from publishers in Canada and England. The novel won the Mayflower Award—the first time that North Carolina's top literary prize went to a woman. Six more novels would follow over the years. Though Harris's husband welcomed his wife's income from writing, depositing the proceeds promptly into his business account, he did not like for her to travel great distances or spend time away from home promoting her works, which made the development of a national audience difficult.

Critics praised Harris's North Carolina folk plays (collected in a 1940 volume prefaced by Frederick Koch) for the writer's skill in presenting rich and poor and black and white characters with an equal focus on their humanity and not on their social status or racial background. Harris explained in an unpublished essay titled "From the Complex" that she was compelled to write, because the lives of the farm people she knew in the region "had too much meaning to be left unrecorded."

Harris stopped writing in 1949 when her husband became ill. At his death a year later, she discovered that he had not made a will. His family, who had never extended much kindness to Bernice, moved quickly to take over the estate, including the banked proceeds from her writing. Bernice was essentially cut off from her late husband's business interests, which were entangled in a partnership with his siblings. She was left with little to live on.

After a long bout of depression, Harris began teaching noncredit classes in creative writing at Chowan College, in Murfreesboro. She also found kinship among other writers through the North Carolina Writers Conference, formed in 1950. From 1951 to 1964, Harris never missed any of the meetings, which were held annually around the state.

Although she lived in the northeastern corridor of North Carolina, where many old plantations sat in ruin and where a romantic longing for the social hierarchy of the Old South sometimes prevailed among her white, literary counterparts, Bernice Kelly Harris would have none of it. According to her biographer, Valerie Yow, she kept on good terms with the historical novelist and literary grande dame Inglis Fletcher, of Edenton, but she did not like the grandiose, magnolia-scented nostalgia in Fletcher's work. In notes Harris made for a talk, which now reside among her papers at the University of North Carolina, she wrote:

> We who read and write and live will not be beguiled by crinoline and broadcloth of Technicolor gentry, or by fly bonnets and linsey-woolsey of the folk either. We will not let authors palm off second-rate writing on us just because their people ride to the hounds on vast estates, or for that matter pitch lowly horseshoes in cramped little yards. We will sift through the external and incidental and focus on human relationships and motivations and behavior. We will not be confused by trends that bear toward the pseudo.—From *Bernice Kelly Harris: A Good Life Was Writing*, by Valerie Raleigh Yow (Baton Rouge: Louisiana State University Press, 1999), 210–11.

Inglis Fletcher gave Harris a hard time for being so "liberal" in her approach to the novel *Janey Jeems*, published in 1946. The novel centers on the life of an

Left to right: Writers Jonathan Daniels, Inglis Fletcher, Bernice Kelly Harris, and Richard Walser at the North Carolina Writers Conference in 1955, an invitation-only event begun in 1950 that continues today. Photo by Bernadette Hoyle, courtesy of Sandy Hoyle Bolick and the North Carolina Collection, Wilson Library, UNC–Chapel Hill.

African American woman but does not directly state the skin color of any of its primary characters. However, when Harris's Weldon neighbor Ovid Pierce wrote a review of the book, he noted, "White people do not enter the story, but their governance and authority is as strong as if they stood upon every page" ("Dark Mixture of Religion, Superstition," *Dallas Times-Herald*, September 1, 1946).

In her intriguing biography, Yow argues that Harris's work might have become as well-known as Eudora Welty's had her life not been so removed from the mainstream. Reading her work is an excellent way to get acquainted with the history of this lesser-known section of North Carolina. Her house still stands at 301 Church Street in Seaboard, and she is buried in the town cemetery, so noted by a historical marker on Main Street (NC 305).

From Seaboard, continue south on NC 305 to the hamlet of Jackson, where Harris's friend and frequent correspondent Mebane Holoman Burgwyn also wrote of rural life, in books aimed at a younger audience. When you reach Jackson, the highway becomes Church Street, intersected by West Jefferson (US 158), the main street in town.

■ JACKSON

Along U.S. Highway Number 1, somewhere south of Richmond, a road forks off to the left and runs parallel to the great highway but closer to the coast. The land begins to flatten out but occasionally the earth dips into low rolling hills and it is surprising to see a home perched higher than the roadbed.

On this highway the little town of Millboro modestly states its name and its speed limit to tourists passing through. It then presents its wide main street for inspection. The highway passes the five blocks allotted to business enterprises and then the conventional residential section with its neat white houses and well-kept lawns. Once outside the city limits another sign urges the transient to COME AGAIN and then one comes again upon the open country where flat fields and occasional low hills are planted year after year with cotton, peanuts, corn and tobacco. Here, too, are scattered tenant houses and the larger landowner homes which remain year after year producing other scattered buildings to cluster about the regal existence of the "Big House."

—From *Penny Rose*, by Mebane Holoman Burgwyn (New York: Oxford University Press, 1952), 7.

Jackson, the seat of Northampton County, here called Millboro, still appears as described by Burgwyn. The passage also refers to the once-predominant phenomenon of sharecropping and tenant farming, a practice that replaced the institution of slavery in the late nineteenth century and that crops up in Depression-era writing throughout the region.

Jackson is proud to claim Burgwyn. She was born and raised in nearby Rich Square, studied education at Woman's College in Greensboro, and did graduate work at East Carolina College (now University). Burgwyn worked for many years as a counselor in the Northampton County schools and wrote seven novels for young people while raising a family on a farm outside town. Her novel *Penny Rose* earned the award for best juvenile book of 1952 from the American Association of University Women. Burgwyn was also one of the many beneficiaries of Bernice Kelly Harris's encouragement, and she was invited to accompany Harris on a trip to New York City in 1953—the first for the older writer, who had stayed home in Seaboard for so many years.

While you're in town, if the timing is right, you may want to make a lunch stop at the Embassy Café, at 124 West Jefferson, where townsfolk trade stories and fill up on fresh seasonal vegetables and various delectable treatments of chicken and pork. The public library at 207 West Jefferson is also a special attraction, with a display of wind and solar whirligigs on the lawn out back.

From Jefferson Street, turn onto Depot Street and head south to reach the next destination. This rural corridor soon becomes Bryantown Road. When you cross Rehoboth Church Road in about four miles, the name changes to Chapel Hill Church Road. In another seven miles you'll cross a bridge. Watch for Chapel Hill Baptist Church on the right. The churchyard is the setting for the following passage:

■ RICH SQUARE

> Lord have mercy. My grandpa is dead. Dead and gone. Braxton Jones was his name. Today we had his funeral at Chapel Hill Baptist Church, right here in Rich Square. . . . The ground was wet like my big sister BarJean's face. I believe she did the most crying. Her and my big brother Coy, who drove down from Harlem together in his new light blue Cadillac. Blue just like the one that my uncle Buddy Bush used to drive when he moved back down here from Harlem five years ago in 1942. Back down to Rehoboth Road where Grandma said he belonged.—From *The Return of Buddy Bush*, by Shelia P. Moses (New York: Simon and Schuster, 2006), 1–2.

Shelia P. Moses—poet, novelist, playwright, and coauthor of comedian Dick Gregory's memoir, *A Callus on My Soul*—was raised on Rehoboth Road, the ninth of ten children. She studied at Shaw University in Raleigh and now lives in Atlanta. She has published three books related to her own family's story in Rich Square: *The Legend of Buddy Bush*, *The Return of Buddy Bush*, and *The Baptism*. Her fourth book, *I, Dred Scott: A Fictional Slave Narrative Based on the Life and Legal Precedent of Dred Scott*, offers young readers a chance to get inside the mind of the enslaved man whose unsuccessful petition to the Supreme Court for U.S. citizenship polarized the country in the years leading up to the Civil War.

To visit Rich Square, continue on Chapel Hill Road and turn left on US 258. This antebellum town was a center of commerce even before enslaved poet George Moses Horton was born on the nearby William Horton Plantation. As a child, Horton was sent to Chatham County, where he tended cattle on another large parcel of his master's land. After teaching himself to read, Horton became well-known in Chapel Hill for his clever poems, and in 1829 he became the first African American in the South to publish a book.

Outside Rich Square, the Chapel Hill Baptist Church and Cemetery figure in a funeral scene in Shelia Moses's novel The Return of Buddy Bush.

Though the nearby town of Scotland Neck is not on our route, readers should know that the Halifax County town, with its curious name, was home for several years to a major twentieth-century poet. Julia Fields was born in Alabama and went to college in Tennessee. Her early poems drew the attention and praise of Harlem Renaissance writer Langston Hughes, the dean of African American poets in the 1960s. Hughes became a mentor to Fields, whose career trajectory continued upward as she moved around the South as the poet-in-residence at a number of colleges and universities, including St. Augustine's and North Carolina State in Raleigh and East Carolina in Greenville. She tired of the academic scene, however, and moved to Scotland Neck to write for several years before settling in Washington, D.C.

Fields's work has been compared to Zora Neale Hurston's for its sensitivities to rural life among African Americans and for its appreciation of southern folklore. Her most anthologized poem recalls scenes and sentiments common to this region:

HIGH ON THE HOG (EXCERPT)
Keep the black-eyed peas
    And the grits,

The high blood-pressure chops
And gravy sops

I want aperitifs supreme
	Baked Alaska—
Something suave, cool
For I've been considered faithful fool
From 40 acres and a mule . . .

I've been
	Sighted enough
	Sever-righted enough
	And up tighted enough
And I want
	High on the Hog

For dragging the cotton sack
	On bended knees
	In burning sun
	In homage to the
		Great King cotton
	For priming the money-green tobacco
		And earning pocket-change
	For washing in iron pots
	For warming by coal and soot
	For eating the leavings from
		Other's tables

I've lived my wretched life
	Between domestic rats
		And foreign wars
	Carted to my final rest
		In second-hand cars

But I've been leeched enough
	Dixie-peached enough
	Color bleached enough
	And I want

High on the Hog!
—From "High on the Hog," by Julia Fields, in
	Negro Digest, September 1969, 55–56.

Retrace your route through Rich Square south on 258 to NC 308 and travel 23.5 miles. Watch for signs to Hope Plantation and turn right on Hope House Road. The Hope Mansion, built in 1803, is on the National Register of Historic Places. It is the restored home of North Carolina governor David Stone (1770–1818) and is furnished with period reproductions and some originals. Governor Stone's library, on the second floor of the mansion, contains 1,400 volumes. The Historic Hope Foundation maintains and interprets this site for visitors at the Roanoke-Chowan Heritage Center (252-794-3140), also on the grounds. Exhibits document the lives of the native peoples who first settled the area, the white settlers who came later, and the enslaved Africans who served them.

This prominent plantation was the likely inspiration for a 1973 novel by Sarah Sawyer Allen, the daughter of a country doctor who grew up in nearby Windsor during the Depression. Entitled *Ginger Hill*, after a fictional tobacco farm that was once a grand plantation, Allen's novel presents daily life among the sharecroppers and the landowning family that employed them—a system that echoed the plantation past. Though Allen is white, she writes convincingly in the voice of her protagonist, Ophelia, the daughter of a West Indian man and an African American woman who works as the cook in the "big house." A number of scenes are powerfully wrought, particularly when a hurricane strikes. In this passage, Ophelia describes the coming of a new season:

> The spring took hold of me and everybody else, putting us under its spell. It covered all the ugly broken things. The trees, battered by the hurricane, grew new limbs and were enfolded by silver-green leaves. The pine trees grew candles, having their own celebration. A glorious feeling covered our bodies, blotting out the dreary, bleak winter evils. The chickens started laying more eggs; the days got longer. Life was beginning again. The freshly plowed fields were black and beautiful with the first little corn shoots bright green against the raw earth. The men began to set out the tobacco plants, and the boys stayed home from school to help.—From *Ginger Hill*, by Sarah S. Allen (Winston-Salem: John F. Blair, 1973), 222.

From Hope Plantation, turn right on NC 308 and follow it into Windsor, where the Cashie (pronounced cash-eye) River comes through town. Follow 308 (South King Street) until it joins up with US 17 Business. Continue on US 17 for nearly five miles and bear right at the fork where Wakelon Road goes off to the

This contemporary painting, depicting life in the era described in Sarah Sawyer Allen's novel Ginger Hill, *was created by artist Erskine Spruill of Greenville. It is part of the exhibition on the local convergence of cultures in the Roanoke-Chowan Heritage Center. © Erskine Spruill, in the collection of the Historic Hope Foundation, Windsor, N.C.*

left. When you reach NC 45, turn right. In 1.5 miles, turn left on Avoca Farm Road, at Merry Hill. Ahead is the setting of George Higby Throop's 1851 novel, *Bertie*.

We were not long in reaching the church. It stood in a grove of noble oaks. It was a plain, wooden structure, without spire, or shutters, or paint. As is usual at a country church in the South, there was a well near by, with the necessary sweep, and bucket, and trough. A few had already arrived; and, scattered here and there among the trees, were the horses, hitched to the overhanging branches, while the carriages stood in a motley group by themselves. Handing the ladies to the church door, we joined the little group outside, now constantly increasing, in which my uncle, the squire, and Uncle Baldy were in quiet conversation. The area around the church, from which the underwood had been thoroughly cleared, was speedily thronged with a medley of vehicles, the majority of which were family coaches; while, among them, you might also see lighter carriages, buggies,

At one time, the Capehart family owned some 5,000 acres along the Roanoke and Chowan rivers. The family—upon whom George Higby Throop based his novel Bertie— *is buried beside this chapel on the Scotch Hall Plantation.*

sulkies, carts and wagons. At intervals, among the trees, were rude deal-tables supported by stakes.—From *Bertie, or, Life in the Old Field, a Humorous Novel*, by Gregory Seaworthy (Philadelphia: A. Hart, 1851), 180.

A winsome Episcopal chapel sits between the botanical extraction plant (Avoca, Inc.) and a sprawling gated community and golf course named Scotch Hall (after the plantation that preceded it). The church is all that is left of the Capehart family plantation that George Higby Throop wrote about in *Bertie* under the pseudonym Gregory Seaworthy. Dates on the gravestones beside the chapel reveal the length of the family's history on this ground.

Schoolteacher George Higby Throop spent a summer with the Capeharts in the mid-1800s serving as a tutor to their children. He drew upon those experiences to write his first novel, *Nags Head*, about a family trip to the coast. His more accomplished second novel, *Bertie*, which is comedic in tone, stereotypically portrays the enslaved people who work for the Capeharts as happy and satisfied and their masters as extremely kind. Nevertheless, the novel is one of only a few pieces of writing from the period that reveal the details of daily life near the confluence of the Roanoke and Chowan rivers in the antebellum era.

The Gingerbread House in Murfreesboro, built around 1877, is an example of the extraordinary architecture in this historic town. Two writers with connections to Murfreesboro are William Hill Brown, author of the first American novel, and— in this century—Alice Eley Jones.

Worth mentioning is the recent determination by scholars that the Scotch Hall land was likely the site of an early fort and settlement, which might have served as a refuge for members of the Lost Colony. The theory has yet to be confirmed.

Retrace your route to NC 45 and turn right toward Colerain, Harrellsville, Cofield, and Winton, a stretch of thirty-three miles. Pick up US 158 in Winton to reach our final stop, in Murfreesboro.

■ MURFREESBORO

In the sixteenth century, explorer John White came up from Roanoke Island to visit this ancient Indian settlement on the Meherrin River. An expedition from Jamestown came through in the seventeenth century. Murfreesboro was incorporated in 1787.

Murfreesboro has the distinction of being the place where the writer of the first American novel died. William Hill Brown's *The Power of Sympathy* was published in 1789. It is a sentimental and heavy-handed story about the dangers to women of seduction and incest. Two years after the book appeared, Brown came to the region from his home in Boston, apparently on business. He died in Murfreesboro at the age of twenty-seven.

Murfreesboro-born writer and scholar Alice Eley Jones has spent a lifetime unpacking some of the lesser-known histories of African slaves, who built many of the elegant old houses here and at Hope Plantation, in Windsor. She is the author of a book on Hertford County and a study of the Meherrin Indians, who still live in the area. Exploring the historic architecture in town is a fitting way to end a tour so full of the remnants of plantation life, the Civil War, and its aftermath.

■ LITERARY LANDSCAPE

Chowan University

One University Place, Murfreesboro

252-398-6500

http://www.chowan.edu

This stately institution, with an administration building to rival Tara in the screen version of *Gone with the Wind*, is adjacent to downtown. Bernice Kelly Harris taught here late in life. Now the Mary Frances Hobson Lecture and Prize for Distinguished Achievement in Arts and Letters is awarded to a distinguished writer, who comes to campus for the annual event. Many past recipients of the prize are featured in this volume of *Literary Trails*: Josephine Humphreys, Michael Parker, Shelia P. Moses, Allan Gurganus, Randall Kenan, Jill McCorkle, and Kaye Gibbons.

Gatesville : Great Dismal Swamp : Elizabeth City : Shawboro : Currituck : Duck : Corolla

Few other natural features in North Carolina have spawned so much writing over the years as the Great Dismal Swamp in the northeastern-most section of North Carolina. Prepare to get your feet wet.

Writers with a connection to this area: Megan Mayhew Bergman, Nathaniel Bishop, Jessie Carty, Jeffery Deaver, Thomas Dixon, Susan Dodd, Robert Frost, Kaye Gibbons, Jim Lavene, Joyce Lavene, Henry Wadsworth Longfellow, Kat Meads, Judith D. Mercier, Travis Morris, Frederick Law Olmsted, J. Saunders Redding, Bland Simpson, Harriet Beecher Stowe, William Styron, Nell Wise Wechter, Eric A. Weil

■ GATESVILLE

In 1672, when George Fox, the leader of the Quakers, visited Gates County, he declared the area barren. Yet the Chowanoke Indians had already occupied this territory for some 800 years. The native people were ultimately ravaged by diseases brought by European explorers, and the survivors were then confined on the first Indian reservation in the United States, established here in 1677. In 1825, the Marquis de Lafayette passed through what is now Gates County, and during the Civil War the area became a hideout for renegades and deserters, who often raided houses and stole from the families left behind by the soldiers who had gone to war. Today, the county's livelihood depends largely on agriculture, forest products, and tourism.

A drive through the county seat of Gatesville brings to mind the gritty perseverance demonstrated by one of the lead characters in *Birds of a Lesser Paradise*, a novel by Rocky Mount writer Megan Mayhew Bergman. Bergman says that she was

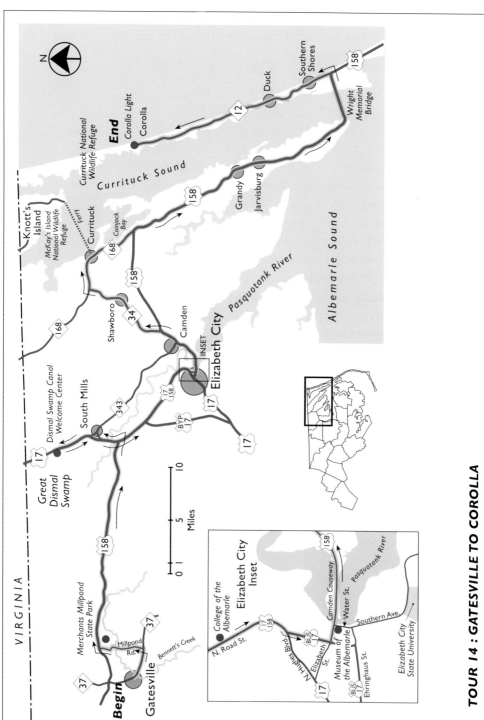

TOUR 14 : GATESVILLE TO COROLLA

inspired by Bland Simpson's expansive memoir, *The Great Dismal*, and by her own youthful curiosity, kindled when her family came through here year after year on the way to the coast.

> Dad was born on the outskirts of the swamp at a time when it was desolate, hard, and flecked with ramshackle hunting cabins. His father had been into timber, and Dad was raised wild—the kind of man who could pick up a snake by its neck with the confidence I'd exhibit picking up a rubber version in a toy store. He was sentimental about his family home and the town. Anything he was used to having around he wanted to keep around. So when the town got too small to sustain a post office, he converted the blue mail drops into composting hubs in the back corner of our lot. He bought the abandoned elementary school at auction for almost nothing—no one wanted to pay the taxes on it, and looters had already taken the copper pipes and pedestal sinks. He rented it out for birthday parties, weddings, and to local artists for studio space. When a developer leveled the city park, Dad reassembled the jungle gym in our side yard near the garden and let the scuppernong vines go wild.
>
> We lived in a dying town with a dwindling tax base. I never thought I'd come back, but the swamp was in me.
>
> —From *Birds of a Lesser Paradise*, by Megan Mayhew Bergman (New York: Scribner, 2012), 38–39.

The mysteries of this boggy landscape are compelling, and there's nowhere better to immerse yourself in its shadowy secrets than nearby Merchants Millpond. From Gatesville, follow Main Street (NC 37) over the Phillip Godwin Bridge across Bennett's Creek. In 3.4 miles, turn left onto Millpond Road (County Road 1400). The state park entrance will be on the right in another 3.7 miles.

This pond, once the site of a gristmill, sawmill, and store, became a 3,250-acre state park in the 1970s and is now a popular spot for canoeing, hiking, fishing, and wildlife observation among the ancient cypresses. It's also possible to canoe down Bennett's Creek from here back toward Gatesville.

Jessie Carty, a poet who grew up in Hertford and Elizabeth City and now teaches creative writing in the Piedmont, taps into a common human response in this sticky wilderness:

SATURDAY AT MERCHANT MILL POND
We had walked at least a mile into the woods.
I had been discussing music with your parents—

In early spring, the cypress knees are surrounded by floating duckweed and water fern that eerily cover the surface of Merchants Millpond, near Gatesville. A poem by Jessie Carty, who was raised in northeastern North Carolina, describes a visit to the pond.

folk songs I first heard your mother play
on her guitar—when I felt the weight at my neck.

I took off my coat, noting the heft was at the collar.
Looking down, there was something in the hood.
I threw the coat and ran. Your sister laughed
as she held the frog whose tongue splayed across his lips.

His legs askew, I would come to laugh as I found
my discarded coat from where it blended in with
the brown leaves on the path. I draped it over my
hunched shoulders. I fell behind you and your family
as we finished the hike. Last in line, I checked my pockets

every few feet for anything else hanging-on.
—From *Paper House*, by Jessie Carty (Rocklin, Calif.: Folded Word, 2010), 33.

Continue north on Millpond Road to pick up US 158 East. In 20.7 miles, take US 17 North in South Mills for another seven miles. Watch for signs to the Dismal Swamp Canal Welcome Center, on the left side of the highway.

The Welcome Center, completed in 2009, offers a dock for boaters coming up the canal—a twenty-two-mile waterway, hand dug by slaves over a twelve-year period and completed in 1805. Interpretive exhibits on the history of the swamp and its connection to the underground railway and the Civil War are inside the Welcome Center, where rangers will also rent bicycles to those wishing to explore the eighteen miles of dirt logging trails or the hard-surfaced bird-watching trail. Canoes and kayaks are also available if you'd prefer to paddle the canal.

> A land riddled with metaphors . . . avoid one and you merely careen off another; I am perhaps half an hour from my destination when a sign lures me into the irresistible reaches of the Great Dismal Swamp.
>
> This ghostly landscape might have been invented to stymie the great. George Washington dropped his venture capital here, founding a lumbering cartel meant to corner the market in cedar shingles. Profits were stingier than projected. A century and a half later, Robert Frost, budding and sappy and bowed by first love, traveled here from New England. His intent was to do away with himself. He ran afoul instead of a boisterous gang of fishermen from Elizabeth City, rowdies who rehabilitated the love-sick youngster's spirit with generous doses of whiskey and fried chicken and boys'-night-out camaraderie. The profitability of the poet's venture was, like Washington's, dubious: Frost went on to marry the young woman who'd spurned him, and the outcome was less than blissful. A swamp is a dark and tangled thing, of course. Its beauty smacks of chaos.
>
> —From *The Mourner's Bench*, by Susan Dodd (New York: William Morrow, 1998), 3.

Novelist Susan Dodd, who lives on Ocracoke Island, manages a quick recap of some of the Great Dismal's history through the mind of her main character, a terminally ill poet and English teacher who is driving south on US 17 with a plan to spend the final months of his life with an old flame. Dodd aptly includes the story of the 1899 visit by Robert Frost, who rode the train south with the idea of disappearing. Instead, the young poet—weary, cold, and hungry—came upon a group of hunters, which he recounted with humor some fifty years later in the long poem "Kitty Hawk":

KITTY HAWK (EXCERPT)
I fell in among
Some kind of committee
From Elizabeth City,
Each and every one
Loaded with a gun
Or a demijohn.
(Need a body ask
If it was a flask?)
Out to kill a duck
Or perhaps a swan
Over Currituck.
—From "Kitty Hawk," in *The Poetry of Robert Frost:*
The Collected Poems, by Robert Frost, edited by Edward
Connery Lathem (New York: Macmillan, 2002), 431.

A poem by a fellow New Englander, Henry Wadsworth Longfellow, prompted Frost's choice of this dismal destination. Longfellow never visited the swamp but was enthralled by its name and the sad fate of those refugees of slavery who sought escape in the thickets:

THE SLAVE IN THE DISMAL SWAMP (EXCERPT)
In dark ferns of the Dismal Swamp
The hunted Negro lay;
He saw the fire of the midnight camp,
And he heard at times a horse's tramp
And a bloodhound's distant bay.
—From *The Poetical Works of Henry W. Longfellow*, by
Henry Wadsworth Longfellow (London: Suitaby, 1888), 21.

The Dismal Swamp reaches well up into Virginia and was believed to be the hiding place of Nat Turner, the leader of a slave revolt in 1831, whose story was brought to life by William Styron in his 1967 novel *The Confessions of Nat Turner*. A much earlier novel, *Dred: A Tale of the Great Dismal Swamp*, by Harriet Beecher Stowe, portrayed Dred, also a revolutionary, who lived as a fugitive in the swamp.

The Great Dismal Swamp Canal was hand dug by enslaved people in the late 1700s and is the oldest continuously traveled, man-made canal in the country. It is one of two inland water routes from the Chesapeake Bay to the Albemarle Sound. The swamp itself figures in the work of Harriet Beecher Stowe, Henry Wadsworth Longfellow, and Robert Frost, among others.

Frederick Law Olmsted, the journalist and landscape architect who designed New York's Central Park and the layout of Asheville's Biltmore Estate, had first-hand experience of the swamp in the mid-1800s and wrote a grim account of his tour:

The Dismal Swamps are noted places of refuge for runaway negroes. They were formerly peopled in this way much more than at present; a systematic hunting of them with dogs and guns having been made by individuals who took it up as a business about ten years ago. Children were born, bred, lived and died here. Joseph Church told me he had seen skeletons, and had helped to bury bodies recently dead. There were people in the swamps still, he thought, that were the children of runaways and who had been runaways themselves "all their lives." What a life it must be! born outlaws; educated self-stealers; trained from infancy to be constantly in dread of the approach of a white man as a thing more fearful than wild cats or serpents, or even starvation.—From *The Cotton Kingdom*, by Frederick Law Olmsted (New York: Mason Brothers, 1862), 155.

Writers still draw upon the Dismal to create a mood of peril or intrigue. In his thriller *The Empty Chair*, Chapel Hill novelist Jeffery Deaver takes his hard-boiled criminologist, Amelia Sachs, into the swamp with a dangerous character, Garrett Hanlon, whom locals dubbed "The Insect Boy":

> Garrett knew the waterways like an expert river pilot and steered the boat up what seemed to be dead ends yet he always managed to find creeks, thin as spiderweb strands, that led them steadily west through the maze.
>
> He pointed out river otter, muskrat and beaver to Sachs—sightings that might have excited amateur naturalists but left her cold. Her wildlife was the rats and pigeons and squirrels of the city—and only to the extent they were useful in helping her and Rhyme in their forensic work.
>
> "Look there!" he cried.
>
> "What?"
>
> He was pointing to something she couldn't see. He stared at a spot near the shore, lost in whatever tiny drama was being played out on the water. All Sachs could see was some bug skipping over the surface.
>
> —From *The Empty Chair*, by Jeffery Deaver (New York: Simon and Schuster, 2000), 263.

Now we turn back toward Elizabeth City on US 17 South to join up with US 158 as the road enters Pasquotank County. The Pasquotank River, which flows into the Albemarle Sound in Elizabeth City, is featured in Rocky Mount writer Kaye Gibbons's fourth novel, *Charms for the Easy Life*. Here in the early twentieth century, the narrator's grandfather operated a ferry and her colorful grandmother worked as a midwife and herb doctor:

> Already by her twentieth birthday, my grandmother was an excellent mid-wife, in great demand. Her black bag bulged with mysteries in vials. This occupation led her to my grandfather, whose job was operating a rope-and-barge ferry that traveled across the Pasquotank River. A heavy cable ran from shore to shore, and he pulled the cable and thus the barge carrying people, animals, everything in the world, across the river. My grandmother was a frequent passenger, going back and forth over the river to catch babies, nurse the sick, and care for the dead as well. I hear him singing as he pulls her barge. At first it may have annoyed her, but soon it was a sound she couldn't live without. She may have made up reasons to cross the river so she could hear him and see him. Think of a man content enough with quiet nights to work a river alone. Think of a man content to

bathe in a river and drink from it, too. As for what he saw when he looked
at my grandmother, if she looked anything like my mother's high school
graduation photograph, she was dazzling, her green eyes glancing from his
to the water to the shore. Between my grandmother, her green eyes and
mound of black hair, and the big-cookie moon low over the Pasquotank,
it must have been all my grandfather could do to deposit her on the other
side of the river.—From *Charms for the Easy Life*, by Kaye Gibbons (New
York: G. P. Putnam's, 1993), 1.

The large tracts of farmland that flank the roads coming into Elizabeth City
allow long-distance views in all directions, inspiring this poem by Eric A. Weil,
who teaches language, literature, and communication at Elizabeth City State
University:

THREE SILOS
We live in utter flatness.
I notice the cuts, ditches
that drain fields of cotton
and corn stretching sunward
like supplicants. The ditches slice
straight across the soil as if a giant
samurai had studied plane geometry.
Where the road tees to town and away,
three ivy-covered silos stand
like sisters in green summer dresses
waiting for their soldier-boys
to return from overseas.
—By Eric A. Weil, in *The Dead Mule School of Southern Literature*,
    February 2010, http://www.deadmule.com/2010/02.

■ ELIZABETH CITY

The best destination for a first-time visitor to this bustling town is the Museum of the Albemarle, on the waterfront at 501 South Water Street (252-335-
1453). Carefully designed exhibits organized by era offer a glimpse of life in the
Albemarle region throughout its history. The museum shop offers a strong collection of regional books and handicrafts, and there's free parking, giving visitors easy access to the downtown sights and restaurants, best seen and savored
under your own steam.

The Museum of the Albemarle, on the waterfront in Elizabeth City, provides a vivid introduction to the history of coastal North Carolina, dating from the aboriginal peoples to the present—referred to by museum curators as the "tourist era."

Two venerable institutions of higher learning are also a significant part of Elizabeth City—the College of the Albemarle, located on US 158 north of town, and Elizabeth City State University, due south from Water Street on Southern Avenue. Both schools have served as professional homes of creative writers over the years.

One of North Carolina's most beloved writers of fiction for young people, Nell Wise Wechter, of Dare County, taught for a time at the College of the Albemarle after a career as a public school teacher and newspaper feature writer. Her locally set books, some of which are still in print, include *Taffy of Torpedo Junction* (1957), *Betsy Dowdy's Ride* (1960), and *The Mighty Midgetts of Chicamacomico* (1974).

At Elizabeth City State, J. Saunders Redding was chair of the English department in the early 1940s when he began *No Day of Triumph*—part memoir and part analysis of the state of black education in the United States, published in 1942. As noted in *Time* magazine, it was the first book by an African American to win North Carolina's Mayflower Cup. (Betty Smith's *A Tree Grows in Brooklyn* was among the contenders that year.)

Elizabeth City is also the birthplace and childhood home of Bland Simpson, the bard of eastern North Carolina's waterways. More than any other writer, Simpson has covered the east with the eye of a poet and the ear of a musician. (As a member of the Red Clay Ramblers, Simpson has recorded a number of albums and cowritten several musicals performed on Broadway.)

Though Simpson has lived most of his adult life in Chapel Hill, where he is a professor of creative writing at the university, his lifetime of travels on the winding rivers and wide sounds that shape the shoreline from Currituck to Calabash has produced more than a few tall tales and powerful insights about the people of the region. Simpson has never tired of writing about his earliest memories of fishing expeditions with his father, which led him to produce a series of guidebooks, made even more vivid by photographs taken by his wife, Ann Cary Simpson. Simpson's travel writing could be excerpted to lend perspective most anywhere along these eastern literary tours, and there's a novel, too, based on a true story that Simpson heard as a boy: *The Mystery of the Beautiful Nell Cropsey*. But only one story must suffice as we head toward the Outer Banks on US 158:

Out beyond Belcross and the potatolands, on U.S. 158 east of Elizabeth City as Camden County is becoming Currituck, there was in my boyhood a small country gas station with a live attraction: Cuff the Bear. He was a big black bear who stood in his shelter, a small hut open in the front from waist height up, looking as if he were going to serve you up a barbeque sandwich or a snow cone. In fact he was addicted to Coca-Colas, and no telling how many six-ounce dopes my family passed his way, Cuff taking the green bottle from you as you quickly retreated. For there was over his window on the world this warning: "Hello. My name is Cuff and I like fingers!" Sometimes Cuff was staked out closer to the highway, chained to a metal rod in the ground. He chugged down a Coke in just a matter of seconds, threw the bottle down, then reached out for more.

I remember my father coming home from court one evening and telling me that Cuff had escaped, gotten away into the swamps. What would happen to him? I asked. My father shook his head—he didn't know. But when he told me that men and dogs were off hunting Cuff, I knew without admitting it that that was the end of the civilized bear. A few days later, Daddy said they'd caught Cuff raiding a hog lot and shot him dead. I cried about all this, for I felt like I knew him, and he'd never so much as taken a nip or swipe at me. By the next time we rode east toward our little shingled shanty at Kitty Hawk, I was merely wistful when I looked at Cuff's old enclosure, empty now but with the I LIKE FINGERS sign still up and in place. Soon that pen was torn down, and for a long time now the station itself has been gone.

Not so some other animal pens that always haunted me, haunt me still: these were the long pony-shed barracks of the migrant laborers who worked the steady and successively maturing crops, coming up from Florida on U.S. 17, the Ocean Highway, in old and overcrowded school buses, encamping all across the coastal plain, passing through Pasquotank and then disappearing after potatoes were in, reappearing I reckon up on Virginia's eastern shore, coming back our way to chop cabbage. I remember them hanging on the stall doors of those pitiful apartments—languorous, exhausted, children half-naked, most of them black but probably in those days some Indians among them too, where nowadays they'd be Mexicans or Haitians, and somewhere back then something strange and rough and ill-fitting lodged in me without intention as I compared the living quarters of these creatures:

Cuff the Bear lived better than the migrants.

—From *Into the Sound Country*, by Bland Simpson (Chapel Hill: University of North Carolina Press, 1997), 189–90.

Continue east on US 158 through Camden and then take NC 34 toward Currituck. Watch for the tiny brick post office sitting beside its newer, prefab counterpart as you pass through the crossroads of Shawboro, hometown of versatile novelist, poet, and playwright Kat Meads, whose aunt was postmistress here for many years. In this scene from Meads's second novel, which is part of a trilogy set in fictional Mawatuck (Currituck) County, local eccentric Clarence Carter climbs on top of the post office with his rifle, one of many stunts he cooked up to convince the Internal Revenue Service that he is crazy and should not have to pay taxes on his sixty-acre farm:

What I'd learned from previous high jinks, I put to use in that post office caper. One, if a person ain't around to see the effect of his put-on, he gives away all the fun. Two, if he ain't there to gauge reaction, how's he gonna see how to go one better next time? Rooftop performance made perfect sense because they see me, I see them seeing me, both sides get a ringside seat. Just perching atop a post office, though, that wouldn't by itself cause folks to stand around gawking, mouths open to flies. So I took my gun up with me to pick off some starlings.—From *when the dust finally settles*, by Kat Meads (Spokane: Ravenna Press Books, 2011), 99–100.

Continue ahead 3.6 miles on NC 34 and turn right on NC 168. In another 3.6 miles, you'll reach the town of Currituck, where a free ferry crosses Currituck Sound to the Knott's Island community and its neighbor, the Mackay Island National Wildlife Refuge. Though not on this tour, Mackay Island does have a literary connection. Once again we come upon Shelby writer Thomas Dixon. (See Tour 9.) With the wealth he acquired from the film script for *Birth of a Nation*, Dixon bought this island as a hunting camp in 1917 and then sold it to Joseph P. Knapp, a New York printing magnate and philanthropist, who also used the acreage for hunting. Knapp, an avid conservationist, would eventually launch the foundation that evolved into Ducks Unlimited, an organization dedicated to the preservation of waterfowl flyways around the globe.

If you're curious to learn more about Currituck County, local writer Travis Morris has assembled *Currituck as It Used to Be*, an excellent collection of oral histories and photos available from History Press.

Head south from Currituck on NC 168 to US 158 and continue to the very tip of the peninsula at Point Harbor, where the Wright Memorial Bridge crosses the Albemarle Sound to reach the Outer Banks. Head north on NC 12 toward Duck.

■ DUCK

This area, commonly known as the North Banks, was once inhabited by only the heartiest of souls, but now it's become a summer destination for thousands. Judith D. Mercier tells the story of Duck's evolution in a fine work of creative nonfiction:

The reputation those nineteenth century Bankers gained isn't extinct just yet. Flashes of it abide here in Duck, those bygone qualities recognizable in a handful of natives who still live in the village. Theirs is a distinctive brand of autonomy, a simple wisdom, a gutsy charisma, a gentle wariness of outside influences and mainland manners, a generous sense of adventure, a resilience in the face of change. Their culture is flavored by this quirky climate, the inconstant land. Their lifetimes are spent seesawing between

In Corolla, the Whalehead Club, at Currituck Heritage Park, is a recently restored, 21,000-square-foot former residence that now operates as a museum. Across the boat basin is the Currituck Light and the Outer Banks Center for Wildlife Education.

the threat of gale force winds and high tides and the surety of having survived them. — From *Duck: An Outer Banks Village*, by Judith D. Mercier (Winston-Salem: John F. Blair, 2001), 33.

Honoring writer Nathaniel Bishop's 1870s travelogue, *Voyage of the Paper Canoe*, which brought the adventurer paddling through these waters, the Paper Canoe is the name of a Duck restaurant, popular with locals, which sometimes serves — what else? — barbecued duck.

Continue north on NC 12 for another fifteen miles to reach the end of the road at Corolla. North Carolina's only red brick lighthouse, the Outer Banks Center for Wildlife Education, and the museum in the Whalehead Club are all within easy walking distance at Currituck Heritage Park. Mystery writers Joyce Lavene and Jim Lavene, who live in the Piedmont, have written a series of novels — among them *A Timely Vision*, *A Touch of Gold*, and *A Spirited Gift* — that feature the Currituck light and the wild Spanish mustangs that roam the dunes and shoreline beyond the pavement.

Page after Page

111 South Water Street, Elizabeth City

252-335-7243

On the waterfront near the Museum of the Albemarle, this shop carries books by local writers and regional favorites. A writers' group meets here monthly, and the store hosts regular readings by visiting writers.

Arts of the Albemarle

516 East Main Street, Elizabeth City

252-338-6455

http://www.artsaoa.com/

This thriving arts center provides programming for Pasquotank, Gates, and Camden counties. Located in the renovated historic Lowry-Chesson Building, the arts center houses the Maguire Theatre, which includes plays on its year-round bill of performances; you'll find the schedule and ticket information on the website. The center's gallery is worth a visit while you're in the neighborhood.

Island Bookstore

1177 Duck Road

(Scarborough Faire Shopping Village)

252-261-8981

http://www.islandbooksobx.com

In addition to the store in Duck, there's one in Corolla (1130 Corolla Village Road) and another in Kitty Hawk (3712 North Croatan Highway). This small chain stocks top regional writers and offers cozy spots for browsing, reading, or striking up a conversation with local folks.

Rocky Mount : Tarboro : Princeville : Parmele : Williamston : Edenton

Prone to floods, this part of North Carolina's coastal plain has evoked many words about water—its beauty and its perils.

Writers with a connection to this area: James Boyd, Grey Brown, Inglis Fletcher, Kaye Gibbons, Eloise Greenfield, Allan Gurganus, Clement Hall, Harriet Jacobs, Jack Kerouac, Shara Lessley, T. R. Pearson, Lucia Peel Powe, Maureen Sherbondy, Thomas Walters, Carole Boston Weatherford

■ ROCKY MOUNT

On the outskirts of Rocky Mount, near a rural crossroads once called Big Easonburg Woods, a small frame house sits in front of a large stand of pinewoods at 8116 West Mount Drive. The sister of Beat Generation novelist and poet Jack Kerouac lived here during the 1950s, and Kerouac stayed with her off and on.

> They all wanted me to sleep on the couch in the parlor by the comfortable oil-burning stove but I insisted on making my room (as before) on the back porch with its six windows looking out on the winter barren cottonfield and the pine woods beyond, leaving all the windows open and stretching my good old sleeping bag on the couch there to sleep the pure sleep of winter nights with my head buried inside the smooth nylon duck-down warmth. After they'd gone to bed I put on my jacket and my earmuff cap and railroad gloves and over all that my nylon poncho and strode out in the cottonfield moonlight like a shroudy monk. The ground was covered with moonlit frost. The old cemetery down the road gleamed in the frost. The roofs

tour 15

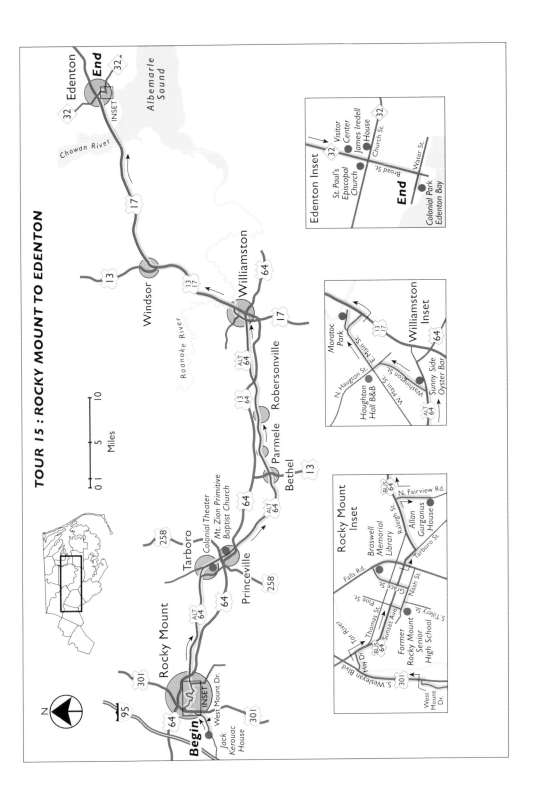

TOUR 15 : ROCKY MOUNT TO EDENTON

N

Miles
0 1   5   10

Rocky Mount

301
95
64
301

Begin
INSET

Jack
Kerouac
House

West Mount Dr.

ALT 64

258

Tarboro

Colonial Theater

Mt. Zion Primitive
Baptist Church

258

64

Princeville

ALT 64

Bethel

13

Parmele

Robersonville

ALT 64

13
64

17

Williamston

64

13
17

Windsor

13

Roanoke River

17

Chowan River

32

Edenton

End

32

INSET

Albemarle
Sound

Edenton Inset

St. Paul's
Episcopal
Church

32

Visitor
Center

James Iredell
House

32

Church St.

Broad St.

Water St.

End

Colonial Park
Edenton Bay

Williamston Inset

Moratoc
Park

N. Haugton St.

E. Main St.

Houghton
Hall B&B

ALT 64

W. Main St.

Washington St.

13
17

64

Sunny Side
Oyster Bar

Rocky Mount Inset

Tar River

Falls Rd.

Pine St.

Thomas St.

Grace St.

Braswell
Memorial
Library

Sunset Ave.

Nash St.

Raleigh St.

Allan
Gurganus
House

Tarboro St.

BUS
64

N. Fairview Rd.

S. Tillery St.

BUS
64

Former
Rocky Mount Senior
High School

S. Wesleyan Blvd.

Nash Dr.

301

West
Mount Dr.

Writer Jack Kerouac often slept on the back porch of his sister's modest house outside Rocky Mount.

of nearby farmhouses were like white panels of snow. I went through the cottonfield rows followed by Bob, a big bird dog, and little Sandy who belonged to the Joyners down the road, and a few other stray dogs (all dogs love me) and came to the edge of the forest.—From *The Dharma Bums*, by Jack Kerouac (New York: Penguin, 1976), 133.

Originally published in 1958, *The Dharma Bums* is representative of Kerouac's free-ranging prose, which influenced a generation of writers in the 1960s and 1970s, among them Tom Robbins, Thomas Pynchon, Richard Brautigan, Bob Dylan, and Ken Kesey. Kerouac has even been called the progenitor of the hippie movement. His rambling travel narrative, *On the Road*, is considered an American classic, though Truman Capote once said wickedly of Kerouac's work, "That's not writing, it's typing." Kerouac came through Rocky Mount a number of times during his itinerant life to visit his mother and sister, who also moved around the country, sometimes following in the writer's footsteps.

Take West Mount Drive east toward town for 3.1 miles and turn left at the major intersection with US 301 (South Wesleyan Boulevard). In 1.1 miles, turn right on May Drive and then take another right on Sunset Avenue, which crosses the Tar River as it heads toward downtown Rocky Mount.

Grey Brown, who served for many years as poet-in-residence at Duke University Medical Center, wrote this portrait of herself, her hometown, and its ubiquitous river:

LIVING ON THE TAR
Perched on Harrison's dock
under the sign of no trespassing
I prayed to the muddy river god,
to the god of the river they named Tar,
I prayed to be made clean in the dirtiest river I knew.
Living in a tobacco town, I prayed to be free of the smell.
I prayed for crystal spirals and no paper mills.
Diving deep with mud on all sides,
I pushed to the bottom as the sun disappeared.
I wanted Mediterranean, I wanted blue sea.
Up from the river, brown legs and belly,
swinging my hair and the stench that followed,
fingernails gray and clear eyes cloudy,
how could the river help, so full of itself?
By mid afternoon I settled for dirty,
fell to roll in leaves like a dog,
dug clay and dipped into algae.
On the edge of the brown, brown river I sat
mud baked and full of my sin.
—From *Staying In*, by Grey Brown (Carrboro:
    North Carolina Writers' Network, 1992), 14.

In seven blocks, turn right on South Pine. In another two blocks, you'll be in front of the original Rocky Mount Senior High School, at 308 South Tillery, where Grey Brown and novelists Allan Gurganus and Kaye Gibbons all went to high school. (The new campus, built in 2012, is on West Mount Drive.)

Gibbons's novels are permeated with the scent of curing tobacco, the summer heat of Wilson, where she was born, and the sight of the Tar River in Rocky Mount, where she came to live with her brother and his wife in 1973, after her mother's suicide and her father's death from alcoholism. Before moving in with her brother, Gibbons spent a short time in a foster home, an experience that informed her first novel, *Ellen Foster*, published in 1987 under the guidance of Louis D. Rubin, who taught English at the University of North Carolina at

The Oldest Surviving
Portrait of the Southern
Writer Allan Gurganus, *by
J. Chris Wilson, was given
to Rocky Mount's Braswell
Library by Catherine and
David Combs. Courtesy of
J. Chris Wilson.*

Chapel Hill. Since then, Gibbons has managed many different voices of North Carolina women from various historical eras in her work.

A striking portrait of short-story writer and novelist Allan Gurganus hangs in the Braswell Memorial Library, at 727 North Grace Street, our next stop. Turn right on Nash and left on Grace. In eight blocks, you'll come to this airy library, which was built in 2002.

In his early years, Gurganus was inclined toward visual art. A local painter, Janice Graveley, coached the young artist, and he went on to study painting at the University of Pennsylvania and the Pennsylvania Academy of Fine Arts. However, while serving in the navy during Vietnam, Gurganus took up writing. Upon his discharge, he enrolled at Sarah Lawrence College to study with short-story master Grace Paley. John Cheever and Stanley Elkin later became mentors at the Iowa Writers' Workshop.

Gurganus's massive first novel, *Oldest Living Confederate Widow Tells All*, which was also serialized for television and won four Emmys, has a number of passages about Rocky Mount, which appears as "Falls, North Carolina." Gurganus's feisty narrator, a ninety-nine-year-old widow named Lucy Marsden, tells her story from a nursing home. She has lived long enough to remember the profusion of antebellum lilacs here and to comment wryly on their struggle to survive in the twentieth century as developers have their way with the landscape:

> At the Big Elk Browse'n'Buy Mall's parking lots' east end, around a few of them stainless-steel lampposts stuck out lonely in the tar, come spring you'll spy green heart-shaped leaves pushing up for air. The strength of things!
>
> Next year in early to mid April, please notice certain purple stunted blooms. A testament to . . . something. Maybe: How stubborn beauty is. Maybe: How this Yankee-operated Mall (my favorite orderly here, he just told me the whole shebang is owned outright by a syndicate from *Japan*) still can't squelch the tints and odors of the region.
> —From *Oldest Living Confederate Widow Tells All*, by Allan Gurganus
>   (New York: Alfred A. Knopf, 1989), 229–30.

Gurganus's work is also full of the tints and odors of the region. His child-hood home, our next stop, is at 526 North Fairview, in a neighborhood of enor-mous trees, including a few sycamores, a variety that turns up in Gurganus's fiction, too.

From Braswell Library, take the first right on Falls Road (the source of the fictional pseudonym), and follow it five blocks alongside downtown. Turn left onto US 64 (Tarboro Street) and in .3 miles turn left onto North Raleigh Street. In .7 miles, watch for North Fairview Road and turn right. The Gurganus family's sprawling ranch house is on the right.

In *White People*, Gurganus's 1991 collection of short fiction, several pieces are set during the 1950s and 1960s in a neighborhood much like this. The stories describe bridge games and cocktail parties—favorite adult pastimes that gave children the scary pleasure of spying on their parents. One character naturally refers to the citizens of Falls as "the Fallen."

A bit farther down Fairview on the left is one of the grocery stores that the writer's father and uncle started in town. Double back on Fairview to US 64 and turn right toward Tarboro, fifteen miles ahead.

The Tar River snakes wildly back and forth in wide arcs beyond the tree line along the north side of this highway. In 1999, the Tar swelled precipitously during rains from Hurricane Floyd, prompting Rocky Mount officials to release water from a dam in an attempt to lessen the impact of the storm. But Rocky Mount was not spared, and the result downriver was also disastrous for Tarboro and Princeville. In all, the flood was declared an event likely to occur only once in 500 years. Few families were untouched, and the flood has since prompted many poems and stories from writers with connections to this area. Raleigh poet Maureen Sherbondy responded with shock at the unforgettable newspaper images of the water's devastation:

LOOSE COFFINS IN CAROLINA
Flood waters rise, dams leak
cemeteries give up their dead.
Do you see the long-buried coffins
floating down Main Street?
Even time cannot hold the departed.

Bones of Smith and Jones drift boxed
past the coffee shop,
maybe they want to return
to this place again,
where the Tar River abandons its edges.

Work crews torch piles of pigs,
wood-hog smoke twists up
in clouds, to pose the question
who will come to this
Southern pig pickin,' while
the natives all stand stranded on roofs.

How do you bury the dead
when the ground won't allow it,
when it won't even show itself,
when the once hard surface

is drowning in water
and will hold nothing down?

See the pigs floating, the chickens too,
see the bodies, now where is that ark?
—"Loose Coffins in Carolina," by Maureen Sherbondy, in
    Independent Weekly, March 29–April 24, 2000, 29.

Though the destruction was grim, new investments have since brought a fine cultural center to Rocky Mount, in what was once the Imperial Tobacco Plant—the Imperial Centre for the Arts & Sciences. Neighboring Tarboro's downtown district has received a face-lift. Continue ahead on US 64 Business.

■ TARBORO

A campaign to restore Tarboro's classic movie house, The Colonial, is ongoing at 514 North Main. The late poet Thomas N. Walters worked here as a young man. His collection, *Seeing in the Dark*, recalls the thrill he experienced from his high perch in the projection booth when glamorous stars such as Smithfield's Ava Gardner shimmered onto the screen:

TARBORO
1939 NEWSREEL
I was the kid who crowed
For the Pathé cock
(the sound gone briefly dead)
That news-ed us bad
And good, mostly bad,
From around the dizzy world
While the Majestic crowd,
Small town,
Knowing each other,
My parents,
Waiting through the Southern
Fall and dark for
Alan Ladd in *Beast of Berlin*,
Laughed in the purple hall
Facing a chimera of cannon,
Jackboots, juggernauts, helmets, smoke.

Tarboro's Colonial Theater was the place to see the Hollywood classics of the 1950s. As a teenager, poet Thomas Noble Walters (1935–83), a much-beloved English teacher at North Carolina State University, ran the projector.

> Firestorms in Polish villages where
> No one laughed at kids
> Who crowed or sang
> Or anything else
> Beneath that sudden strangled rooster
> Jerking, slumping atop the globe.
> —From *Seeing in the Dark*, by Thomas N. Walters
>   (Durham: Moore Publishing Company, 1972), 10.

Continue through town on Main Street to the bridge over the Tar River. On the far side is Princeville, the town that nearly drowned when Hurricane Floyd struck.

The Mt. Zion Primitive Baptist Church in Princeville was erected in 1896 and has survived more than a hundred years of floods, including the devastation from Hurricane Floyd. In Princeville: The 500-Year Flood, *High Point writer Carole Boston Weatherford tells this town's story.*

■ PRINCEVILLE

Carole Boston Weatherford, a poet and writer of books for children, offers a bit of town history:

> Years ago, on the front porch of a house that still stands, Mama's great-grandpa John told her how Princeville began.
>
> When the Civil War ended in 1865, ex-slaves left Tarboro, North Carolina plantations and settled near the Union Army camp on low, flat, swampy land on the Tar River's south shore. Eventually the Union troops departed, but the freed slaves stayed. They named their community Freedom Hill— after the little hill where Union soldiers had declared the slaves free. By 1885, the town had been granted a state charter and had changed its name to Princeville, for carpenter Turner Prince, a town founder. The town was the first in the South founded and governed by ex-slaves.
>
> Over the years, the floods came and went. In 1919, the Tar River rose to the railroad bridge. By 1923, though, the sun was once again shining on

Princeville. Julius Rosenwald, the president of Sears, Roebuck, gave money to build a school for the town.

—From *Princeville: The 500-Year Flood*, by Carole Boston Weatherford (Wilmington: Coastal Carolina Press, 2001), 13.

Princeville always struggled, but when the last dike that had been built failed and the muddy Tar took the town completely under, the toll was unbearable. It was here that coffins floated out of their graves. Townspeople were displaced and dozens of buildings were condemned. Some people never returned—a story that prefigured the Hurricane Katrina disaster in New Orleans. Today, the spirited citizens of Princeville have a new town hall and community center, though lingering remnants of the flood can still be seen.

■ PARMELE

From here, the tour follows US 64 Alternate through the agricultural towns of Bethel, Parmele, and Robersonville before arriving in Williamston. If you're traveling here in April or May, chances are you'll find plenty of pick-your-own strawberry stands, where you can gather up a pile of juicy red berries to carry along.

Though Parmele (some sixteen miles beyond Princeville) is a quiet cross-roads, it lands on the literary map as the birthplace of children's writer Eloise Greenfield, the winner of many honors, including the Phyllis Wheatley lifetime achievement award and the Hope S. Dean Memorial Award from the Foundation for Children's Books. Greenfield has written biographies for young readers of Rosa Parks, Mary McCloud Bethune, and Paul Robeson, and her poetry books often describe the childhood pleasures of rural life.

Parmele also pops up in a mouthwatering essay by novelist T. R. Pearson, whose signature run-on sentences just fit the menu he describes. In the 1950s, the Pearson family of Winston-Salem regularly rented a pink vacation house in Kitty Hawk, and on the way, they would stop at the Baptist church in Parmele to picnic:

> We had ham biscuits off a cakeplate and deviled eggs off a deviled egg plate and fried chicken off a regular dinnerplate and pimiento cheese sandwiches out from a Tupperware box and potato salad like Gonny made it with considerable mustard and we had green beans too that did not my sister and me ever eat any of and sweetened ice tea out of Dixie cups, sweetened iced tea over rock ice that we all sucked on and spat and sucked

In spring, strawberry picking is the exercise of choice in eastern North Carolina. This pick-your-own enterprise is between Parmele and Robersonville, on the route that novelist T. R. Pearson followed with his family every year to get to Kitty Hawk.

on again like we wouldn't ever at the table.—From "When We Used to Go Where We Went," by T. R. Pearson, in *A World Unsuspected*, edited by Alex Harris (Chapel Hill: University of North Carolina Press, 1987), 144.

If you haven't brought your own picnic, save your appetite for Williamston, where a most unusual eatery comes highly recommended by writers who have documented the restaurant's steamy way with seafood since the 1930s.

■ WILLIAMSTON

In mid-September of 1933, after Labor Day when the weather gave the slightest suggestion of switching cooler, everybody in Martin County and several counties around had to make the first run of the season to the

As novelist Lucia Powe describes it, when oysters are in season, diners drive for many miles to get a seat at the Sunny Side Oyster Bar, in Williamston.

Sunnyside Oyster Bar for the first R-month oysters brought up from Nags Head.

Everybody was vying to get some before anyone else did. They'd brag about how many bushels they ate and how large, fresh, and delicious the oysters were. Somebody always had to tell the old thing about "the bravest man who ever lived was the first man who ate an oyster." Then somebody else had to say, "Or the hungriest!"

Roosevelt Jones was their favorite person to open oysters. Most ordered theirs raw. Some wanted them steamed just a little, and some, a lot. The sauce, of course, was the secret. And the owner would never tell how he made it. Tomato sauce, horseradish, lemon juice, Texas Pete hot sauce, and Worcestershire were obvious. But nobody could figure out what the secret ingredient was. Some guessed crushed cucumbers and others spring onions. Still others guessed a touch of beer. However, one could purchase a quart jar full and take it home for shrimp or whatever. One woman, a bank president's wife from Raleigh, would phone down and have the owner send her two quarts by a highway patrolman coming toward Raleigh before she had her large parties or church affairs.

—From *Roanoke Rock Muddle*, by Lucia Peel Powe (Raleigh: Pentland Press, 2003), 164–65.

Lucia Powe, from Georgia, married a Williamston attorney and lived for three decades in Martin County, the setting of her novel. The book includes a few local recipes. Powe's daughter runs a bed-and-breakfast in town, at 203 North Haughton Street.

You can read more about the Sunny Side Oyster Bar in Bland Simpson's travelogue, *Into the Sound Country*. This one-of-a-kind restaurant serves only steamed oysters, shrimp, clams, and crab legs. The sole side dish on the menu is steamed broccoli with cheese sauce (unless saltines and beer qualify as sides). Sunny Side nearly closed in 1991, but devoted patrons came to the rescue. It is open in months that contain the letter R and is located at 1102 Washington Street.

Before leaving Williamston, feast your eyes on the Roanoke River at Moratoc Park (102 River Road). Besides the giant Atlantic cedars that have survived here, the site also has a boardwalk for fishing and a restored schoolhouse and historic tobacco barn.

River Road will carry you directly to US 13 East/US 17 North toward Edenton, some thirty-five miles ahead. Once across the sound, take Exit 227 into Edenton, following NC 32. In half a mile, turn right onto North Broad Street. Our first stop is St. Paul's Episcopal Church, at the intersection with West Church Street.

■ EDENTON

On Sunday morning he attended the dark brick church. All of Edenton that mattered was there in broadcloth and bombazine, decorously sweltering under the noonday sun. They moved sedately along the magnolia shaded walk between the broad heraldic tombstones and through the shadowed archway, where they paused while the old pew-opener in white hair and black gown, shuffling up and down the carpeted brick aisle, opened the low little doors with their brass name-plates. Ranged in their mahogany box pews, they sat, waving fans of partridge wing and ivory, inclining velvet bonnets, caps of Irish lawn; smoothing down waistcoats, fluffing up stocks. The church was filled with the subdued flutter of conscious elegance . . . —From *Drums*, by James Boyd (New York: Charles Scribner's Sons), 1925, 80.

Southern Pines novelist James Boyd's description of St. Paul's goes on to offer an interpretation of the finer points of social stratification during the early years of elegant Edenton's development. Enslaved people attended services with their owners and sat in the gallery above. "House-slaves and body-

The Chowan County Courthouse and the adjacent jail date back to the era when rebellious slaves were imprisoned and punished by being put in stocks and publicly whipped. Edenton writer Harriet Jacobs (1813–97) describes such events in her memoir, Incidents in the Life of a Slave Girl.

servants, they knew well how to deport themselves and how to dress. Their chief concern in life was that no one, black or white, should mistake them for field hands" (80).

Among these churchgoers many years later, after the American Revolution, was Harriet Jacobs, who wrote *Incidents in the Life of a Slave Girl*, a memoir published in 1861 under a pseudonym. As a young woman, Jacobs suffered the sexual advances of her master, Dr. James Norcom, a noted Edenton physician who is buried in this churchyard. Jacobs hoped to stymie Norcom's attentions when she became involved with Samuel Sawyer, a white lawyer with whom she bore two children, who were duly baptized at St. Paul's. But Norcom would not be deterred. Jacobs finally escaped, hiding in a tiny attic room in her grand-mother's house for nearly seven years. That residence, no longer standing, was on Edenton's West King Street, just blocks away from her master's office.

When Jacobs first disappeared, Norcom jailed her children, brother, and aunt for two months to try to force her out of hiding, but Samuel Sawyer intervened. He bought his own children from the doctor. Jacobs, still in hiding, watched them play every day from a peephole she drilled in the attic.

In 1837, Sawyer was elected to Congress, and finally, in 1842, Jacobs made her escape by boat from Edenton Bay, following the maritime underground railroad to Philadelphia. She remained a fugitive until 1852, when a friend bought her freedom. By that time, she had reunited with her children and her brother. Her memoir—one of the first to tackle the taboo of sexual abuse by slaveholders—made her a celebrity. She used the book as a platform to raise funds for other refugees from slavery, before and after the Civil War.

St. Paul's has another literary connection. Clement Hall, who served as church rector in the early 1700s, kept a journal describing his itinerant preaching duties across the region. He also published a book of aphorisms in 1753— *A Collection of Many Christian Experiences, Sentences, and Several Places of Scripture Improved*—which was inspired by the hardships of stewarding the not-so-faithful settlers. Clergy representing the Church of England were not generally popular among the rough-hewn folk who had expressly migrated to North Carolina to find religious freedom from the king's church—its strictures and levies.

Clement Hall was well liked, however, in comparison with his successor at St. Paul's—the enterprising Daniel Earl. Parson Earl spent most of his time on Bandon Plantation, some twelve miles north of Edenton, where he launched a school and a herring fishery. Earl neglected the church and its parishioners so severely that an unknown poet left this commentary tacked to the church door: "A weather-beaten church, / A broken-down steeple, / A herring-catching parson, / And a damn set of people."

In the twentieth century, writer Inglis Fletcher and her husband acquired Bandon Plantation, where she wrote a dozen novels about the early history of the state. *Raleigh's Eden* (1940)—the first in her Carolina Series—was sparked by the writer's curiosity about her own Tyrrell County ancestors. Fletcher won the first North Carolina Award for Literature and helped to establish the North Carolina Writers Conference and the Elizabethan Gardens in Manteo. Sadly, the Bandon Plantation house burned in 1963, but the smokehouse, schoolhouse/office, and a dairy building have been moved to Edenton, to the grounds of the James Iredell House, at 105 East Church Street.

Edenton's historic architecture is an aesthetic feast. Maps and self-guided walking tours (which note locations related to writer Harriet Jacobs in addition to the one on West King Street) are available at the visitors' center at 108 North Broad. To reach our last stop, proceed to the end of Broad on the waterfront and turn right toward Colonial Park to see the recently completed restoration of the 1886 Roanoke River Lighthouse.

One of the last lighthouses of its kind in the United States, this square frame building was stationed out in the river and guided water traffic until 1941. It

Built in 1886, this restored lighthouse in Edenton once marked the entrance to the Roanoke River and is the subject of a poem by Shara Lessley. It helped to guide boats traveling upstream to Plymouth and Williamston.

was then moved ashore, where it served as a residence until 1995. It sat empty until the state acquired the building in 2008 and moved it to the Colonial Park site for restoration. A poem by 2009 North Carolina Arts Council fellowship winner Shara Lessley tells the story:

THE BEACON

Edenton Bay, North Carolina

From a temporary storage prop her dead
eye calls to the boats, watching through
a Fresnel lens as waves summon the shore-

line, then break like glass across the pier-
side shamble of sea-lice. Anything
less would dissolve in such mist, lost

to the Sound's dark appetite for fish-bone,
freshwater crab. When a barge sinks, it coughs
up foam; when a lighthouse is grounded,

it drowns. Surrounded now by tapered
hedgerows she drinks the tourists'
shadows, their cameras' fainting spell

of sparks, ember glints like those that fell
from her hinges as Confederates scuttled her
40 dizzy miles up the Roanoke to thwart

another Union blockade; streams of men
and boys taking hold of her rectangular frame,
grunting and charging, charging then pressing

forward the thick pairs of stilts rising
from her base. No cry, but their pick-axes'
wind-streaked swing, the river licking

reeds down to the root-tip, baiting
a Northern Harrier into some darker harbor
where another generation will fight

a quieter war for her history—drawing
metal and wood onto the auction block—
then haul the lighthouse off on a rented truck

toward the manicured grass of Colonial
Park where she'll rest till funds are raised.
Under splintered sun, the brown-blue

bay baiting her back as her lantern turns
the color of fog; her clapboards becoming
the wind, becoming the wreckage.
—By Shara Lessley, in *Crab Orchard Review* 16, no. 2 (Summer/Fall 2011): 116.

■ LITERARY LANDSCAPE

Imperial Centre for the Arts & Sciences

270 Gay Street, Rocky Mount
252-972-1266
http://www.imperialcentre.org
   A stunning example of adaptive reuse, this facility has several galleries, special history and science exhibitions, an outdoor theater, and a growing perma-

nent collection from some of the state's finest artists. It is also the site of readings and performances by writers.

Martin County Arts Council

124 Washington Street, Williamston

252-789-8470

http://www.martincountyarts.com/

This all-volunteer arts council is renovating the historic Flat Iron Building to serve as an arts center. It supports the Martin Community Players, who perform a play each fall and a musical each spring.

The Garden of Readin' Bookstore

302 South Broad Street, Edenton

252-482-7465

http://edentoncoffeehouse.com/bookstore

As part of the Edenton Coffee House Bakery & Café, this used bookshop is a good place to pick up a bargain and breakfast or lunch.

Fountain : Greenville : Washington : Bath : Belhaven : Lake Mattamuskeet : Columbia : Creswell

The past prevails in this tour, where North Carolina's oldest town is still bathing in orange sunsets and new shoots of hope are rising from old fields.

Writers with a connection to this area: Alex Albright, Gerald Barrax, Rachel Carson, David Cecelski, Henry Churchill DeMille, William DeMille, Julie Fay, Edna Ferber, Alex Haley, Linda Leigh Hargrove, John Hoppenthaler, Erica Plouffe Lazure, H. Joe Liverman, Suzanne Newton, Ovid Pierce, Dorothy Spruill Redford, Marty Silverthorne, Bland Simpson, Ronald L. Speer, William Styron, Luke Whisnant

■ FOUNTAIN

An old country store—the center of gossip and other essential transactions—begins the tour. Situated at the intersection of US 258 and NC 222 in the old town of Fountain, the repurposing of the R. A. Fountain General Store is the brainchild of East Carolina University literary scholar and writing professor Alex Albright and his colleagues. Though the place is still outfitted with a riotous assortment of original goods for sale— including regional books—it is probably best described these days as a music and literary venue, open in the evenings on most weekends (http://rafountain.com). Marty Silverthorne, of Greenville, offers a metaphorical appraisal of the place:

GETTIN' THE HOLY GHOST AT R. A. FOUNTAIN
Daddy's dead but not tonight off Exit 63
at R. A. Fountain General Store reared
back in an old church pew. Stage lights
fall on empty mikes, upright piano,

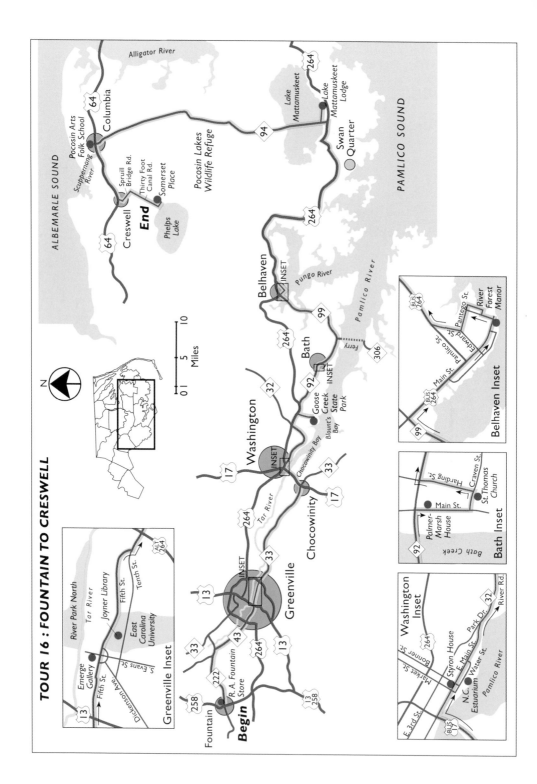

TOUR 16 : FOUNTAIN TO CRESWELL

The R. A. Fountain General Store, between Wilson and Greenville, is a destination for Americana music, literary readings, and good company.

thumping bass. The steel picks up, rings
around the general store, in and out of
a nail keg, across worn frets of a ladder back.

The young crooner cries *Waltz across Texas*,
Daddy dances in the Sea of Galilee,
Mama pats her foot and hums.
The tenor sets Acuff's *speckled bird* flying.
Daddy can't be held down by dirt,
runs the aisles in R. A. Fountain,
dances with axe, maul, handsaws.

It's Mama's music too; the young boy
pulls his hat off, slicks back black hair,
he's Elvis turning a hymn into
a *hunka, hunka* heaven. Mama rises
from the pew, shouts "who are these

children bringing the dead out of the dark;
they must be Moses' children
freeing us from our own Folsom."

The spotlight falls on mikes at rest,
after waltzing Luke the Drifter
over oiled hardwood. Daddy came
back from the drink box with a Coke,
Tom's Peanuts, a cone of hand churned
chocolate ice cream for Mama.
He dropped peanuts down
the slender neck of the bottle,
baptizing them in dark syrup.
Mama savored chocolate from the cone.

If Mama's heart had windows
you'd see a house of broken panes.
Daddy and Mama raise their hands
grasping a life line, a saint pulling
them into salvation as if they
saw the light and were lifted
on the wings of a snow white dove.
—Used by permission of Marty Silverthorne

From Fountain, take NC 222 for nine miles to its meeting with NC 43 and follow 43 another ten miles. It becomes Fifth Street and goes directly to the campus of East Carolina University and the Joyner Library. You are now at the literary epicenter of eastern North Carolina.

■ GREENVILLE

The early risers at the Pelt County Farmer's Market arrived yawning in ball caps and sweatpants, holey work shirts and flip flops, milling about for local eggs and a few heads of lettuce or a sweet potato pie. Dozens of bodies moved from stall to stall in an easy, cordial way under the pavilion, out of the grasp of the morning's steamy heat. Somewhere in the din, a toddler asked for strawberries, even though it was past Labor Day. What was left of the season was mostly tough-skinned root food: Potatoes. Sweet potatoes. Squash and more squash. A few farmers sold hand-jarred pesto

Right to left: North Carolina Literary Review *founding editor Alex Albright, founding art director Eva Roberts, and W. Keats Sparrow receive the Roberts Award for Literary Inspiration for their work in creating the* Review. *Presenting the award are Shelby Strother (then president of the Friends of Joyner Library) and the journal's current editor, Margaret Bauer. Photograph by Jim White, © 2007; courtesy of* North Carolina Literary Review.

and comb-in honey. — From "Freezer Burn," by Erica Plouffe Lazure, used by permission of the author.

A graduate of East Carolina University's master's program in creative writing, Erica Plouffe Lazure offers a culinary oxymoron. The combination of hand-jarred pesto and comb-in honey captures perfectly the simultaneous presence of new school and old school in Greenville. Once a major tobacco center, this increasingly cosmopolitan college town has experienced growth at warp speed. The new industries are education and medicine. Nevertheless, there is yet the occasional scent of livestock and tobacco in the air, and if you're traveling by car, running up on some lumbering mechanical farm implement with giant studded tires is a predictable hazard on Pitt County back roads.

East Carolina University has built an impressive literary program. The ditch work began in the 1950s, under the muscle of novelist Ovid Pierce (see Tour 12) and the imagination of Kinston-born Keats Sparrow, a scholar of early North

Carolina literature who served as chair of the English department for many years.

In 1992, Sparrow tapped Alex Albright to become founding editor of the *North Carolina Literary Review*. The result is an annual compendium of literary news, fresh scholarship, poetry, fiction, creative nonfiction, and reviews. Sparrow's dream was a publication to serve writers that would parallel the *North Carolina Historical Review*. He got his wish and more. The *North Carolina Literary Review*, now edited by Margaret Bauer, has become as important to the state's writers as Grier's Almanac once was to rural farmers. The journal *Tar River Poetry*, published for more than thirty years, also comes out of East Carolina. The current editor, Luke Whisnant, is a poet and fiction writer whose 1992 novel, *Watching TV with the Red Chinese*, was made into a movie in 2008. *Down in the Flood*, a collection of his short stories, published in 2006, draws upon the local landscape and eastern North Carolina weather for some of its drama.

Maury York, who works in Special Collections at East Carolina University's Joyner Library, wanted to go beyond the production of publications and came up with the idea for an Eastern North Carolina Literary Homecoming. First held in 2004, it's now an annual festival sponsored by the library.

Beyond the university, Greenville's pleasures are many—galleries, diverse restaurants, a large river park on the banks of the Tar, several museums, and a number of neighborhoods with homes on the National Register of Historic Places. Fifth Street is a great place to start your exploration. The Pitt County Arts Council at Emerge Gallery at 404 South Evans Street offers classes for children and adults that focus on the visual arts; it's also a nice stop right in the heart of downtown Greenville.

From the East Carolina campus, head out of town on Fifth Street to its end at Tenth Street and turn left. This road (NC 33) runs sixteen miles to Chocowinity, parallel to the Tar River. In Chocowinity, turn left onto US 17 Business North and soon you'll cross a bridge—the most attractive gateway into the Beaufort County seat of Washington.

■ **WASHINGTON**

Where the Tar becomes the Pamlico River sits Little Washington, as it is often called, founded in 1776. Playwright Henry Churchill DeMille, whose career in the New York theater was short but successful, was born here in 1853. Before his untimely death from typhoid fever at the age of thirty-nine, DeMille, with his writing partner, David Balasco, wrote some of the most popular plays of the nineteenth century, including *The Wife* and *Lord Chumley*. His son, Cecil Blount

The Tar River becomes the Pamlico River at "Little Washington," as it is commonly known, in Beaufort County. The father of novelist William Styron grew up here, and his father, Alpheus Styron, once ran a moonlight excursion boat from Washington to the Outer Banks.

DeMille, turned *Lord Chumley* into a silent film in 1914 starring Lillian Gish—one of seventy movies over the course of his career. Cecil B. DeMille would go on to found Paramount Studios.

Cecil's younger brother, William, followed more closely in his father's footsteps, working as a successful playwright until Cecil coaxed him into the movie business in Hollywood. A building with the family name inscribed at the top of its facade is located in downtown Washington, at the corner of Market Street and Ward Lane. The DeMille family plot, where Henry is buried, is in Washington's Oakdale Cemetery.

Several purveyors of cruises along the Washington waterfront offer an enchanting view of town from the river. The North Carolina Estuarium, also on the waterfront, provides environmental education in the form of exhibits, aquaria, and environmental artworks that explain a range of natural phenomena. The Inner Banks Artisans Center, at 158 West Main, is an innovative reuse of an old building that now houses studios, galleries, and shops run by artists.

As might be expected, weather and water are much on the minds of Pamlico poets. John Hoppenthaler, who teaches English and creative writing at East Carolina, has published two collections of poetry: *Anticipate the Coming Reservoir* (2008) and *Lives of Water* (2003), both from Carnegie Mellon University Press.

THE WEATHER DOWN HERE
Washington, NC

for Christy

A quick stop at Food Lion for beer & whole wheat buns,
then Hog Heaven for pints of barbecue, baked beans,

& slaw. Idling in the take-out lane, I'm taken
by gangrenous clouds closing fast from the east.

In Beaufort County, storms are upon us in minutes; roiling
cells shear through skillet-flat fields of tobacco & cotton.

In lightning's flicker, the family plots of farmers appear
visited by God. They startle me like you do, dear, like

Cumulonimbus on the horizon. Come gather after; slip
your hand into my pocket & kiss my sunburned neck.

Recite with me again the capricious
　　　　　　　　　　　　　nature of our Carolina weather.
—Used by permission of John Hoppenthaler

Hoppenthaler's poetic endorsement of Hog Heaven might lead to a need for further investigation. The restaurant is northwest of downtown at 1969 West Fifth Street (US 264).

One block inland from the Washington waterfront, West Main Street (NC 32) heads southwest. As you leave town, watch for the intersection of Main and Bonner streets. The two-story house on the northwest corner of this intersection was the boyhood home of novelist William Styron's father. The author's grandfather, Alpheus Styron, born on Portsmouth Island, settled here after the Civil War. Alpheus launched a number of business enterprises in Washington. For a time, he manufactured his own brand of smoking tobacco, called Mocking Bird, and later he launched an excursion boat that took tourists on moonlight cruises to the Outer Banks.

Continue east on Main, which becomes Park Drive and then curves inland as

River Road/NC 32. Just before the intersection of US 264/NC 99, watch for Camp Leach Road. If you're up for a walk in a lush spot, turn right, and in two miles, you'll be in Goose Creek State Park, where boardwalks wind through the marsh and the bird-watching is sublime.

Poet and East Carolina University professor Julie Fay lives on Blount's Bay, across the Pamlico from Goose Creek State Park. Fay has published four poetry collections and coedited a volume of writing by people who weathered Hurricane Floyd. This poem about a mother's worry takes shape as a pantoum (a poetic form that originated in Malaysia). The lines circle and return like birds on the Pamlico:

PAMLICO RIVER
All winter we've been wheezing
gasping nights for breath.
Lace-edged, brackish, never freezing,
outside, the river crests.

Gasping nights for breath,
I sit upright, listen:
outside, the river crests
inside, your breath glistens.

I sit upright and listen
for it: are you still or still breathing
inside? Your breath glistens
with the humidifier's misty heaving

Are you? Still? You are still breathing!
We'll learn the names of birds
with the humidifier's misty heaving
background music to our words.

We learn to name the birds:
now you, at four, know grebes'
background music. Our new words:
coots' velvet necks, white beaks.

You, at four, know grebes,
grosbeaks, finches, buffleheads
and coots' velvet necks, white beaks.
We watch them mornings from the bed.

Grosbeaks, finches, buffleheads,
the busy estuary thrives.
We watch mornings from the bed
the river nursery, *en masse*, rise.

Today, snow geese V'd north overhead
lace-edged, brackish, never freezing
the river overflowed its bed
to end the winter of our wheezing.
—From *Blue Scorpion: Poems*, by Julie Fay (Kirksville, Mo.:
  Truman State University Press, 2005), 85.

Retrace your route from the state park to US 264/NC 99 and turn right. As
US 264 forks to the left, bear right on NC 99/92 to Bath.

■ BATH

I stood at the top of the arch of Peaceful River bridge and took a last look
downriver toward our house. There it sat, brighter and bigger than any of
the others lining the shore—the color of margarine. It was an architectural
spectacle, thanks to Dad, who had said, when we first came to Shad four
years ago, that if the Foster Lodge and Tourist Home was going to be profit-
able, we would have to call attention to it in some way.

The problem was that most of the people coming across the bridge lived
in Shad already and were not looking for overnight lodging.

Five-time winner of the North Carolina Juvenile Fiction Award from the
American Association of University Women, novelist Suzanne Newton grew
up in Bath and Washington. In *Ruebella and the Old Focus Home*, the narrator's
family lodge in Shad (Bath), described above, is ultimately taken over by a group
of senior citizens. Their leader, a Mrs. Smithers, explains the idea:

An Old Focus Home. We knew the time would come when it wouldn't be
advisable for any of us to live alone. Rather than entering a nursing home
or a retirement home, we hit upon the idea of pooling our resources and
opening our own place. Not a rest home, mind you, but a place where
all of our various talents and interests might be put to good use. An un-
rest home, you might say, where our lives would find their final focus and
meaning.—From *Ruebella and the Old Focus Home*, by Suzanne Newton
(Philadelphia: Westminster, 1978), 1, 40.

The Museum of the Albemarle, in Elizabeth City, displays a scale model of the James Adams Floating Theatre. The two photos behind the model show the exterior and interior of the barge that inspired Edna Ferber's 1926 novel, Show Boat.

North Carolina's oldest town (1705) and first port, Bath is also the location of the state's oldest surviving church building (St. Thomas), the first public library in the Carolina colony, and the sometime-residence of infamous pirate William Teach—Blackbeard.

In 1925, novelist Edna Ferber spent a week in Bath doing research on the remarkable James Adams Floating Theatre—a lumbering, two-story barge, 134 feet long and 32 feet wide. Tugboats pushed the wooden palace from town to town, docking it so that eager audiences could watch live melodramas on its stage. Ferber's encounter with the acting troupe in Bath inspired her novel *Show Boat*, later translated into a musical with the same name and made immortal by Jerome Kern's classic ballad "Ol' Man River."

Among the many historic buildings in Bath, the Palmer-Marsh House served as temporary quarters for writer Edna Ferber when she came to meet the cast and crew of the James Adams Floating Theatre, which locals called "the Opry barge."

Ferber was a member of the elite Algonquin Round Table in New York. Coming from the big city to tiny Bath and spending two nights in the shabby Palmer-Marsh House (now spruced up on Bath's Main Street) were not her happiest hours. When the boat finally arrived, Ferber immersed herself in the workings of the theater and conducted colorful interviews. She then left town and hurried to France to write the novel from copious notes, having taken the name of her lead character, Suzanne Ravenal (Mrs. Robert Palmer), from the epitaph on a grave at St. Thomas Church.

■ BELHAVEN

Continue on NC 99 for eighteen miles to Belhaven, a port city on the north shore of the Pungo River, at the mouth of Pantego Creek. (The River Forest Manor at 402 East Main Street is a grand inn that writer Bland Simpson and photographer Ann Cary Simpson chose for their honeymoon.) This is a great place to stretch your legs and observe the comings and goings on the water. Before you leave town, check your gas tank—there's not much chance for a refill in the next seventy miles.

On the far side of Belhaven, pick up US 264 East for a thirty-three-mile me-

Bird-watching on Lake Mattamuskeet is always rewarding. In addition to the resident herons, "a fortune of swans"—as writer Bland Simpson once put it—arrive every November on their way south.

andering ride around the many inland bays to North Carolina's largest natural lake—Mattamuskeet. Though NC 45 peels off of US 264 and goes to Swan Quarter, where a state ferry could float you to Ocracoke, this tour heads instead to NC 94, a raised road that bisects the huge lake.

■ LAKE MATTAMUSKEET

The winter never seemed barren of them. I cannot remember ever looking up without seeing at least a V of snow geese flying between the lake and crop fields where they grazed among the stubble or a pair of the tundra swans, their wings spanning six feet or more, flying between the lake and salt marshes of Swan Quarter Bay. On my morning walks, I watched them by the thousands feeding on the wild asparagus and duckweed that grows so abundantly on the lake's bottom. The lake was sixteen miles long and six miles wide, but its depth was never more than three or four feet, allowing a verdant garden of aquatic grasses to grow. To reach the grasses, the birds turned tail feather up and stretched their long necks be-

A resort for hunters in the 1930s, Mattamuskeet Lodge is slated for renovation as a lodge, meeting site, and museum in Hyde County. Writer Rachel Carson stayed here in the mid-1940s.

neath the water.—From "The constant, haunting music of the geese," by David Cecelski, in *North Carolina Literary Review* 20 (2011): 21.

David Cecelski, environmental writer and historian, spent a year observing the wildlife in and around this body of water. He was intrigued to discover that writer Rachel Carson had come to Mattamuskeet in the mid-1940s, long before her books made her famous, to write a report on the lake for the U.S. Fish and Wildlife Service. She stayed at Mattamuskeet Lodge on Headquarters Road at the south end of the lake, just off NC 94. The lodge, opened in 1937, once housed hunters and an unsuccessful pumping station intended to drain the lake to create new farmland. The structure, now undergoing renovation, belongs to the state. Still, the main attraction here is the annual spectacle of thousands of birds, large and small, that pass along this flyway for several months, beginning in early November.

Continue north on NC 94 for thirty-four miles to Columbia.

North Carolina's smallest county in terms of population is Tyrrell, pronounced TERR-il.
The county seat, Columbia, located on the Scuppernong River, draws writers, storytellers,
and artists from all over to teach at the Pocosin Arts Folk School, near the waterfront.

■ COLUMBIA

This tiny village on the Scuppernong River is headquarters to the amazing Pocosin Arts Folk School, a grassroots arts and environmental organization that has helped to showcase and preserve local music, storytelling, and handcrafts. The river view from Columbia's handsome downtown boardwalk is undisturbed by artifice, save for the bridge—a nonessential asset according to one of Bland Simpson's cousins, who once said, *"Oi don't care if they burn the bridge over the Scuppernong River and tear it down, just so long as Oi'm on this soide!"* (*Into the Sound Country*, by Bland Simpson [Chapel Hill: University of North Carolina Press, 1997], 33).

Two writers from Tyrrell County—physician Joe Liverman and popular columnist Ronald Speer—are among a stable of regional writers published by Columbia's first-rate independent press, Sweet Bay Tree Books. Liverman and Speer have delivered joyful memoirs that capture the local rituals of crabbing, fishing, minding the weather, mending nets, building boats, and growing fresh produce.

From Full Circle Seafood to Vineyards on the Scuppernong Winery—both on US 64—to Southern Dreams Gallery of local photography, next door to Pocosin

Arts on Main Street, this town and nearby Somerset Place are worth a weekend of exploration.

To reach our last stop, take US 64 West over the Scuppernong to Exit 558 and follow the state signs to Somerset Place.

■ CRESWELL

Formerly an environmental engineer, Linda Leigh Hargrove grew up in Creswell, earned a master's degree from North Carolina State University, and now writes novels about race and class in America. In *Loving Cee Cee Johnson*, Hargrove's main character is a jaded television reporter from Raleigh who has lied about her origins in the impoverished community of "Pettigrew," where the descendants of slaves still struggle to carve out a living. Just as she arrives in her hometown to cover a juicy story, a tornado rips through the countryside, forcing Cee Cee into a series of encounters with family and neighbors that help her reconcile the past with her present life.

Few places in North Carolina bear witness to the early story of racial subjugation and its long-term fallout as powerfully as Somerset Place, the state historical site on the outskirts of Creswell. Among North Carolina's most prosperous plantations, Somerset belonged to the Josiah Collins family, which owned 300 skilled slaves.

When Alex Haley's book *Roots* came out in 1977, Columbia-native Dorothy Spruill Redford, then living in Portsmouth, Virginia, began researching her family's genealogy. Her young daughter, Deborah, had asked about the family origins. Redford's research yielded a long list of families, including her own, who had been enslaved at Somerset. She invited all the relations she could find—black and white—to a homecoming on these grounds, which would be followed by many more. Some 3,000 descendants and others connected to Somerset came to the ceremonies in August 1986—the first such event on any former plantation in the United States. North Carolina governor Jim Martin attended, as did Alex Haley.

Not quite satisfied with the reconciling power of such a gathering, Redford then took on the management of Somerset in 1988 (a state position) and set about raising money. Her goal was to erect on excavated foundations reproductions of buildings that no longer stood on the property—work spaces, living quarters, and a small hospital where the enslaved people were treated for illnesses and the injuries that came from digging miles of drainage canals. (The canals are still in use.)

Writer Dorothy Spruill Redford (in white) greets guests during a 2001 homecoming of the descendants of the enslaved workers and the plantation owners at Somerset Place, in Creswell. The "big house" that belonged to the Josiah Collins family is in the background.

Redford also researched the history of Native Americans, who had preceded the white settlers and whose burial canoes were recovered from nearby Lake Phelps. She documented her work in *Somerset Homecoming*, published by Doubleday in 1989 and reissued by the University of North Carolina Press in 2000. In 2005, Arcadia Press published her second book, *Generations of Somerset Place: From Slavery to Freedom*.

This powerful site, now fully interpreted, is a proper spot to reflect on the wisdom in this poem by Gerald Barrax. (Barrax, a recipient of the North Carolina Award for Literature and an inductee into the North Carolina Literary Hall of Fame, taught for many years at North Carolina State University, where he also edited the international journal *Obsidian: Literature in the African Diaspora*.)

TO WASTE AT TREES
Black men building a Nation,
My Brother said, have no leisure like them
No right to waste at trees
Inventing names for wrens and weeds.

But it's when you don't care about the world
That you begin owning and destroying it
Like them.

And how can you build
Especially a Nation
Without a soul?
He forgot that we've built one already—
In the cane, in the rice and cotton fields
And unlike them, came out humanly whole.
Because our fathers, being African,
Saw the sun and moon as God's right and left eye,
Named Him Rain Maker and welcomed the blessings of his spit,
Found in the rocks his stoney footprints,
Heard him traveling the sky on the wind
And speaking in the thunder
That would trumpet in the soul of the slave.

Forget this and let them make us deceive ourselves
That seasons have no meanings for us
And like them
We are slaves again.
—By Gerald Barrax Sr., in *North Carolina Literary Review* 20 (2011): 95.

◼ LITERARY LANDSCAPE

Wine and Words
220 West Main Street, Washington
252-974-2870
http://wineandwords.biz/Washington
Specializing in histories, mysteries, gourmet food, and wine, this shop is a
welcome stop in downtown Washington.

Ocracoke Island : Portsmouth Island : Hatteras Island : Pea Island

The necklace of islands that shift and shelter the North Carolina mainland—known as the Outer Banks—has long been a source of fascination, drama, and wisdom. According to the writers along this tour, living on an island can teach you what is most essential and what can wait.

Writers with a connection to this area: Alton Ballance, Jan DeBlieu, Daniel Defoe, Philip Gerard, Becky Gould Gibson, Homer Hickam, Margaret Hoffman, Ben Dixon MacNeill, Scott Owens, Michael Parker, Nicholas Sparks, David Stick, William Styron, Carole Boston Weatherford, Nell Wise Wechter, David Wright, Lee Zacharias, David Zoby

■ OCRACOKE ISLAND

On the map, Ocracoke Island looks like a rod and reel thrown back over the shoulder, about to be cast. The reel is at the south end where the villagers live, and the rod is the long, narrow spit of land that stretches toward Hatteras. Three different ferry routes can take you to the island—across the Pamlico Sound from either Swan Quarter or Cedar Island or from the tip of Hatteras Island to the continuation of NC 12 on Ocracoke. Once you arrive, the best way to experience the village is on foot or bicycle. There are marsh trails to paddle and long walks to be had on the beach. Because it takes a while to get to Ocracoke, staying for several days is the best idea; there is plenty to explore. Most any map you pick up on the island will lead you to the sites described.

It begins in darkness. Before dawn, before the laughing gulls wake, before the Governor Edward Hyde, which departs the island for Swan Quarter at 6:30 every morning,

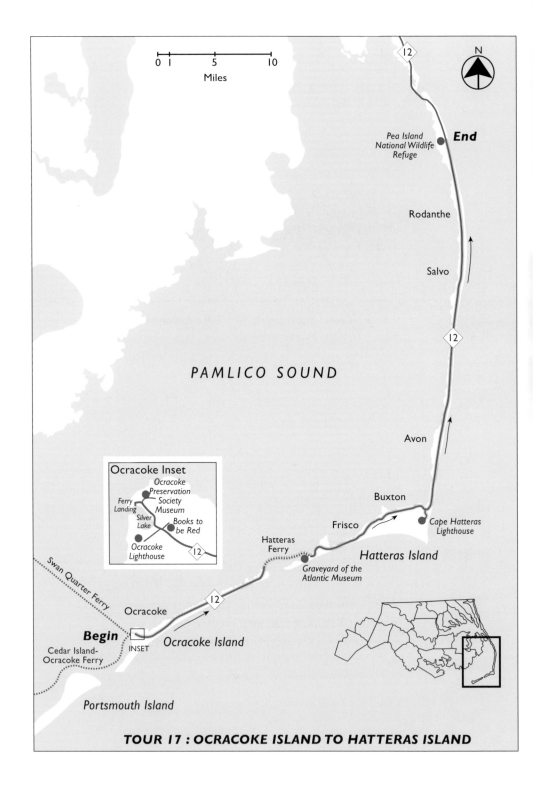

0 1   5   10
Miles

N

12

Pea Island National Wildlife Refuge

End

Rodanthe

Salvo

PAMLICO SOUND

12

Avon

Ocracoke Inset

Ocracoke Preservation Society Museum

Ferry Landing

Silver Lake

Books to be Red

Ocracoke Lighthouse

12

Buxton

Cape Hatteras Lighthouse

Frisco

Hatteras Ferry

Hatteras Island

Graveyard of the Atlantic Museum

Swan Quarter Ferry

Ocracoke

12

Begin

Cedar Island-Ocracoke Ferry

INSET

Ocracoke Island

Portsmouth Island

TOUR 17 : OCRACOKE ISLAND TO HATTERAS ISLAND

The Ocracoke Lighthouse has been photographed in all seasons by island resident Ann Ehringhaus, author of Ocracoke Portrait. *Courtesy of Ann S. Ehringhaus.*

sends a smudge of smoke skyward and sounds its deep horn. While the hull of the moon is still caught in a black sky freighted with stars. At the ocean breakers will be spilling their thunderous white spume, but here at the harbor the water is calm, glass at the surface, a bottomless sheen the color of jet. Across the harbor a few yellow bulbs still burn, but already there is a faint bluing at the horizon; the sky's black ink is dissolving into indigo, its brilliant plot of stars disappearing. The light is as swift as a swallow. You cannot go to it; you must wait for it to come to you.

Always I am up early here. For years I have crept through a dark cottage and across the screened porch with my camera and tripod to wait on a deck built high above a shelf of shallow water across from the Coast Guard Station just inside the harbor. Nearly always it is May, and though the summer season is another one, two, or three weeks away, vacationers have begun to crowd the village. By noon the road from the ferry dock to the foot of the harbor will clog with bicyclists and pedestrians strolling

Novelist Lee Zacharias writes of Ocracoke Island at dawn when the first ferry departs for Swan Quarter: "Here at the harbor the water is calm, glass at the surface, a bottomless sheen the color of jet."

from motel to museum to the Slushy Stand and shops, the Pelican and Jolly Roger, but at this hour I am the only visitor awake. Hidden inside the sleeve of night, I might be a spy. All photographers are spies.
—From "Morning Light," by Lee Zacharias, in *Crab Orchard Review* (Winter/ Spring 2007): 237.

Greensboro novelist and photographer Lee Zacharias has observed the changes on Ocracoke Island in her annual pilgrimages since 1990. More and more visitors have discovered this island, where families with only a dozen or so surnames among them have lived for generations. Newcomers who have the means to build second homes or refurbish old ones can afford the increasing property taxes more easily than the natives. Yet vestiges of old Ocracoke can still be found—in the brogue spoken by the islanders, at the David Williams House Museum near the harbor, at the oldest operating lighthouse in North Carolina near Silver Lake, and all along the tree-shaded back lanes of Ocracoke village.

Alton Ballance is a native son. He explains in his memoir, *Ocracokers*, that locals these days must work multiple jobs to keep up with the cost of owning the land they've inherited. Every islander must also share in the multiple demands of survival in such isolation, where food, mail, and high-tech medical care are available only by boat, or helicopter in an emergency. Ballance, who served for a time as assistant principal and a teacher at the Ocracoke School (kindergarten through high school), now creates programs at the North Carolina Center for the Advancement of Teaching, housed in the old Coast Guard headquarters at the mouth of the harbor. He also runs a bed-and-breakfast near the house where his mother and grandmother were born and where he now lives.

> East Howard Street. Ocracokers say it's about the only place left in the village that resembles "the way things used to look around here." When the village roads were paved during the 1950s East Howard Street was left unpaved. . . . Steady traffic has pressed the sand and dust hard, forming two ruts that wind past old houses, tiny graveyards, ancient live oaks, towering pines, and twisted cedars. Fences are so close to the sandy land that you can reach out and touch some of them as you drive through. . . . Many people say it's one of the darkest places on the island. When I was growing up, I walked through East Howard Street to get to school, which is located near the Methodist Church. Like other kids, when the walk was at night, I often found myself taking the rut farthest from the graveyard. — From *Ocracokers*, by Alton Ballance (Chapel Hill: University of North Carolina Press, 1989), 111.

As Ballance's description implies, when islanders die on Ocracoke, they are generally buried in family plots near their houses. On such a small island, mortality is therefore always in plain view. Vigilance, self-preservation, and preparation — for harsh weather, illness, or death — are second nature to Ocracokers. Winston-Salem poet Becky Gould Gibson explores this mind-set as she imagines the life of a nineteenth-century fisherman's wife. In the following excerpt, the woman is finishing her kitchen chores in order to turn again to sewing a new burial shroud, because the harsh Ocracoke elements have rotted the silk one she had stored. Earlier in the poem, her husband asks, "How many times will you make a dress / you'll only wear once?"

A WOMAN'S SHROUD:
 Ocracoke, North Carolina, circa 1890 (Excerpt)
The mackerel were ready to pack.
This morning she'd scaled them,

David Stick, writer and historian of the Outer Banks, collaborated with photographer Aycock Brown on books documenting the region. Left to right: Jon Blizzard, Aycock Brown, and David Stick. Courtesy of Outer Banks History Center, J. Foster Scott Collection, North Carolina Department of Cultural Resources.

> stripped the viscera, soft
> purple coils bloodying her hands.
> She salted the last layer.
> Preserver, destroyer!
> Same salt that kept these mackerel
> took her silk. Here salt
> invaded everything, even death.
> The last grains glittered
> as she squared on the cover,
> nailed in each side.
> —From *First Life*, by Becky Gould Gibson
>   (Greenville, S.C.: Emrys Foundation, 1997), 41.

Among Ocracoke's early hazards were the predations of notorious pirate Edward Teach, or Blackbeard. His memory yet plays in the imaginations of children who visit the beach and marshlands of the island. Blackbeard met his end at the hands of Lieutenant Robert Maynard in a bloody confrontation in Ocracoke Inlet. Outer Banks literary and historical expert David Stick explains that Blackbeard's legend is more than a bit larger than life:

> A quick tally of the writings that Blackbeard the Pirate has inspired, the treasure he is believed to have hidden on the Outer Banks, or the living Bankers who claim descent from him or his crewmen suggests that he plied local waters for decades with a fleet as large as the Royal Navy. The truth is that Edward Teach or Blackbeard was not born in North Carolina or even in North America and his activities around the Outer Banks lasted less than a year. —From *An Ocracoke Reader*, edited by David Stick (Chapel Hill: University of North Carolina Press, 1998), 119.

Stick's many carefully researched books on North Carolina's coastal history — and especially his *Reader* — are useful sources of Outer Banks lore. In the *Reader*, Stick excerpts *A General History of the Pyrates*, written in 1724 by Captain Charles Johnson, a pseudonym of Daniel Defoe, author of *Robinson Crusoe*. For a more contemporary page-turner, consider Margaret Hoffman's colorful 1998 novel, *Blackbeard: A Tale of Villainy and Murder in Colonial America*.

■ PORTSMOUTH ISLAND

A historical novel by Greensboro writer Michael Parker, winner of the 2006 North Carolina Award for Literature, also parries with pirates and takes readers out into the waters off Ocracoke to nearby Portsmouth Island. Parker's narrative began as a compelling short story, "Off Island," about the last three people who as late as the 1970s inhabited Portsmouth — a destination that requires the services of Ocracokers to visit by boat. A few hardy souls still lease cabins from the National Park Service, which they occupy as getaways in good weather. Others come to explore, and still others come for the annual Portsmouth Homecoming to honor their forebears who once lived in the ghost village where the Methodist church and a few other landmarks still stand. Parker explains the slow demise of the island's population:

> After so many storms hit the island the people started to move away. Back pews and balcony of the church thinned so much the preacher asked the couple dozen of them still in attendance to spread out so it would look like he'd drawn a crowd. Weeks later the preacher himself went off island, hymnals he said he needed, and never came back. Woodrow watched

Michael Parker's 2011 novel, The Watery Part of the World, *is based on the history of Portsmouth Island. At the 2010 Portsmouth Homecoming, descendants of the island's original inhabitants gathered for a picture in front of the Methodist church. Courtesy of photographer Ann S. Ehringhaus.*

those last to arrive leave first, and in time the descendants of families who had been around as long as the wild island ponies, rumored remnants of seventeenth-century Spanish explorers shipwrecked along the Outer Banks, packed it in for Salter Path, Beaufort, Elizabeth City, anyplace not stuck out here in this six square miles of sea oat and hummock afloat off the cocked hip of North Carolina.—From *The Watery Part of the World*, by Michael Parker (Chapel Hill: Algonquin Books of Chapel Hill, 2011), 21–22.

To flesh out the novel, Parker added another intriguing era in the island's history to his short story. He postulates the answer to an unsolved mystery: What happened to Theodosia Burr Alston, the highly educated daughter of U.S. vice president Aaron Burr and the wife of the governor of South Carolina?

In 1813, Alston boarded the schooner *Patriot* in Georgetown, South Carolina, bound for New York. When the boat was never seen again, most believed that Alston and all the others on board had been lost at sea off the treacherous North Carolina coast. When the novel begins, however, we find Alston abandoned on the shore of Portsmouth by the pirates who captured her. She must now figure out how to live among a ragtag assortment of runaways on the island. The novel, which takes its title from a phrase in *Moby Dick*, moves seamlessly between the early 1800s and the 1970s.

There's one other surprising literary connection to this still-diminishing landmass near Ocracoke. Portsmouth Island figures in the genealogy of novelist William Styron. According to biographer James L. W. West, Styron's paternal grandfather, Alpheus Whitehurst Styron (1848–1920), whom the writer never met but physically resembled, was born on the island in 1848, when some 500 residents lived here and oysters and wild game were plentiful. Visiting sailors and their vessels also thronged the village and port. Two schools and two churches were the social centers of Portsmouth; the Styrons were members of the Methodist Episcopal congregation.

When you're ready to leave Ocracoke, head up NC 12 for the short ferry ride to Hatteras and consider these lines from Hickory poet Scott Owens:

BARRIER ISLANDS (EXCERPT)
None of us leave much of a mark
on islands known to be temporary
themselves, migrating west,
shaped and reshaped by blue-green
waters of the Atlantic, patrolled
by timeless squads of gull
and tern, grackle and skimmer.
Footprints are washed or blown away
by nightfall, words drowned in wind
and waves, everything else
consumed by time or boundless sea.
—Used by permission of Scott Owens

■ HATTERAS ISLAND

South of the ferry landing, an essential first stop on Hatteras is the Graveyard of the Atlantic Museum. Built to withstand winds of 135 miles an hour, the facility is not only an architectural feat but also a valuable repository of many of the stories attached to the strategically significant shores of Hatteras Island.

The literature of Hatteras is rife with military dramas played out in the rough waters here, beginning with the earliest shipwrecks of British and other vessels and the pirates who plundered them. Later, the sinking some sixteen

The Graveyard of the Atlantic Museum is built to withstand hurricane-force winds. A Fresnel lens once used in the Hatteras Lighthouse is among the artifacts on exhibit. Many writers have set their work on Hatteras Island.

miles southeast of Hatteras of the *Monitor*, an ironclad ship deployed by Union forces during the Civil War, would eventually lead to the creation in 1975 of the first national marine sanctuary in the United States.

During the world wars, discoveries of German U-boats off the Outer Banks were major events, as were the test bombings conducted in 1923 by General Billy Mitchell, for whom the Hatteras Airport is named. In all, some 650 boats have wrecked in this maritime graveyard, which runs from Diamond Shoals at Cape Lookout north to Pea Island. Fittingly, on the night of April 14, 1912, the Hatteras Weather Bureau Station was the first to receive and record the message from the R.M.S. *Titanic*: "Have struck iceberg."

These stories of danger and disaster have fascinated writers for generations. Wilmington novelist Philip Gerard set his book *Hatteras Light* during World War I when Bankers were enlisted to help the U.S. Navy defend the waters off Hatteras:

There wasn't a free cutter anywhere on the coast, from the Keys to the Virginia Capes. There was submarine activity off New York and Massachusetts. A wolfpack, it was rumored. Thirteen vessels lost in a single week, five of them fighting for ships of the line. There were priorities and no help for Hatteras but his own cigar boat. Halstead had all the torpedoes, ammunition and depth charges he wanted, and a truck to deliver them to the slip. They had given his dead engineer a medal. They were big on medals these days. Halstead himself might even get one, but the thought did not cheer him. Their freedom with decorations only meant that things were getting worse. The war was coming home at last. — From *Hatteras Light*, by Philip Gerard (Winston-Salem: John F. Blair, 1997), 112.

Other writers have recounted stories of Germans landing on Hatteras during World War II—from Nell Wise Wechter's *Taffy of Torpedo Junction*, a juvenile novel published in 1957 and still in print, to Homer Hickam's 2005 novel, *The Keeper's Son*, set on fictional Killakeet Island. Both take place in 1941, when the attack on Pearl Harbor heightened the determination of Bankers to protect their shores from German spies and the U-boats that were disrupting merchant and military traffic up and down the coast.

From the museum, proceed north on NC 12 to the widest part of Hatteras, at the town of Buxton, and follow the signs to the tallest lighthouse in the country. In 1999, the 4,400-ton Hatteras Lighthouse was moved in one piece nearly 3,000 feet away from the site of its original construction. It now stands in a location less vulnerable to the roaring Atlantic.

Ben Dixon MacNeill, a journalist, lived in Buxton on a hill near the Hatteras Lighthouse during the latter years of his life. There he wrote *The Hatterasman*, an Outer Banks classic that is part fact and part fiction and that is based on the writer's years of listening to the natural-born storytellers of the island. One of those characters was the lighthouse keeper, Bannister Midgett, who retired from his post in 1916.

As a matter of fact and record Bannister Midgett read widely and wrote fluently, but in privacy. It was only in public and in the discharge of official duty that he assumed the posture of an unlettered man. It saved him a lot of such bother as is inherent in the keeping of records, the carrying on of official correspondence, and the like. These he ignored, and when a harassed official would finally come down to inquire of him why he had not observed such and such an order, or replied to urgently official letters, he would say that he had not been able to read them. — From *The Hatterasman*, by Ben Dixon MacNeill (Wilmington: Publishing Laboratory, 2008), 223–24.

Pictured is Rodanthe in 1952, long before the village became the subject of a novel by New Bern writer Nicholas Sparks. Courtesy of Outer Banks History Center, Aycock Brown Collection, North Carolina Department of Cultural Resources.

MacNeill was originally from Laurinburg and a distant cousin of poet John Charles McNeill, whom he knew as a boy. His determination to write this book came from his rescue in 1926 by the surfmen of the Cape Hatteras Lifeboat Station. MacNeill's sporty roadster was caught in the rising tide as he was likely driving an ailing Josephus Daniels down the coast—a story he shares in the book's preface though he does not identify his passenger. MacNeill was a protégé of Daniels who served as secretary of the navy under Woodrow Wilson and was publisher of the *Raleigh News and Observer*.

In 1937, MacNeill decided to give up the newspaper business. He moved to Manteo, where he became publicity director for Paul Green's play *The Lost Colony* in its first season. When his health began to fail, MacNeill moved to Buxton to write the book he'd thought about for years following his watery rescue. *The Hatterasman* was published in 1958 and reissued in a fiftieth anniversary edition by the University of North Carolina at Wilmington. As David Stick wrote in an entry for William Powell's *Dictionary of North Carolina Biography*, MacNeill told a visitor in May 1960 during the last week of his life: "I am in the place in this world where I most want to be." If you climb the lighthouse, you can see the glory he was talking about.

From Buxton, continue north on NC 12 for twenty-five miles, passing through the communities of Frisco, Avon, Salvo, and Chicamacomico, now better known as Rodanthe. Nicholas Sparks set his 2002 novel, *Nights in Rodanthe*, here. A movie version starred Diane Lane and Richard Gere. The combination of the book and the movie put Rodanthe on the nation's cultural map. Not long after the filming here, the house portrayed as the Rodanthe Inn nearly collapsed into the Atlantic. Now called Serendipity, the six-bedroom structure was moved and restored to look exactly as it did on film. It's available for rent. See it on Beacon Road East, on the ocean side of NC 12 just past the Hatteras Island Pet Resort, on the left. Continue north for another seven miles to reach the Pea Island National Wildlife Refuge.

■ PEA ISLAND

Jan DeBlieu adopted the Outer Banks as her home in 1985 and established her reputation as an incisive environmental writer with her first book, *Hatteras Journal*, a memoir of island life. Though she lives in the slightly tamer territory of Manteo now, DeBlieu's 1998 book, *Wind*, won the John Burroughs Medal, an award of the John Burroughs Association (housed at the American Museum of Natural History) to honor outstanding natural history writing. Here she writes of Pea Island:

> I stand on the observation platform in full sun. The cold front, offshore now, has lessened its grip; the wind is lighter and more easterly than predicted. But that has not stopped the birds. To the west I spot a sharp-shinned hawk beating out its familiar pattern: flap-flap-glide, flap-flap-glide. A second sharpie follows a few minutes later. A period of quiet, then a merlin flies low down the center of the island. It swerves slightly to the east, as if spooked by the sight of me, but still passes close enough that I can see the nostrils in its fierce, hooked beak. — From *Wind: How the Flow of Air Has Shaped Life, Myth, and the Land*, by Jan DeBlieu (New York: Shoemaker Hoard, 2005), 72.

Pea Island was the site of Station 17, one of some two hundred posts that the U.S. Life-Saving Service (a precursor of the Coast Guard) established at intervals along the Atlantic seaboard in the nineteenth century. Each station had a trained squad of surfmen prepared to rescue mariners in trouble. The teams

The Pea Island Lifesavers were the only all-African American lifesaving team on the Atlantic coast at the turn of the twentieth century. The Lifesavers are the subject of a children's book by High Point writer Carole Boston Weatherford. Courtesy of the North Carolina Office of Archives and History, North Carolina Department of Cultural Resources.

were skilled at navigating the roughest of waters in their narrow boats. When sending a crew into the waves was too dangerous, the surfmen fired cannons loaded with rope designed to unfurl and land aboard the stranded ships, creating a literal lifeline to shore for stranded passengers and crew.

Among these posts, only Station 17 had an all–African American crew, led by Richard Etheridge. In the 1890s, Etheridge and his Pea Island Lifesavers managed to rescue everyone aboard the *E. S. Newman.* The act was unheralded until one hundred years later, when the crew of Station 17 posthumously received the Gold Life-Saving Medal. High Point writer Carole Boston Weatherford tells the story of Etheridge and the challenge of leading the only African American crew in the history of the Life-Saving Service in *Sink or Swim: African American Lifesavers of the Outer Banks*, a children's book.

Scholars David Wright and David Zoby also tell the story in *Fire on the Beach.*

The social breakthrough that Richard Etheridge managed is metaphorically echoed in this passage describing the hurricane that shifted the landscape when Etheridge was only four years old:

> Richard Etheridge was born a slave on the beaches north of Pea Island on January 16, 1842. He grew up knowing the tides and currents, the channels and shoals, and early on, he learned the savage power of storms. The hurricane of September 7, 1846, blew so strongly that winds and flood waters from the Pamlico Sound burst through Bodie Island and opened an inlet near Richard's childhood home. The storm caused the tide to rise nine feet higher than normal. Farther north, it carried away the market house and destroyed the warehouse of the Nags Head Hotel, littering its stores for a half a mile along the beach. . . . According to lore, Jonathan Williams's ship, the *Oregon*, on a return trip from Bermuda to its home dock of Edenton, on the Albemarle Sound, was caught in the storm surge—thousands of metric tons of rushing water—that cut the inlet open through Bodie Island, leaving the ship stranded but intact on a sandbar in the newly opened channel. Area residents began calling it Oregon Inlet. The same hurricane opened Hatteras Inlet the next day.—From *Fire on the Beach*, by David Wright and David Zoby (New York: Scribner, 2001), 24–25.

■ **LITERARY LANDSCAPE**

Books to be Red
34 School Road, Ocracoke
252-928-3936

It's easy to while away the better part of an afternoon in this old house near Ocracoke School, where most any title that touches on the Outer Banks is within reach. Local art and unusual gifts also fill the walls and shelves.

Ocrafolk Music and Storytelling Festival
Ocracoke Island
http://www.ocracokealive.org/home.cfm
http://www.ocracokealive.org/ocrafolkfestival.cfm

For more than a decade, the Ocrafolk Festival has celebrated traditional music and storytelling during the first weekend in June.

Kitty Hawk : Kill Devil Hills : Nags Head : Wanchese : Manteo : Fort Raleigh City

Whether you are heading south on US 158 from Kitty Hawk or coming north on NC 12 from Oregon Inlet, this section of the Outer Banks contains landmarks seared into the minds of North Carolinians starting in their grade school years—the Wright Brothers Memorial, the enormous dunes of Jockey's Ridge, the pounding surf of Nags Head, and the Mother Vine of Manteo.

Writers with a connection to this area: Philip Amadas, Arthur Barlowe, Inglis Fletcher, Paul Green, Thomas Hariot, William Least Heat-Moon, Marjorie Hudson, Gwen Kimball, Charles Kuralt, Steven Lautermilch, Margaret Lawrence, Sir Walter Raleigh, Susan Rose, Muriel Rukeyser, Anne Rivers Siddons, Betty Smith, Marsha White Warren, Liza Wieland

tour 18

The very first words written from America in the English language amounted to a real estate promotion. In 1584, Sir Walter Raleigh sent Philip Amadas and Arthur Barlowe to scout out a place for a settlement. In a vast sound behind Barrier Islands, the Outer Banks of North Carolina, my home state, they found the green haven of Roanoke Island. They ignored the mosquitoes and the heat and the sand spurs and the possibly hostile Indians. They emphasized the good fishing in the waters and the abundance of grapes on the land. In their report to Queen Elizabeth, they kept coming back to those grapes. They summed up Roanoke Island by mentioning the grapes one more time and concluding, "It is withal, Madam, the Goodliest Land Under the Cope of Heaven." Except for the Elizabethan English, doesn't that sound familiar? The surveyors arrived the next year, and they started laying out the first English

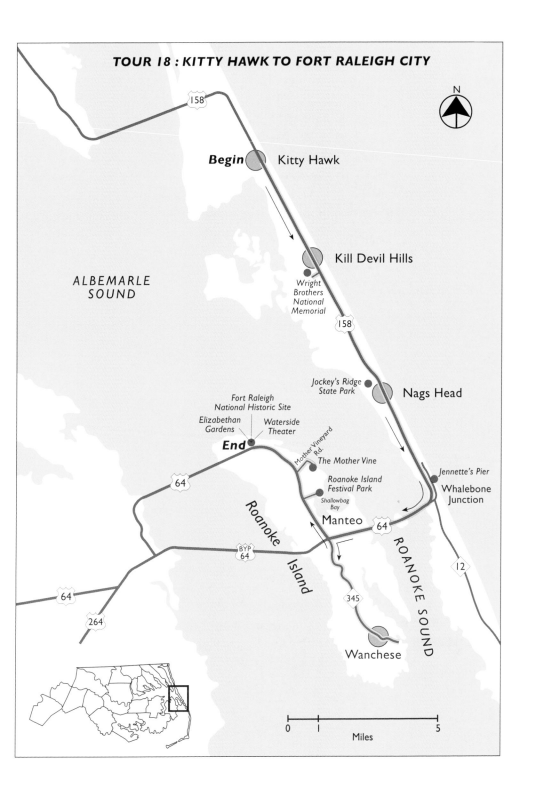

TOUR 18 : KITTY HAWK TO FORT RALEIGH CITY

N

Begin Kitty Hawk

Kill Devil Hills

Wright
Brothers
National
Memorial

158

ALBEMARLE
SOUND

158

Jockey's Ridge
State Park

Nags Head

Fort Raleigh
National Historic Site

Elizabethan   Waterside
Gardens   Theater

End

Mother Vineyard Rd.

The Mother Vine

Jennette's Pier

64

Roanoke Island
Festival Park

Shallowbag
Bay

Whalebone
Junction

Roanoke

Manteo

64

Island

BYP
64

ROANOKE SOUND

12

64

345

264

Wanchese

0   1   5
Miles

colony in the New World.—From an address by Charles Kuralt at Scenic America's National Conference, May 12, 1997, Baltimore, http://www .scenicflorida.org/kuralt.html.

With these words from North Carolina's beloved raconteur, we move onto the last stretch of highway in *Literary Trails*. Charles Kuralt was born in Wilmington, spent time as a boy on his grandparents' tobacco farm in Onslow County, went to high school in Charlotte and college in Chapel Hill, and, with some stops along the way, began his long career as a journalist for CBS. Because of his love for the coast (his parents retired to Kitty Hawk from Charlotte), a trail that connects several wildlife refuge areas in northeastern North Carolina bears his name. His words quoted here were among the last he delivered publicly. Charles Kuralt died on Independence Day in 1997.

■ KITTY HAWK

In Kitty Hawk, the Wright Brothers National Memorial is at Milepost 7.5 on US 158. This landscape—the site of the first contact between the aboriginal people of the coast and its would-be English settlers and the site of the first human flight, conducted here by the Wright brothers—is infused with a pioneering spirit. Many stories, poems, and speculations have been written about the place over four centuries—some from unexpected sources, such as twentieth-century political activist and poet Muriel Rukeyser, who offered this note about the inspiration for her poem "The Outer Banks," excerpted here:

This country, the Outer Banks of North Carolina, is a strong country of imagination: Raleigh's first Settlements, in which Thomas Hariot the scientist served a year in the New World, were here; the Wright Brothers flew from here; Hart Crane's "Hatteras" is set among these sand-bars, these waters. Several journeys here, the last one for the sake of the traces of Thomas Hariot (toward a biography I was writing) led me to this poem:

THE OUTER BANKS (EXCERPT)
Horizons of islands shifting
Sea-light flame on my voice
                        burn in me
                              Light
flows from the water from sands   islands of this horizon
The sea comes toward me across the sea.   The sand

moves over the sand in waves
between the guardians of this landscape
the great commemorative statue on one hand
    —the first flight of man, outside of dream,
         seen as stone wing and stainless steel—
and at the other hand
    banded black-and-white, climbing
the spiral lighthouse.
—From *The Collected Poems of Muriel Rukeyser*
  (New York: McGraw-Hill, 1938–78), 469.

Rukeyser, who published *The Traces of Thomas Hariot* in 1971, was fascinated by Hariot's enthusiasm for the natural world and his pioneering spirit. Ahead of Galileo by a few months, Hariot made the first drawing of the moon through a telescope. His passionate words about the New World were among the first to describe what would become North Carolina. His mathematical and navigational skills helped the second English expedition, headed by Ralph Lane, to find their way here in 1585. Hariot joined Lane's group at the bidding of Sir Walter Raleigh, whom he would later help to write *The History of the World*. Hariot was also useful to Lane's crew, because he had mastered the Algonquin language by spending time in London with Manteo and Wanchese, the indigenous men who had traveled to England the year before, when Philip Amadas and Arthur Barlowe returned from the first English expedition.

◼ KILL DEVIL HILLS

The pioneering spirit of the Outer Banks persists among those who live here today. For those of us who make occasional pilgrimages for vacation, the transience of the landscape and the volatility of the weather remind us how quickly life can change in response to natural or human intervention. Here is a vacation memory from the late poet Susan Rose, of Chapel Hill:

AT KILL DEVIL HILLS HOTEL
   10:15 A.M., August 6, 1945
Across the Beach Highway the Memorial stands,
symbol of a dream—that they could fly,
no thought of anything but cycle parts,
wing struts, winter winds, sloping sand,
their goal—to keep the fragile craft in flight.

At the Wright Brothers Memorial at Kitty Hawk, a bronze casting of the
first airplane is accessible even to the youngest pilots.

The flag blows out straight in the steady breeze.
The granite pylon reaches up, proclaims
that man has made a conquest over air
with "Dauntless Resolution, Genius, Faith."
Or such is the view we see from Nags Head beach

where the sun beats down on children holding back
the surf with fortresses. Their parents watch,
play porpoise with them, read in the shadow of the dunes.
We lean into our cars to hear the news
from Hiroshima, "Enola Gay." We stare

at sand that changes with a shifting wind
and tide, brings oil in shore from tankers hit
far off. Clouds darken the pylon, dim-out the scene;
we pick up shovels, pails, seize towels against
the chill, move close and take our children's hands.
—"At Kill Devil Hills Hotel," by Susan Rose, from *North Carolina's 400 Years:
Signs along the Way*, edited by Ronald H. Bayes (Durham: Acorn, 1986), 35.

Continue through Kill Devil Hills to the entrance of Jockey's Ridge State Park, at Milepost 12 on US 158. A character in Georgia writer Anne Rivers Siddons's 1991 novel *Outer Banks* is yet another pilgrim to North Carolina who, after a long absence, comes back to find that unchecked commercial development on the beach and a craze for hang gliding from the high dunes have taken over:

I passed the great hulks of Jockey's Ridge on my right. On the highest ridge, antlike people lined up black against the setting sun. Great, prehistoric shapes like pterodactyls flew black against the orange sky, and I realized that the people of the Banks still sailed their kites, but such kites as I had never seen or imagined. I ground through Kill Devil Hills behind an RV from Portland that said on its bumper, "Hell, Yes, I Do Own the Whole Damned Road." I passed the fishing pier, clotted with people, and went through Nag's Head, as bad as Kill Devil Hills. The air was thick and warm now, the fresh, streaming salt cut off by beetling condos and high rise motels, and I violated one of my own strictest rules and switched on the car's air conditioner, even while the top was down. It did little good. I hesitated, and then smiled grimly. Why not? What did it matter now? I turned the air on full blast. —From *Outer Banks*, by Anne Rivers Siddons (New York: HarperCollins, 1991), 282.

Novelist Margaret Lawrence looks back further, attempting to imagine the grief of the native people who made the decision to abandon their historic homelands along these islands and move inland in the late sixteenth century, away from the strange English settlers who brought mysterious diseases and customs from across the ocean:

Leaving an island forever is like dying. It is the surrender of a personal kingdom. Of self-reliance, solitude, ritual, magic. The safe hiding place of the soul.

In their secret hearts, they all know they will never return. The move takes a little over two weeks and they go secretly, working at night, the women weeping quietly as they fill the big war canoes with cooking pots, fishnets and spears, baskets of corn and beans from the storehouse, strings of dried pumpkin, family heirlooms, furs and heavy robes from the bed-places. When their torches are seen by the English soldiers, they pretend to be night-fishing.

On the last night, they take the reed mats from the cedar house poles and the men knock down the poles to be ferried over and set up on the

Students on a field trip climb the hot sands of Jockey's Ridge—an image described by writer Anne Rivers Siddons in her 1991 novel Outer Banks.

mainland. Last of all, under a guard of four with Tesid in command, goes the stolid black statue of God.

Airstalker enters one of his famous trances, hoping for a vision. The night is cold, but Naia and her children sleep on Ena's grave under the big yellow pine at the rim of the cove, in the hope that his spirit will come and wake them with a blessing.

It is their last chance. The dead cannot cross over water.

—From *Roanoke*, by Margaret Lawrence (New York: Bantam Dell, 2009), 77.

■ NAGS HEAD

Before we cross over water toward the towns of Wanchese and Manteo, consider one last stop at Jennette's Pier, at Milepost 16.5 in Nags Head. Construction began in 2009 on this 1,000-foot-long environmental education and fishing facility, exactly seventy years after the Jennette family built the original pier. Damaged by one hurricane after another and rebuilt, the pier demanded a new approach following the devastating blow from Hurricane Isabel in 2003. A group of private donors working with the North Carolina Aquarium reimagined the pier and helped to build today's all-concrete structure incorporating green design. It combines a long and sturdy fishing platform with environ-

Kill Devil Hills poet Steven Lautermilch describes a sunset on the Outer Banks as "leaving the altar of this blue hour / in between twilight / and night." Jennette's Fishing Pier is an excellent spot to witness the sun set to the west over Roanoke Sound while also watching the light change over the roiling Atlantic.

mental exhibits, an aquarium stocked with the species of fish you can expect to catch here, and other presentations and workshops about marine life and ocean ecology. Three wind turbines provide up to half the power for the entire facility, while rooftop photovoltaic cells light the pier at night. With geothermal heat and air and a complex water recycling system, this pioneering edifice is a model for future coastal facilities. It's a fine destination to watch the sun rise or set, with or without a rod and reel in hand. This poem by Steven Lautermilch, a resident for many years of Kill Devil Hills, profiles a native fishing expert—the blue heron:

BLUE HERON
Long before dawn, solitary,
you were working the water,
casting the net of your reflection,

hauling in the river until,
come evening, even the sun
is spooked and hides, wary

as a speckled trout or shy flounder,
slippery hermit of the wandering eye,
under the whiskey milk of the bay.

Call it a day, creek
farmer,
before you catch your death.

The harbor lights
are coming on now,
and the lovers.

Can't you see the young moon,
nudging the sea gate,
already climbing the walls?

It wants to see you break your
trance, step on water
and walk on air,

that long s-curve of neck
guiding you home, the arrow
of your prayer like a shot in the dark,

leaving the altar of this blue hour
in between twilight
and night.
—From *Fire Seed & Rain*, by Steven Lautermilch
    (Fayetteville, N.C.: Methodist University Press, 2008), 11.

From Whalebone Junction, where NC 12 and US 158 converge at the terminus of US 64, take 64 West (the Virginia Dare Trail) over the sound toward Roanoke Island.

■ WANCHESE

William Least Heat-Moon, a travel writer of Irish and Osage Indian descent, made his pilgrimage to Roanoke Island in the 1980s and turned first toward the fishing village of Wanchese at the south end. Heat-Moon was promptly enlisted by local fishermen to help unload a boat. He reflected on the Indian men whose names remain a part of this place now occupied by servants to the food industry and vacationers:

In 1584, Philip Amadas and Arthur Barlowe, the leaders of Raleigh's first colonial exploratory expedition, returned to London from Roanoke with tobacco, potatoes, and a pair of "lustie" Indians to be trained as interpreters. Their names were Manteo and Wanchese. The Virgin Queen and the courtiers in their lace ruffs were fascinated by the red men. Months later when the Indians returned to the sound, Manteo, the first man baptized by the British in America, was on his way to becoming a proper English gentleman. But Wanchese, after seeing London, came back an enemy of "civilized" society. Four hundred years later, the towns carrying their names, sitting at almost opposite ends of the island, still show that separation.

Wanchese, smelling of fish and the sea wind, was on the lower tip of Roanoke. . . . The town had a craft shop now, but mostly it was splintered pilings and warped gangways and fish barrels. The small houses, built by seamen used to working in limited quarters, were made even smaller by the expanse of marsh weed and scrub loblolly stretching away to the sound. Rusting boilers and winches and broken hulls bobbed up like buoys from the waving grass; on lawns, under the crimson violence of camellias, fishermen had set admiralty anchors rusted to fragility or props painted red, white, and blue. From any home the boatmen could look to the wharf and see the white wheelhouses trimmed only in black, and the booms with lines and nets dripping like kelp.

—From *Blue Highways: A Journey into America*, by William Least
Heat-Moon (New York: Little, Brown, 1999), 53, 59.

In the other direction, heading toward the middle of Roanoke Island on US 64, is Manteo, a quaint village situated around Shallowbag Bay. To reach the waterfront, take Budleigh Street to the right.

The first English colony is duly commemorated here by the *Elizabeth II*, a replica of the explorers' ship. Across a small bridge nearby is Roanoke Island Festival Park, where a museum, a re-created Indian town and English settlement, and outdoor and indoor theaters combine to tell the story of the colony. For more recent history, stroll around the narrow streets of Manteo to appreciate the range of architectural styles that have withstood storms over decades, and in some cases, centuries. If you're interested in boats, the George Washington Creef Boathouse, named for the inventor of the shad boat, is a handsome museum on the waterfront.

From downtown, take Ananias Dare Street back toward US 64 and turn right. In slightly less than a mile, turn right on Mother Vineyard Street and follow it around a sharp curve to the residence at Number 255. Though the prop-

More than 400 years old, the Mother Vine was described by the earliest writers who visited the shores of Roanoke Island. Threatened in the early twenty-first century by an accidental spraying of herbicide, it has been nursed back to health by its caretakers, the Wilson family of Manteo.

erty is private, from the street you can see the massive vine that is believed to be the oldest cultivated grape in the country, planted more than 400 years ago, by either native people or the first settlers on the island.

Let's say there's a scuppernong vine, its trunk the size of an elephant's leg—no, the size of a baobab tree. Its tendrils extend across miles and miles of coastal drift, along sand and even into the water. Bronze globes float in the brine when the tide is gentle, become crushed and pulpy in pounding storms. Let's say it's August and the Gulf Stream is warm, and it is bringing things to shore that the shore has never seen: gold signet rings; Spanish amphoras filled with wine; the bones of Englishmen. Let's say there's sex in this story, and beautiful virgins, and the root of the vine goes deep beneath the sand to the river of time. And the river of time connects all things, sifts and dissolves all memories of scented vines, all bones, all intentions into one slow moving tide of myth; we dip our feet in it. Myth is the language in which we live, that soaks and permeates everything we know and most of what we don't know.—From *Searching for Virginia Dare: A Journey into History, Memory, and the Fate of America's First English Child*, by Marjorie Hudson (Winston-Salem: Press 53, 2007), 3.

Chatham County writer Marjorie Hudson takes on the story of Virginia Dare—the first English child born on these shores, the daughter of Ananias Dare and John White's daughter Eleanor, the child who disappeared with the rest of the Lost Colony. Blending lyrical fiction with historical research and her own family history, Hudson reminds us of how faulty and selective memory can be and of how we build our reality around it anyway. She makes clear what good fiction makes clear: there is no way to know what *really* happened to the Lost Colony, but a story can still get at truth.

Thomas Hariot, the explorer, saw grapevines on his visit to the New World with Ralph Lane's expedition. Like Amadas and Barlowe the year before, he wrote in 1585 that the grape was sure to be the single most promising asset of the colony and predicted a future in winemaking for the settlers. Perhaps North Carolina, which has more than one hundred wineries, the majority of which were established in the first decade of the twenty-first century, is finally catching up to Hariot's vision.

In case you don't know the Lost Colony story, let's review: John White's group from England was the third to land here, after the expeditions by Barlowe and Amadas and by Lane. White led his group, which included his daughter Eleanor, who was pregnant, into a settlement that Ralph Lane's group had abandoned. Lane's group had comprised military men—no women—and they were soon in constant conflict with the native peoples. Eventually, with their supplies dwindling, the Lane party took off for England with the help of Sir Francis Drake. They left behind some buildings that could be occupied, and once the John White group was settled and White's granddaughter, Virginia Dare, was born and baptized, he set off to England for more provisions.

White's plan to come back with supplies, however, was delayed for three years, because of England's ongoing clash with the Spanish Armada, the wishes of the temperamental queen, and the sheer complexity of making such a trip. When White finally did return, his family and the other settlers were gone. Only the word CROATOAN, carved in a tree on the site of the settlement, remained. Storage trunks White had buried had been dug up and emptied. The colony could not be found.

The mystery of the Lost Colony, told and retold, inspired Paul Green's play of the same name, which debuted in 1937. Green's idea to stage it on the site of the disappearance would open a new chapter in theater (and North Carolina) history.

Backtrack to US 64 and turn right. Watch for signs to Fort Raleigh National Historic Site on the right in less than a mile.

■ **FORT RALEIGH CITY**

"Along there is where they probably landed," Green said, pointing off toward the water, and Bonnie felt the same excitement, a tightness in her throat, that she always experienced when she stood on ground where great events had taken place. It was as though something flowed from the earth, from the scene itself, directly to her; as though the trees, the earth, and the sea were speaking of those human happenings so fateful to generations to come.—From *The Puzzle of Roanoke: The Lost Colony*, by Gwen Kimball (New York: Duell, Sloan and Pearce, 1964), 57.

The sentiment of Gwen Kimball's character toward this place is part of the genius of *The Lost Colony*—the play that itself has taken on the status of legend. Commissioned by Roanoke Island residents to celebrate the 350th anniversary of Virginia Dare's birth, *The Lost Colony* opened on July 4, 1937, in the middle of the Depression. Hearing of its success, President Franklin Roosevelt came to see the show that August.

In the ensuing years, some 5,000 actors and theater technicians have launched their careers here. Prominent actors such as Colleen Dewhurst and Lynn Redgrave have portrayed Queen Elizabeth—just for the experience. Before the career of a young Andy Griffith took off, he played the role of Sir Walter Raleigh, and novelist Betty Smith spent a summer at the Waterside Theater as a Native American maiden. The stage is larger than that of most Broadway houses, and the cast and staff number around 200—an enormous production.

The show's only hiatus was four years during World War II, because of U-boat activity off the Outer Banks. Not that the production hasn't been threatened. In 1947, Waterside Theater burned to the ground and had to be quickly rebuilt. In 1960, the theater was nearly washed away by Hurricane Donna. In 2007, the Irene Rains Costume Shop—named for the seamstress who had saved the costumes from the 1947 fire—burned. Costumes going back to 1937 were lost, along with more recent designs by Tony Award–winning costumer William

Andy Griffith portrayed Sir Walter Raleigh in The Lost Colony *outdoor drama on Roanoke Island. Queen Elizabeth, played here by Lillian Prince, is receiving tobacco leaves brought back from the first expedition to the North Carolina coast. Courtesy of the Hugh Morton Collection of Photographs and Films, North Carolina Collection, Wilson Library, UNC–Chapel Hill.*

Ivey Long, who has been designing the show since 1988 and working on it for forty-two seasons. Marsha White Warren, a poet and the executive director of the Paul Green Foundation, who also led the North Carolina Writers' Network for many years, wrote this tribute to the first costumer:

INVINCIBLE IRENE

    Irene Rains—Costumer for The Lost Colony *from 1938 to 1984*

The Armada
    bore down on the
    coast of England
    and the colony was lost.

Three and a half centuries pass
    and a young woman
    begins to sew silk
    brocade, the buttoned brass

Betty Smith, author of A Tree Grows in Brooklyn, *spent a summer performing as an Indian maiden in Paul Green's symphonic drama* The Lost Colony. *Courtesy of the Roanoke Island Historical Association.*

embroider the story told
   retold
   of why they came
   and why they were lost.

Relentless as the storms
   that battered the band at Roanoke
   she pieces together history
   with petticoats

that billow like
   sails in steady wind.
   Costume colors
   once clear and bright

now faded tapestry
   woven tight
   will last her lifetime.

Fire tested The Lost Colony *production twice in its first seventy-five years. Shreds of burned costumes from the last blaze, in 2007, are on display in the company offices.*

Each summer she migrates to Manteo
   a bird once plumed
   now softened, worn
   Irene reigns queen

behind the scene.
   Her fingers gnarl with age
   her jerkin pockets spill
   with hooks and thread

a needle marks the place
   where breasts once full
   were hugged away
   by the actors she dressed.
—"Invincible Irene," by Marsha White Warren, from
   North Carolina's 400 Years: Signs along the Way,
   edited by Ronald H. Bayes (Durham: Acorn, 1986), 9.

The thousands of miles represented along these literary tours must now come to an end. A reflective walk through the Elizabethan Gardens, adjacent to the Fort Raleigh site and Waterside Theater, seems appropriate.

In the Elizabethan Gardens in Manteo, this Carrara marble statue imagines Virginia Dare as a grown woman. Carved in Rome in 1859 by Maria Louise Lander, the statue spent two years on the bottom of the Atlantic Ocean off the coast of Spain following a shipwreck. Rescued from the depths, it was sent to sit in the State Hall of History in Raleigh but was ultimately removed as being too controversial. The statue then went to live with playwright Paul Green in Chapel Hill, until he returned Virginia Dare to her birthplace at Fort Raleigh.

Created by the Garden Club of North Carolina at the urging of novelist Inglis Fletcher and several other women, these elaborate gardens with their formal symmetry stand in striking contrast to the wild vines and ample understory that the first explorers tried and failed to tame. A final telling of the tale, this time from Liza Wieland, who lives on the Albemarle Sound and teaches writing at East Carolina University, claims artistic license in its rendition of the message on the tree. Wieland, as writers will do, takes the mystery of that single word, "Croatoan," and plants a garden of meaning. Let her poem carry us home, back to the present: lost and found.

GONE TO CROATAN:
the first words written in the new world,
on tree bark, a message, an invitation.
You know the story: the lost colony
at Roanoke, North Carolina, the first child,
Virginia Dare, the gray-eyed Algonquins
who appeared later, how these first immigrants,
debtors, serfs, eluded their English masters
and while Governor John White was away,
they disappeared into Great Dismal Swamp.
Chose chaos, the academics say, *intentionally*,
went native, *dropped out*, *began the tradition*.
Not the first words written, my husband argues,
the first words posted, maybe. Now I live
four miles away, across the river, called Neuse,
which appears to me on some days "croatan,"
meaning yellow-brown, weak tea-colored
and they've returned, still named Dare, Lee,
Salter, Willis, with their ruddy skin and gray
blue eyes squinting against sunlight on stucco
come back to pour concrete, pump out the septic,
install the gas line, finance the loan, teach the children.
In her school called Croatan, my daughter learns
to put her head down, on her crossed arms,
when she's finished the morning's work,
to stare into darkness. That's how they see
she's mastered the numbers, the letters,
the glue. She can understand
this, I know, this blindness of her own

making, even at four years old, sense
the way knowledge leads to death.

Two months ago, she fell in love, desperately,
with one of the boys, followed him everywhere,
listened so hard when he talked she couldn't
eat her lunch or hear another living voice,
didn't want to, she told me, not ever again.
So her teachers, descendants of Croatan
separated this boy and my daughter,
kept them from sitting together
or walking in the same group.
She cried every afternoon, while they waited
calmly, saying, tears won't get you anywhere.
Her heart is so rich, her teacher told me later,
I tell her to spend it on her momma.
And she did, she does, she's over him now.

What did you learn in Great Dismal Swamp?
I want to ask the Dares, the Salters, the Whites,
who ran away from their father, the governor.
Plenty about living, they'd say, needing not so much,
serving no master or civilization, practical dissent.
Alternatives to wage labor, *scuffling*, it's called.
The Rastafarians do it, sell homemade brooms
and cosmetics because they believe, they expect
at any moment to return to their native Africa.
But what did you learn about love?
I want to ask. Is that why you came back?
Because you found that love is chaos too,
but it won't let you disappear, drop out,
go native. It pleads, it cries, stay here.

Not the first words written, but maybe
the first Dear John letter, my husband says
and laughs at his joke, but it scares me
how the yellow brown river, the Neuse
lies between us, shallow, insubstantial as tears,
between my daughter and Great Dismal Swamp.
Nearly every week she says this:

I want to go there, go to the Indian Forest,
and I know one day I'll turn my back
then later find the note scrawled on paper,
those first last words, taped to the door.
—From *Near Alcatraz*, by Liza Wieland
   (Cincinnati: Cherry Grove Collections, 2005), 25–27.

■ LITERARY LANDSCAPE

Duck's Cottage Downtown Books

105 Sir Walter Raleigh Street, Manteo
252-473-1056
http://www.duckscottage.com
After the popular Manteo Booksellers took a devastating hit from Hurricane Irene in 2011, two partners from Duck decided to expand their offerings to Manteo. They have opened this new shop in the location that Manteo Booksellers occupied. The store has a strong selection of regional reading.

Dare County Arts Council

300 Queen Elizabeth Avenue, Manteo
252-473-5558
http://www.darearts.org
This arts council hosts regular open mic nights in partnership with different venues throughout the county. It also offers workshops on writing and other literary events.

ACKNOWLEDGMENTS

How fortunate we are in North Carolina to live in a state that supports a project as ambitious and unusual as the *Literary Trails* series. Such enterprising ideas to draw out and celebrate the cultural treasures of our state come regularly from the North Carolina Arts Council and its parent agency, the North Carolina Department of Cultural Resources. That is why North Carolina is known as "The Creative State." We owe this distinction to many in state government, but perhaps most of all to Mary B. Regan, who has been the chief architect of the cultural infrastructure we enjoy today. Mary retired as director of the Arts Council in early 2012 after thirty-nine years of ceaseless innovation and quiet but powerful leadership. There is no program in the arts in North Carolina that she has not touched, and her graceful hand is yet in this guidebook. Thank you for your courage and inspiration, Mary.

Our effervescent secretary of the North Carolina Department of Cultural Resources, Linda A. Carlisle, the steady and seasoned Wayne Martin, who has succeeded Mary as the Arts Council's executive director, and *Literary Trails* project director Rebecca Moore have lent their enthusiasm and critical eye to this work, for which I am most grateful. Special thanks go also to staff members David Potorti and Ardath Weaver, who have helped with research and ideas all along the way.

The original idea for this project was sparked by a *New York Times* travel story that novelist Josephine Humphreys wrote about traveling down US 17 through South Carolina's Low Country. The Arts Council's deputy director, Nancy Trovillion, read Humphreys's piece and asked, "Why can't we bring literary perspectives to *all* of North Carolina?" Congratulations, Nancy. Your amazing vision has, I hope, been realized.

Debbie McGill, who was the first editor of this manuscript, was contracted by the Arts Council and helped me find just the right word and construction while encouraging me to keep improving every sentence.

Donna Campbell, photographer, has navigated this literary journey over eight years and 10,000 miles. Her keen eye and exquisite composition grace these pages.

Special thanks to my mother, Virginia Reed, and my brother, G. Ray Eubanks, and to Cindy Campbell, Donna Campbell's sister.

My dear friend and fellow writer Wayne Goodall helped in the research early on, and she took delight in exploring possible excerpts with me for this third book. Nancy Hardin gathered up all the permissions to excerpt poems and prose works.

This book has required all kinds of resources and ideas from people across the eastern region. In particular, I appreciate the willing advice and stories from Sally Buckner, Marjorie Hudson, Donnie Jernigan, Randall Kenan, Carrie Knowles, Sandy Landis, Nicki Leone, Michael Malone, Margaret Maron, D. G. Martin, Carol McLaurin, Darlene McLaurin, Sarah Merritt, Kathryn Milam, Deborah Martin Mintz, Feather Phillips, Bland Simpson, Steve Smith, Ben Steelman, Shelby Stephenson, Joey Toler, Marsha Warren, Karen Wells, and Valerie Raleigh Yow. Special acknowledgment goes also to Robert Anthony and Keith Longiotti at the North Carolina Collection in Wilson Library at the University of North Carolina at Chapel Hill. Maurice York and Ralph Scott at Special Collections in Joyner Library at East Carolina University helped enormously with photo permissions. Kim Cumber at the North Carolina Division of Archives and History was also extremely professional and quick to respond to our requests for images.

Then there were the total strangers: A woman named Crystal stopped what she was doing at the public library in Fairmont to drive with us to find the grave of *New Yorker* writer Joseph Mitchell in one of three possible town cemeteries. On another day, Officer Twine of the Seaboard police finished writing a speeding ticket (not for us, fortunately) and then took us to Shirley Stevens's house so that she could help us identify the whereabouts of the former home of writer Bernice Kelly Harris. Jerome Tyson in Little Washington directed us to the DeMille plot in that city's enormous cemetery, while both Ali Morrow and Jerry Parnell actually made special trips to help verify the inscription on the 1898 Memorial in Wilmington. There are, of course, many more stories—enough to last a lifetime.

Thanks to Ann Ehringhaus, Jill McCorkle, Tom Rankin, and Lee Zacharias for sharing their fine photos.

At the University of North Carolina Press, I have had the privilege of working with David Perry, Paul Betz, Heidi Perov, Caitlin Bell-Butterfield, Vicky Wells, Dino Battista, Gina Mahalek, Jennifer Hergenroeder, Susan Garrett, and the dependable folks at Longleaf Services. Michael Southern prepared the amazing maps, and Dorothea Anderson once more served as copyeditor. You all are the best.

Finally, the biggest appreciation must go to all the writers, past and present, who have made three books' worth of contributions to our state. Between the second volume of this series and this one, we lost both Doris Betts and Reynolds Price. I hope this series helps to preserve their gifts and kindnesses and the memory of all writers in North Carolina who have helped put the many distinctions of our state into words.

A NOTE ON THE NORTH CAROLINA
LITERARY TRAILS PROGRAM

North Carolina Literary Trails is a cultural tourism program of the North Carolina Arts Council, an agency of the Department of Cultural Resources. *Literary Trails of Eastern North Carolina*, the third volume in a series of guidebooks, is a journey through forty-five counties where you'll discover some of the people and places shaping the coastal region—including many off the beaten path. North Carolina's literary heritage continues to surprise and delight us.

Our tour guide for the literary trails is Georgann Eubanks—writing coach, communications consultant, and North Carolina Arts Council Literary Fellowship recipient. Her generosity of spirit and her willingness to share her talents are legendary among writers, aspiring writers, and people who didn't even know they wanted to be writers until they met Georgann. Her fondness for the written word and keen eye for narrative allow her to share with residents and visitors an exciting way to see this state on roads less traveled.

The beautiful photographs illustrating the guidebook were taken by Donna Campbell, who graciously donated both her talent and her time for the three volumes of the literary trails project. Also an award-winning documentary producer, Donna captures her love of North Carolina and its story in every photograph.

If you haven't already discovered the literary highlights in the rest of the state, be sure to read volume one, *Literary Trails of the North Carolina Mountains*, and volume two, *Literary Trails of the North Carolina Piedmont*.

Because new books and authors emerge constantly in our state, it is impossible to be all-inclusive of North Carolina's literary treasures in print guidebooks. The tours that make up the trails were developed to be representative of the following priorities:

—historic sites where North Carolina authors have lived and worked;
—sites that can be visited by the public that figure prominently in the published poetry, fiction, creative nonfiction, and plays of North Carolina writers and other writers who have spent significant time here;
—libraries with notable publicly accessible collections of manuscripts, books, and other literary artifacts related to North Carolina authors;
—bookstores, universities, local arts councils, and other venues where North

Carolina authors take part in public programming or are represented in exhibits, events, performances, and other local activities; and

—other local amenities related to each tour itinerary as recommended by contemporary writers familiar with the area.

Our companion website, http://www.NCLiteraryTrails.org, provides up-to-date information about literary North Carolina. Many writers not included in this guidebook are listed on the website by region. In addition, you'll find current news about writers across North Carolina. You'll also find videos of North Carolina writers reading from their work and interviews with them. Click here, too, for footage of the state's poet laureates.

NCLiteraryTrials.org offers profiles of writers and a calendar of literary festivals. Plus, it's easy to share our content and provide your own. Facebook, YouTube, and Twitter are only a click away at NCLiteraryTrails.org.

We also invite you to visit the online *North Carolina Literary Map* at http://library.uncg.edu/dp/nclitmap. A project of the UNC-Greensboro Libraries in association with the North Carolina Center for the Book, the map highlights the literary heritage of the state by connecting the lives and work of authors to real and imagined geographic locations. The map is searchable by region, author or genre of writing, and focuses on works written about North Carolina by authors who live (or have lived) in the state, as well as those who have made significant contributions to its literary landscape.

We hope these resources spark an interest in your own creative life.

The N.C. Arts Council also invites you to go on to explore Blue Ridge music, African American music, and North Carolina crafts. Our cultural trails portal, http://www.NCArtsTrails.org, is your starting point to see North Carolina through the eyes of its artists. Discover Creative North Carolina by adding http://www.NCArtsTrails.org to your travel planning.

PERMISSIONS

Unless otherwise indicated, the copyright holder is the author.

POEMS

Adcock, Betty: "Topsail Island," from *White Trash, an Anthology of Contemporary Southern Poets*, ed. by Nancy C. McAllister and Robert Waters Grey (Boson Press), copyright © 1996.

Albrecht, Malaika King: "Grave Rubbing with my Daughters at Bethesda Cemetery," copyright © 2012.

Ammons, A. R.: "Alligator Holes Down Along About Old Dock," copyright © 1994, from *The Complete Poems of A. R. Ammons* (W. W. Norton). Used by permission of W. W. Norton & Company, Inc.

Ammons, Shirlette: "Living Will," from *Matching Skin* (Carolina Wren Press), copyright © 2008.

Applewhite, James: "Collards," from *James Applewhite: Selected Poems* (Duke University Press), copyright © 2001.

Baddour, Margaret Boothe: "How We Deal with Dusk" (excerpt) from *Scheherazade and Other Poems* (St. Andrews College Press), copyright © 2009.

Barrax, Gerald, Sr.: "To Waste at Trees," from *North Carolina Literary Review* 20, copyright © 2011.

Beadle, Michael: "Town Too Small for Maps" (excerpt), copyright © 2006.

Brantley, Russell: "Play Ball: 1936" (excerpt), from *Fetch Life* (Stratford Books), copyright © 2000. Used by permission of Robin Brantley.

Brown, Grey: "Living on the Tar," from *Staying In* (North Carolina Writers' Network), copyright © 1992.

Buckner, Sally: "Raleigh, Moving Through the Years," copyright © 1992.

Carty, Jessie: "Saturday at Merchant Mill Pond," from *Paper House* (Folded Word), copyright © 2010.

Clark, Jim: "Old Mill Road" (excerpt) copyright © 2004.

Dupree, Edison: "Record," from *Prosthesis: Poems* (Bluestem Press), copyright © 1994.

Fay, Julie: "Pamlico River," from *Blue Scorpion: Poems* (Truman State University Press), copyright © 2005.

Rukeyser, Muriel: "The Outer Banks" (excerpt), from *The Collected Poems of Muriel Rukeyser* (McGraw-Hill), copyright © 1965. Reprinted by permission of International Creative Management, Inc.

Schmidt, Susan: "Green Thought in Green Shade," copyright © 2012.

Sherbondy, Maureen: "Loose Coffins in Carolina," *The Independent Weekly*, March 29–April 24, 2000, copyright © 2000.

Silverthorne, Marty: "Gettin' the Holy Ghost at R. A. Fountain," copyright © 2012.

Stephenson, Shelby: "The Farm That Farms New Houses" (excerpt), from *Rambler*, March–April 2006, copyright © 2006.

Stephenson, Shelby: "Hogs," from *Greatest Hits 1978–2000* (Pudding House Publications), copyright © 2002.

Stephenson, Shelby: "Blue Country Rising," from *Turnstile* 2, no. 1 (reprinted in *Greatest Hits 1978–2000*), copyright © 1990.

Warren, Marsha White: "Invincible Irene," from *North Carolina's 400 Years: Signs along the Way*, ed. Ronald H. Bayes (Acorn Press), copyright © 1986.

Weil, Eric A.: "Three Silos," from *Dead Mule School of Southern Literature*, February 2010, copyright © 2010.

White, Michael: "Coup" (excerpt), from *North Carolina Literary Review* 18, copyright © 2009.

Wieland, Liza: "Gone To Croatan:" from *Near Alcatraz* (Cherry Grove Collections) copyright © 2005.

Wilson, Emily Herring: "Easter at Holden Beach Fishing Pier," from *Solomon's Seal* (Cedar Rock Press), copyright © 1978.

PROSE

Brantley, Russell: excerpt from *The Education of Jonathan Beam* (Macmillan), copyright © 1962. Used by permission of Robin Brantley.

Church, Kim: excerpt from "Cafeteria Lady," *Prime Number Magazine* 11, copyright © 2011.

Delany, Sarah L., A. Elizabeth Delany, and Amy Hill Hearth: excerpt from *Having Our Say: The Delany Sisters' First 100 Years* (Dell Publishing), copyright © 1993. Used by permission of Amy Hill Hearth.

Donald, David Herbert: excerpt from *Look Homeward: A Life of Thomas Wolfe* (Little, Brown), copyright © 1987. Used by permission of Aida Donald.

Godwin, Gail: excerpt from *Evenings at Five* (Random House), copyright © 2003. Used by permission of Ballantine Books, a division of Random House, Inc.

INDEX

Page numbers in italics refer to photographs and captions. Page numbers in boldface refer to maps.

Andrews Press, 74; Scots Plaid Press, 49; Sweet Bay Tree Books, 289
Pulphead: Essays (Sullivan), 119
Pungo River, 286
Purslane (Bernice Harris), 227, 229
The Puzzle of Roanoke: The Lost Colony (Kimball), 320
Pynchon, Thomas, 258

Quail Ridge Books and Music, 8–10, *9*
Quakers, 241
"Quarantine" (Gibbons Ruark), 223–24
Quarter Moon Books (Topsail Beach), 191

Race relations: in Baldwin's *The Fire This Time*, 168; in Chesnutt's *The Marrow of Tradition*, 60; and Dixon, 73, 158; in Hargrove's *Loving Cee Cee Johnson*, 290; and Bernice Harris's folk plays, 230; in Humphreys's *Nowhere Else on Earth*, 78–80; in Melton McLaurin's *Separate Pasts*, 144–45; and Native Americans, 78–80; in Neely's *Blanche Passes Go*, 19; in Wilmington, 122, 125–28, *125*. *See also* African Americans; Civil rights movement; Ku Klux Klan; Segregation
Rachel Carson National Estuarine Sanctuary, 195
Raeford, **2**
R. A. Fountain General Store (Fountain), 275, 277–78, *277*
Rafting. *See* Boating, rafting, and tubing
Ragan, Samuel Talmadge, 44–46, *45*, *47*, *74*, 190
Ragan Writers at Weymouth, 46
Railroad depots, 42
Railroads, 35, 78–79, 213

Railton, Stephen, 183
Rain Song (Wisler), 159, *160*
Raleigh: Armistead Maupin House, 11–12, *12*; bedroom communities of, 137; bookstores, 8–10, *9*, 30; Broughton High School, 14–15, *15*; *Education Wall*, 22–23, *23*; K&W Cafeteria, 10–11; maps of, **2**, **6**; Meredith College, 28; North Carolina Museum of Art, 5, 7, *8*; North Carolina Museum of History, 30; North Carolina State Archives, 30; North Carolina State Capitol Building, 23–24; North Carolina State Fairgrounds, 28–29; Oakwood Cemetery, 19–20; Price and Tyler Houses, 17; Quail Ridge Books and Music, 8–10, *9*; Reader's Corner, 30; St. Augustine's University, 20–22, *21*; St. Mary's School, 13–14; Shaw University, 24–25; and state government, 5, 23–24; Tompkins Hall, 26–28, *27*; Wake County Public Libraries, 30; "Wakestone," 15–17; William Peace University, 18–19; WRAL-TV, 25–26
Raleigh, Walter, 78, 209, 308, 311, 317, 320
Raleigh Fine Arts Society Literary Contest, 10
Raleigh Medal of Arts, 24
"Raleigh, Moving Through the Years" (Buckner), 29
Raleigh News and Observer, 33, 63, 214, 221, 304
Raleigh–Pamlico Sound Railroad, 213
Raleigh's Eden (Fletcher), 271
Ran, Nâzım Hikmet, 49
Rand, Tony, 66
Randolph-Macon College, 33
Raney (Edgerton), 41

Rankin, Tom, 66

Rash, Ron, 9–10, 180

"The Raven" (Poe), 171–72

Raven Rock, 41

Reader's Corner (bookstore), 30

The Rebel, 224

"Record" (Dupree), 181

"The Red and the White" (Long), 109–10

Red Barn Studio (Wilmington), 119

Red Clay Ramblers, 251

Redding, J. Saunders, 250–51

Redford, Dorothy Spruill, 290–91, *291*

Redgrave, Lynn, 320

Redheaded Stepchild, 47

Reed, Donna, 55

Reflections in a Golden Eye (McCullers), 53, 63–64, *64*

Reflections in a Golden Eye (movie), 64

Rehder, Jessie, 115, 221

Reid, Christian, 113

Rescuing Patty Hearst (Holman), 117

Research Triangle Park, 31, 36

Resilience (Elizabeth Edwards), 20

Restaurants: Baker's Kitchen (New Bern), 183; Candy Sue's Café (Lumberton), 88; Captain Bill's Waterfront (Morehead City), 199; Eddie's Café (Newton Grove), 147; Edenton Coffee House Bakery and Café, 274; Ella's (Calabash), 102; Embassy Café (Jackson), 233; Hog Heaven (Washington), 282; Inlet View Bar and Grill (Shallotte), 106; K&W Cafeteria (Raleigh), 10–11; McCall's BBQ and Seafood Restaurant (Goldsboro), 158; Melvin's (Elizabethtown), 89; Paper Canoe (Duck), 254; Ralph's (Roanoke Rapids), 222–23; Sanitary Fish Market (Morehead City), 199; Seafood

Hut (Calabash), 102; Sunny Side Oyster Bar (Williamston), 268, *268*, 269; Wilber's Barbecue (Goldsboro), 158

"The Resurrection of Christ" (Sedaris), 7

The Return of Buddy Bush (Moses), 233, *234*

Revolutionary War, 43, 89

Rhine, J. B., 46

"Rhythm" (Moore), 24–25

Richmond Temperance and Literary Society Commission, 71

Rich Square, **228**, 232, 233, 239

Rigsbee, David, 159–61, *185*

Ripa, Dean, 124

Rivenbark, Celia, 169

River Forest Manor (Belhaven), 286

The River Less Run (Tim McLaurin), 41, 113

River Time (Lembke), 205

Riverton, **69**

The River to Pickle Beach (Betts), 42

River Way Outdoor Adventure and Education Center, 99

R.M.S. *Titanic*, 302

The Road to Wellville (movie), 119

Roanoke (Lawrence), 313–14

Roanoke-Chowan Heritage Center, 236, *237*

Roanoke Island, 78, 239, 308

Roanoke Rapids, **212**, 220, 221–23

Roanoke Rapids High School, 222

Roanoke River, 220, 238, 269

Roanoke River Lighthouse (Edenton), 271–72, *272*

Roanoke Rock Muddle (Powe), 267–68

Roanoke Sound, *315*

Robbins, Tom, 258

Robert Ruark Inn, 110

Roberts, Eva, *279*

Roberts, Nancy, 77